TEST MATCH GROUNDS

OF THE WORLD

TEST MATCH
GROUNDS
OF THE WORLD

Contributing writers

**Mihir Bose · John Coffey
Tony Cozier · Michael Owen-Smith
Jack Pollard · Mahinda Wijesinghe
Marcus Williams**

WILLOW BOOKS
Collins
8 Grafton Street, London W1 1990

Willow Books
William Collins Sons & Co Ltd
London · Glasgow · Sydney · Auckland
Toronto · Johannesburg

© Jollands Editions 1990

A CIP catalogue record for this book is
available from the British Library

ISBN 0 00 218282 3

Editorial planning by Jollands Editions
Designed by Janet James
Set in Garamond
Typset, printed and bound in Great Britain by
Butler & Tanner Ltd, Frome, Somerset

Photographic Acknowledgements

Thanks are due to the following individuals and organisations for allowing their copyright material to be reproduced in the book: All-Sport/Adrian Murrell 85b, 122, 123, 124, 129, 130, 139, 141, 154, 164, 171, 173, 179, 190, 191, 202, 223; All-Sport/Simon Bruty 156; Associated Press 188, 189; *Daily Telegraph* (Sydney); Patrick Eagar 8, 13, 35b, 43, 50a, 50b, 52, 57b, 58a, 58b, 61, 68, 69, 74b, 82, 83, 85a, 112b, 116, 117, 118, 120, 127, 135, 136, 137, 142, 143, 145, 146, 160, 194, 204, 209, 210, 212, 213, 215, 220; Patrick Eagar/Jan Traylen 97; Bill Frindall Collection 138, 167, 170, 193; *Hobart Mercury* 27; Hulton Deutsch Collection 18/9, 23, 49, 56/7, 62, 65, 78, 91, 93a, 93b, 95, 96, 104, 106/7, 174, 186b; Illustrated London News Picture Library 77, 92, 119, 148/9, 152/3, 169, 176/7, 180/1, 181r, 197; Ken Kelly 64; Library Board of Western Australia 38/9, 40; J. W. McKenzie 153r; Roger Mann Collection 46, 76, 112a, 125, 133, 134, 178, 182, 184, 185, 186a, 200l, 200r, 205, 217a, 217b; MCC 25, 32/3, 71l, 71r, 74a, 159, 199; Melbourne Cricket Ground Museum 31; Pat Mullins Collection 21; National Museum, New Zealand 157; *New Zealand Herald* 150; Nottinghamshire CCC 114; Jack Pollard Collection 26, 35a; Queensland Cricketers' Club 22; South Australian Cricket Association 16; Surrey CCC 89; Sport & General 80, 106b.

Key – a above, b below, l left, r right

Contents

Test Match Grounds of the World
15 March 1877 to 31 December 1989

Test centre	Ground	Tests	First day
Melbourne (A)	MCG	81	15.3.1877
London (E)	The Oval	72	6.9.1880
Sydney (A)	SCG (No. 1)	75	17.2.1882
Manchester (E)†	Old Trafford	57	10.7.1884
London (E)	Lord's Cricket Gnd	84	21.7.1884
Adelaide (A)	Adelaide Oval	47	12.12.1884
Cape Town (SA)	Newlands	24	25.3.1889
Port Elizabeth (SA)	St George's Park	12	12.3.1889
Johannesburg (SA)	Old Wanderers	22	2.3.1896
Nottingham (E)	Trent Bridge	38	29.6.1899
Leeds (E)	Headingley	52	29.6.1899
Birmingham (E)	Edgbaston	26	29.5.1902
Sheffield (E)	Bramall Lane	1	3.7.1902
Durban (SA)	Lord's	4	21.1.1910
Durban (SA)	Kingsmead	19	18.1.1923
Brisbane (A)	Exhibition Ground	2	30.11.1928
Christchurch (NZ)	Lancaster Park	28	10.1.1930
Bridgetown (WI)	Kensington Oval	25	11.1.1930
Wellington (NZ)	Basin Reserve	24	24.1.1930
Port-of-Spain (WI)	Queen's Park Oval	39	1.2.1930
Auckland (NZ)†	Eden Park	31	14.2.1930
Georgetown (WI)	Bourda	21	21.2.1930
Kingston (WI)	Sabina Park	27	3.4.1930
Brisbane (A)	Woolloongabba	32	27.11.1931
Bombay (I)	Gymkhana	1	15.12.1933
Calcutta (I)	Eden Gardens	26	5.1.1934
Madras (I)	Chepauk (Chidambaram Stm)	20	10.2.1934
Delhi (I)	Feroz Shah Kotla	22	10.11.1948
Bombay (I)	Brabourne Stadium	17	9.12.1948
Johannesburg (SA)	Ellis Park	6	27.12.1948
Kanpur (I)	Green Park (Modi Stadium)	16	12.1.1952
Lucknow (I)	University (Gomti) Ground	1	23.10.1952
Dacca (P*)	Dacca Stadium	7	1.1.1955
Bahawalpur (P)	Dring (Bahawal) Stm	1	15.1.1955

Test centre	Ground	Tests	First day
Lahore (P)	Lawrence Gardens (Bagh-i-Jinnah)	3	29.1.1955
Peshawar (P)	Peshawar Club Gnd	1	13.2.1955
Karachi (P)	National Stadium	28	26.2.1955
Dunedin (NZ)	Carisbrook	8	11.3.1955
Hyderabad (I)	Fateh Maidan (Lal Bahadur Stadium)	3	19.11.1955
Madras (I)	Corporation (Nehru) Stadium	9	6.1.1956
Johannesburg (SA)	Wanderers Stadium	11	24.12.1956
Lahore (P)	Lahore (Gaddafi) Stadium	23	21.11.1959
Rawalpindi (P)	Pindi Club Ground	1	27.3.1965
Nagpur (I)	Vidarbha CA Gnd	3	3.10.1969
Perth (A)	WACA Gnd	17	11.12.1970
Hyderabad (P)	Niaz Stadium	5	16.3.1973
Bangalore (I)	Karnataka SCA (Chinnaswamy) Stm	9	22.11.1974
Bombay (I)	Wankhede Stadium	13	23.1.1975
Faisalabad (P)	Iqbal Stadium	13	16.10.1978
Napier (NZ)	McLean Park	1	16.2.1979
Multan (P)	Ibn-e-Qasim Bagh Stadium	1	30.12.1980
St John's (WI)	Recreation Ground	4	27.3.1981
Colombo (SL)	P. Saravanamuttu Stm (Colombo Oval)	3	17.2.1982
Kandy (SL)	Asgiriya Stadium	4	22.4.1983
Jullundur (I)	Burlton Park	1	24.9.1983
Ahmedabad (I)	Gujarat Stadium	2	12.11.1983
Colombo (SL)	Sinhalese Sports Club Ground	2	16.3.1984
Colombo (SL)	Colombo Cricket Club Ground	3	24.3.1984
Sialkot (P)	Jinnah Park	2	27.10.1985
Cuttack (I)	Barabati Stadium	1	4.1.1987
Jaipur (I)	Sawai Mansingh Stm	1	21.2.1987
Hobart (A)	Bellerive Oval	1	16.12.1989

† Rain prevented play until 11.7.1884 at Manchester and until 17.2.1930 at Auckland
* Bangladesh since 16.12.1971

Preface and Acknowledgements

Test cricket has taken place on 62 cricket grounds: seven in Australia, seven in England, sixteen in India, five in New Zealand, eleven in Pakistan, seven in South Africa, four in Sri Lanka and five in the West Indies. Between them, these grounds have staged 1132 official Test matches. It may therefore seem surprising that this is the first book to devote itself to telling their stories.

The book is arranged alphabetically, first by country then by Test match centre, London's two Test venues – Lord's and the Oval – being treated as separate centres. Seven of the 52 centres have staged Tests on more than one ground: Bombay, Brisbane, Colombo, Durban, Johannesburg, Lahore and Madras. For each country, an introduction is followed by a description of the ground/s at each Test centre, at the end of which appear tabulated results of the Tests played there. The prefix of the reference numbers in these tables relate to the match numbers first adopted by Bill Frindall in *The Wisden Book of Test Cricket*.

One of the joys of editing this book has been to work with a team of contributing writers whose enthusiasm for the project lasted from beginning to end. I offer my grateful thanks therefore to Jack Pollard (Australia), Marcus Williams (England), Mihir Bose (India and Pakistan), John Coffey (New Zealand), Michael Owen-Smith (South Africa), Mahinda Wijesinghe (Sri Lanka) and Tony Cozier (West Indies).

Thanks are due to many others, notably Philip Bailey for help with the tables, Dick Brittenden, Michael Doggart at Collins, Patrick and Annabel Eagar, Stephen Green and his staff at the MCC Library, Elaine Hart at the Illustrated London News Picture Library, Keith Humphrey at Butler & Tanner, Janet James and Roger Mann. A separate list of photographic acknowledgements appears elsewhere.

Tim Jollands
Bath
December 1989

The Members' Stand at Sydney.

Australia

JACK POLLARD

Australian cricket began in Sydney's Hyde Park in 1803, 20 years after white settlement began, between teams made up of civilians and officers from the supply ship *Calcutta*. First-class matches were not played until 1851 when Victoria met Tasmania at Launceston. Since then 26 grounds have been used for first-class cricket in Australia, five of which have emerged as outstanding Test match venues, and a sixth at Hobart, Tasmania, which had its first Test in December 1989.

The first-class game began precariously at a time when Australia comprised a series of colonies peopled mostly by sullen convicts. Free settlement was still in its infancy. Federation of the colonies into one nation was still half a century away when the Gentlemen of Van Dieman's Land, the official name for Tasmania until 1855, accepted a challenge from cricketers across Bass Strait at Port Phillip.

The Launceston players persuaded Governor Denison to allot them a piece of land near the city's racecourse where they set to work preparing a field for the contest. They then sent news to Hobart that Melbourne's team were coming and the Derwent club agreed to send players north to strengthen the Van Dieman's Land XI.

Unfortunately, the official responsible for informing the Melbourne players of the acceptance of their challenge forgot to post the letter, and when the steamer from Port Phillip berthed in Launceston the welcoming players were dismayed to find that the Victorians were not on board. They had to be content that year of 1850 with playing a North Van Dieman's Land *v* South Van Dieman's Land match.

The following year the letter of acceptance got through and the Gentlemen of Van Dieman's Land looked a surprisingly smart outfit as they defeated the Gentlemen of Port Phillip by three wickets on 11 and 12 February at Launceston Oval. The Victorians blamed their defeat on the stormy passage they had had across Bass Strait, but most observers said the difference between the two sides was the shrewd captaincy of the heavily bearded Tasmanian 'keeper John Marshall, who was then in his 56th year. Marshall continued in these games until he was 58 and remains Australia's oldest first-class cricketer.

A return match was played in Melbourne in March 1852, on a pitch at South Yarra, and this time Victoria won by 61 runs. By the time they played the third match at Launceston, however, the friendly relations between the two teams had cooled. The Tasmanians objected to the Victorians fielding professionals, who were employed as ground bowlers in Melbourne. This conflict prevented further Tasmania *v* Victoria matches for four years and in this period the initial matches between Victoria and New South Wales began.

New South Wales first met Victoria on 26 March 1856, at Melbourne Cricket Ground (MCG), when New South Wales won by three wickets. First-class cricket reached Sydney on 14 January 1857, on the Sydney Domain, where New South Wales won the return match by 66 runs. The Domain remained the venue for Sydney's big matches until 1871, but the cricketers often had to fight for the right to play there against citizens who claimed it was public parkland.

No charge for admission could be made, although leading players of the colony enjoyed parading on the Domain with their ladies and the Governor invariably attended major games. Cows roamed free over this rough, uneven paddock and cowpats usually had to be removed before play could begin.

A remarkable feature of these early matches was the betting. The *Sydney Morning Herald* reported that £5000 changed hands when New South Wales won, including one bet of £1000 to £1600, astonishing sums when free settlers' wages were lucky to reach £100 a year.

The New South Wales Cricket Association (NSWCA) was formed at a meeting in the open on the Domain on 13 December 1859 and one of its first objectives was to find a more suitable ground for important matches. The search was still going on when H.H. Stephenson brought the first England touring team to Sydney early in 1862, and their meeting against XXII of New South Wales had to be played on the Domain.

The Melbourne Cricket Ground was already well-established on its site in Richmond Paddock when the Albert Ground opened in the Sydney suburb of Redfern on 29 October 1864. The Albert Ground was a magnificent venue, a favourite of W.G. Grace, fenced all round, possessing the best facilities for players and spectators, and in a central location.

Unfortunately, the Albert Ground was built as a money-making venture by a company which overcharged the NSWCA, causing them to restrict matches there and continue using the Domain. But by 1871 inter-Colonial matches had become so popular that the association was forced to move to the Albert Ground where all spectators had to pay.

After the winding-up of the company which owned the Albert Ground and the closure of that site, the NSWCA moved to a ground at Moore Park originally used as a rifle range by troops from nearby Victoria Barracks. The association renamed the Garrison Ground the Association Ground and opened it for special events in 1878 when Victoria met New South Wales.

Meanwhile the South Australian Cricket Association (SACA), aware that inter-Colonial cricket and matches against England teams flourished in neighbouring colonies, won a long struggle for control of the place that became Adelaide Oval. The first major match there was in March 1874, when W.G. Grace's English tourists agreed to extend their itinerary to play XXII of South Australia, whom they beat by seven wickets.

South Australia made its first visit to Melbourne in 1883 but were not judged strong enough to play on the Melbourne Cricket Ground and were relegated to the East Melbourne Ground, where Victoria defeated them by an innings and 98 runs.

Queensland cricketers could only envy the opening of major grounds in the south, enduring primitive conditions as their main matches moved from Eagle Farm to Queen's Park, Brisbane's Albert Ground, Breakfast Creek, Bowen Bridge Road and the Exhibition Ground, a natural amphitheatre built for agricultural shows but with poor facilities for cricket. First-class cricket arrived at the Exhibition Ground in April 1893 when Queensland beat New South Wales by 14 runs. Agricultural society members used their passes for free entry to Exhibition Ground cricket matches and this loss of revenue forced cricket officials to concentrate their activities on the Woolloongabba Ground. The Gabba, first used in 1895, took over as Brisbane's main arena in November 1931.

In Western Australia, the Association Ground at East Perth was opened for play on 3 February 1894 and soon became generally known as the WACA (pronounced 'Whacker'), but it was not until January 1906 that South Australia lost the initial first-class match there by 103 runs.

For a variety of reasons first-class cricket has also been played at Fremantle Oval; Unley Oval in Adelaide; South Melbourne; and on two Hobart grounds – the Railway Ground and (in 1987) lower down Mount Lofty at Bellerive. None of them are sites to delight lovers of leafy cricket fields.

Test cricket began in Australia in 1877 and in the seasons that have followed 248 Tests have been played on contrasting grounds, each with its own character, each a severe test of even the greatest players' skills and adaptability. In the late 1980s these are cricket fields for TV heroes, arenas rich with memories of brilliant feats, venues that have enhanced cricket's international prestige.

Today Australians like to think that no top-class cricketer's education is complete without a spin round the Australian Test circuit. The Gabba usually offers steamy tropical heat, and the likelihood of nasty black clouds suddenly appearing from the Pacific Ocean to hurl rain on surrounding galvanized-iron roofs with the sound of machine-gun fire. Before covered pitches were introduced, Gabba rainstorms could have the stumps floating in half an hour and later, when the sun came out, produce the most vicious 'sticky' wickets in Christendom.

Across the continent, further from the Gabba than London is from Moscow, the WACA Ground on the banks of the Swan River provides its own vagaries as to weather. Here the distinctive wind known as the Fremantle Doctor, which some say has its origins in far-away Durban, blows in from the Indian Ocean with soothing regularity to cool spectators and players and help swing bowlers and those seeking a little drift.

A few hours by air across the Great Australian Bight, Adelaide Oval, which surely must have been shaped by a rugby player, offers huge boundaries on the straight hit, short boundaries square of the wicket, and a background of cathedrals and gardens. Here the seagulls from St Vincent's Gulf and the Great Southern Ocean hold court on a ground that many consider the world's finest, rivalling even the fields of Worcester, Chesterfield or Cape Town for beauty.

There are plenty of gulls, too, on Melbourne Cricket Ground, a concrete mausoleum of enormous proportions that tests the game's biggest hitters and consistently produces cricket's biggest crowds. Melbourne was the birthplace of all Test cricket but today the MCG trees have gone, along with the grape vines that climbed over the wooden pavilions and the famous well into which W.G. Grace loved to drop a bucket to taste the icy cold water.

A far sadder loss has been the Sydney Hill, virtually replaced in the 1980s by a hideous electronic scoreboard, floodlight towers standing as dark and ugly witnesses over terrain that once attracted thousands to hear the unique voice of 'Yabba' (Stephen Harold Gascoigne) barracking players out on centre field. Australian cricket has paid a high price for progress, with only Adelaide Oval left among its established Test grounds with any claims to charm. Adelaide has a National Trust preservation order on its old world scoreboard which prevents administrators copying other States by erecting an electronic scoreboard and then deluging spectators with non-stop advertising.

Australia's newest Test ground, Bellerive Oval, across Bass Strait on the banks of the River

Derwent, provides some spectators with spectacular views right down to Bruny Island. Bellerive
staged its first Test on 16 December 1989 between
Australia and Sri Lanka. The ground boasts seven
small grandstands, an electronic scoreboard, 500
members and a hill that accommodates half the
ground's capacity of 15,000.

The five mainland Test grounds have stands
exclusively reserved for ground members who pay
big annual subscriptions for the privilege of watching big cricket. Melbourne has 51,200 members,
4400 of them women, and a 16-year waiting list;
Sydney has 20,000 members, including 1000
women, and a 13-year waiting list; Adelaide 9200
members, 500 of them women, and a 10-year
waiting list; Brisbane 9600 members, 6000 of them
from the Queensland Cricketers' Club and a two-
year waiting list; Perth 9300 members and a one-
year waiting list. Melbourne, Sydney and Perth
have lighting for night cricket, a facility lacking at
Adelaide and Brisbane.

Adelaide

ADELAIDE OVAL

Adelaide Oval is a delightful cricket venue, sitting
amid gardens and lovely trees in front of church
spirals with a serenity that belies its acrimonious
past. Overlooked by the purple peaks of the Mt
Lofty ranges, the ground ranks with Newlands in
Cape Town, one or two Caribbean grounds, and
the most charming English fields as the most
attractive in world cricket, but no other Australian
ground has endured as many bitter disputes as has
Adelaide since it opened in 1873.

The arguments started when the South Australian Cricket Association secretary H. Yorke
Sparks opened a public subscription to develop the
ground. Sparks marked out the boundaries – which
later became the official limits of the ground – with
surveyor H.M. Addison, bought some chain for
£17 which he donated to the association, and then
threaded the chain through iron stakes. Clearly,
Sparks could not cut or hook as the boundaries are
uncommonly short square of the wicket.

There was an immediate public outcry from citizens who claimed Sparks was infringing on parkland and the original lease stipulated that the SACA
could not charge for admission to the ground. John
Darling, whose son Joe later captained both South
Australia and Australia, introduced the Bill in the
State parliament to grant the association a lease on
12 acres for the oval. But after this was passed the
Adelaide city council demanded an annual rent too
high for the association to pay. A long, drawn-out
debate ended with the council settling for £7 per
annum for the first seven years and £14 per annum
thereafter for a further seven years.

A contract for ploughing, levelling and planting
was let to a Henry Copas at an estimated cost of
£85, but the work cost £190 and after protracted

argument in the courts the association was ordered to pay £157. There was just as long a debate over whether to plant couch, English clover or rye grasses on a surface that was mostly clay.

G.W. Gooden, the ground's first curator, was also a fine cricketer and he plunged into his duties with rare enthusiasm, gradually removing the thistles and weeds. Water was not laid on and he had to carry it from a single tap outside the fence to prepare the playing strip. The first match organized by the SACA, between British and Colonial-born teams, had to be played at St Peter's College on 11 November 1872 because the oval was not ready. The State government agreed to set aside £300 in 1873 to build a pavilion at the ground, but the SACA still depended heavily on the help of important citizens to pay its way. Gooden was layed off through the winter as the SACA could not afford his salary and the weeds grew undisturbed.

In 1874–75, 38 club matches were played on the ground, plus matches between Marrieds and Singles, British and Colonial-born. The feature of the season, however, was a match between XVIII of Adelaide and what was virtually the Victorian Second XI. Halfway through the second day conditions for this match became so bad that players got between the shafts of a roller and hauled it up and down to flatten out bad bumps in the pitch.

Near the end of that season the sponsors of the tour of Australia by W.G. Grace's England team offered to play the final tour match in Adelaide. The association hesitated over whether it could afford the £800 guarantee requested by the sponsors and while they were working on their finances the cricket club at Kadina, a hundred miles down Yorke Peninsula, stepped in and put up the money. England won a farcical match against XXII of Kadina by an innings and 9 runs in the most primitive conditions Grace said he ever encountered.

The SACA sent emissaries to Kadina to invite England to add another match to their tour. Having completed his agreed 14 matches for his sponsors, Grace felt free to negotiate independently for the Adelaide appearance and the parties settled for £110 plus half the gate receipts. This was the first major promotion on Adelaide Oval and the first involving an overseas team.

The SACA coaxed the government to declare a

public holiday for the second day of the match. Twenty-Two of South Australia made 63 and 82, England 108 and 73 for 3 to win by seven wickets. Grace was given out with his score at 6 when Alexander Crooks dashed around the boundary and took a spectacular one-handed catch before falling over the chains. Argument ensued when Grace claimed the ball had been caught on the far side of the chains but the umpires held firm and Grace departed. The SACA made £300 profit from the match and Crooks was promoted to general manager of the Commercial Bank of South Australia. He proved to be a better fieldsman than a banker: he was sent to prison for fraud.

The first inter-Colonial match on Adelaide Oval saw South Australia (182) defeat Tasmania (72 and 97) by an innings and 13 runs on 10 and 11 November 1877. Victoria appeared on the ground for the first time in 1881 when they defeated South Australia by 151 runs, scoring 191 and 174 to 163 and 51. The following year South Australia (119 and 200) surprised even their most ardent supporters by beating Victoria (106 and 182) by 31 runs. But the first Test on Adelaide Oval, from 12 to 16 December 1884, was only the fifth first-class match at the ground. Billy Murdoch's 1884 team, the fourth white Australian side to tour England, were joined on their voyage home by the eighth England team to visit Australia, captained by Arthur Shrewsbury. The Australian side was regarded as a powerful outfit and a keen contest was expected but only Percy McDonnell, Jack Blackham and George Giffen arrived in time for serious practice before this, the 17th Test.

There was consternation when the Australians demanded half the gate takings and threatened not to play when they were offered 30 per cent. They then offered to play for 40 per cent of the takings if the extra 10 per cent went to charity. This was

also rejected and when it seemed that the match would be abandoned the SACA gambled by agreeing to pay both teams £450 each. The Australians accepted this but the Englishmen were disgusted, believing their higher tour expenses entitled them to a larger share than their opponents.

Argument continued when Fred Spofforth disagreed with his Australian team-mates and withdrew from the match. Murdoch then increased the tension by refusing to allow James Lillywhite or Alfred Shaw, England's managers, to umpire despite their long experience. There was no time to get an experienced umpire from Sydney or Melbourne and the SACA had to use locals I. Fisher and J. Travers. Some of their decisions further upset the players.

Percy McDonnell scored his second successive Test century (124) when cricket replaced disputation and at 220 for 4 Australia seemed strongly placed at the end of the first day. Then Billy Bates took five wickets and Australia were all out for only 243. England replied with 369, William Barnes, the Nottinghamshire batsman, contributing 134. Barnes survived thunderstorms before lunch and after lunch had to lie down on the pitch with the rest of the players while a ferocious dust storm passed over the ground. With England leading by 126, McDonnell appeared likely to hit his team out of trouble, rushing to 83 at better than a run a minute before Giffen, troubled by lumbago, ran him out. Giffen struggled to 47 but with Alick Bannerman absent hurt, Australia folded for 197. England scored the 66 needed to win for the loss of two wickets. The Australians continued their demands for 50 per cent of the gate for the next Test at Melbourne but this time the Victorian Cricketers' Association, promoters of the match, refused and a completely new Australian side had to take the field and be soundly beaten.

George Giffen, a clean-living postman, was Adelaide Oval's first authentic hero but he suffered from the delusion that selectors mistreated his brother Walt. George sometimes refused to play for sides that omitted Walter and even dropped out of tours to England because his brother was not selected. The truth was that Walter was not in the same class as George, who headed the South Australian batting averages seven times between 1887–88 and 1902–03 and topped the bowling averages 11 times. George toured England five times, refused to tour twice when selected, but Walter only went once.

George Giffen gave the finest display of his career at Adelaide Oval in 1891–92 when he scored 271 for South Australia against Victoria and then took 16 wickets for 166 runs, a feat noted English cricket historian Harry Altham said was 'surely the greatest all-round performance in recorded cricket history of any class'. Giffen, a right-arm off-spinner, took five wickets or more in an innings 48 times. He captained Australia in four of his 31 Tests, but was so used to carrying the entire South Australian attack that he proved a poor national captain. To George, changing the bowling meant that he switched ends.

While George Giffen, the Jarvis brothers, the Victorian-born Slight brothers, Alick and Bill, and the Gooden brothers, Henry and Jim, did their best to promote South Australian cricket on the field, they were supported behind the scenes by a dynamic character named John Creswell. From 1883 to 1902 as secretary of the SACA, Creswell worked tirelessly for the improvement of Adelaide Oval and during his term new stands and gardens were built.

Creswell was responsible for bringing the English professional Jesse Hide to Adelaide for five years as coach to the SACA at a cost of £200 a year. Hide, born at Eastbourne, played for Sussex in 1876 and 1877 before he moved to Adelaide. He was a steady right-hand batsman, an outstanding field at point, and a useful right-arm fast-medium bowler, but he also had a thorough knowledge of the preparation of pitches which proved invaluable to Adelaide Oval curators. At a time when some Australian groundsmen used rollers made of wood, Hide had to convince groundstaff they would not bruise the turf by rolling it.

In the 1880s and 1890s, Creswell's belief that great players would emerge if they were given top-class pitches proved correct. A steady flow of superb cricketers began their careers at Adelaide Oval. There was Jack Lyons, a spectacular hitter, who first played for South Australia in 1884–85 and toured England three times; Clem Hill, one of the greatest left-hand batsmen, who made his State debut in 1892–93; Joe Darling, another left-hander of the highest quality who followed Hill into the State team in 1893–94; and the irrepressible fast bowler Ernie Jones, who made his debut in the same season as Hill and later became famous for bowling a delivery through W.G. Grace's beard. Between them they brought colourful cricket to Adelaide Oval and gave South Australia strength that was unexpected in such a thinly populated State. Hill made 45 first-class centuries after prodigious scoring as a schoolboy for Prince Alfred College, Adelaide, for whom he once made 360 retired. He was Australia's worst 'nervous nineties' victim, with scores of 96, 97, 98, 98 and 99 in Tests against England. In the Third Test at Adelaide in 1901–02, England's John Tyldesley tried to persuade Hill to continue batting as he walked off on 98. 'Go back, Clem, I took that catch standing on the cycling track,' said Tyldesley. Hill kept going towards the pavilion, explaining to Tyldesley that the captains had agreed the fence and not the bike track that ringed the field should be the boundary. Hill made 97 in the second innings of that match, his third successive Test dismissal in the 90s.

Joe Darling was 14 when he scored 252 for Prince Alfred College against St Peter's on Adelaide Oval in 1885, batting for six hours. Joe was the sixth son of Hon. John Darling MP, the South Australian grain king. John Darling at first objected to Joe's addiction to cricket and sent him to manage one of the family's wheat farms when Joe finished school. But when Joe returned to Adelaide and forced his way into the State and Australian teams John became his biggest fan.

Thrilled by Joe's innings of 178 on Adelaide Oval in the Third Test against Stoddart's England team in 1897–98, the elder Darling went to the dressing-room and gave Joe a cheque representing a pound for every run he had scored. John Darling followed his son round Australia's other major grounds but Joe scored so well that his father reduced his cheques to a pound for every run *over* 100. 'Have to be a bit canny with Joe – he bats better when the silver is up,' he said.

Adelaide Oval regulars argued for hours over whether Hill or Darling was a better cricketer. The record suggests that Clem was the superior batsman with 17,216 first-class runs to his credit at 43.47, including four double-centuries, highest score 365 not out on Adelaide Oval in 1900–01 when he hit an eight and 35 fours. Darling made 10,637 runs at 34.42, with 21 first-class centuries, top score 210, but he also made a major contribution as Australia's captain on three of his four tours of England. Joe toured in 1896 and as skipper in 1899, 1902 and 1905.

When Jesse Hide left to return to England, Charlie Checkett took over as curator at Adelaide Oval. Checkett took advice from Clem Hill, a noted authority on horseflesh, when the mare that pulled

The first grandstand at Adelaide Oval, opened in November 1882. The horse is long-serving Queenie.

the Oval roller had to be replaced and bought a huge animal named Queenie. He was well advised, for Queenie remained in the job for more than a quarter of a century. John Creswell was always buzzing in and out of the ground in between his duties in rifle shooting, lawn bowls, manager of the company that built Plympton greyhound track, secretary of the Adelaide Chamber of Commerce, secretary of the Wine Growers' Association and South Australia's representative to the English Board of Trade. It was Creswell who suggested that Checkett set aside a marquee for smokers at the Oval, which one newspaper commented was 'very popular among those addicted to the weed'. No wonder they named an Adelaide Oval stand after Creswell.

Towards the end of his career with South Australia, when he took over from Darling as captain, Clem Hill often had the Adelaide Oval curator Alby Wright in his team. Wright had served his apprenticeship at the Adelaide Oval under Charlie Checkett, where he bowled at the nets to the State team twice a week. He became such a skilful right-arm leg-break bowler that he was often drafted into the State team in a period when the side was desperately short of bowlers. He first turned out for South Australia in Adelaide on a pitch he had helped prepare in December 1905 against New South Wales. He took 5 for 150 from 40.2 overs. His good form continued and he took 5 for 42 in 1906–07 against Victoria and 6 for 91 against New South Wales.

Wright took 106 first-class wickets at 30.81, but he was most famous for his ineptitude with the bat. In 1905–06 he established a world record for unsuccessful batting by scoring six successive ducks. The roars that resounded around Adelaide Oval when Alby got off the mark surpassed those reserved for century-makers. He dropped out of the State side in 1909–10 claiming that playing cricket interfered with his duties as a curator, but in 1910–11 he was pressed into service again. When South Australia opened the bowling with him at Sydney against New South Wales, Alby took 5 for 75 and 6 for 103. He retired for good at the end of the 1911–12 season to look after his pitches and to take care of Queenie, the mare in the specially padded boots. Alby was quite upset when Queenie had to be replaced by a motorized roller.

South Australia was fortunate in those years before the First World War to have the services of the distinguished English all-rounder John Neville Crawford. With a brilliant Test career ahead of him, Crawford quarrelled with the Surrey committee who barred him from playing county cricket with their side. Crawford took a job teaching at St Peter's College in Adelaide and had five superb seasons in the South Australian side.

Crawford's father, a parson, and his two brothers, R.T. and V.F.S. Crawford, were all noted for their big hitting and in Adelaide Crawford did not let the family reputation down. He was a magnificent driver of the ball and many of his best front-foot shots cleared the long boundaries at the far ends of the Adelaide Oval. None of the Adelaide Oval regulars were surprised when Crawford put on 289 in 69 minutes with Victor Trumper in 1914 for an Australian XI against South Canterbury in New Zealand.

At Adelaide in 1911–12, Crawford made 110 at a run a minute for South Australia against an England attack comprising Sydney Barnes, Frank Foster, Wilfred Rhodes, Jack Hearne and Frank Woolley. At Adelaide in 1911–12 he made 126 for South Australia against Victoria, and at Adelaide in 1912–13 he made 163 against Victoria. Crawford also had five wickets in an innings six times on the Adelaide ground, best figures 8 for 86 against Victoria in 1912–13.

After the First World War Clarence Everard ('Nip') Pellew, one of four Pellews to play for South Australia, gave Adelaide Oval fans plenty to applaud whether he was fielding or batting. 'Nip' was without peer in the outfield, picking up and throwing on the turn with such vigour that he frequently tore the heels from his boots. A right-hand middle-order batsman, he scored a century in the lunch to tea session in March 1920 for South Australia against Victoria on his way to a score of 271.

Just as impressive an athlete was Vic Richardson, who had 20 seasons in the South Australian team, making his debut in 1918–19. Richardson represented his State in five sports. He was one of cricket's greatest fieldsmen and his aggressive right-hand batting featured a superb hook shot. After he retired they named the Richardson Gates, near where his hook shots used to land, in his honour.

Richardson captained South Australia from 1921 until 1935 when Don Bradman took over. Any doubts about Bradman's popularity at Adelaide Oval were dispelled when in his first three innings

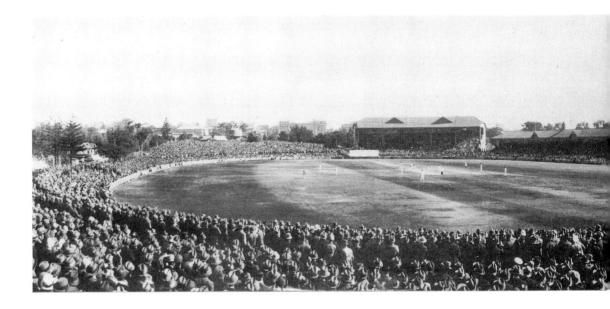

for South Australia he scored 117, 233 and 357 –
he added 109 before lunch on the second day.
Bradman's 369 for South Australia against Tasmania in 1936, including 356 in 181 minutes for
the third wicket, remains the highest score on the
ground.

Bradman's prolific scoring in England in 1930
(974 runs in seven Test innings at 139.14), in Australia in 1930–31 against West Indies (447 runs at
74.50), and against South Africa in 1931–32 (808
runs at 202.00) caused critics to claim that he would
ruin cricket. One expert suggested that he should
be credited with 100 without having to bat.
Between September 1931 and August 1932 he
scored well over 7000 runs at an average of well
over 100, most of them in non-first-class matches,
but he was in such dominating form that England's
chances in the 1932–33 series in Australia obviously
depended on curbing his scoring.

Douglas Jardine's solution was Bodyline. This
unfair method of attack in which batsmen protected
themselves against persistent bouncers at the risk
of edging the ball to a packed legside field created

Some 37,000 spectators – all, apparently, in hats – watching the second day's play of the Fourth Test against England on 2 February 1929.

such ill-feeling that players on both sides barely
spoke to each other. The first two Tests saw the
Australians badly knocked about as the anger of
Australian players and spectators grew.

The climax to the whole sorry affair came in the
Third Test at Adelaide after the Australian captain
Bill Woodfull had been struck over the heart and
Bert Oldfield's skull was fractured. The entire
future of international cricket was at stake as the
Australian and English cricket authorities
exchanged ill-worded cables. Diplomats became
involved in Whitehall. The feeling was so intense
that the Australian Prime Minister's office in
Canberra had fears that in the midst of a crippling
economic Depression English loans to Australia
would not be renewed.

On the Saturday of the Adelaide Test 50,962
people crammed into the ground, with mounted
policemen circling the Oval to prevent them invad-

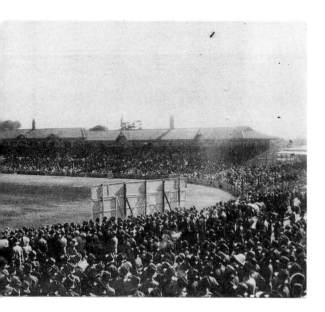

ing the field. This remains the largest crowd ever in Adelaide and all of them seemed emotionally involved. Finally the Australian Board of Control withdrew charges of unsportsmanlike conduct against Jardine's players and the MCC in turn agreed not to cancel the tour. Today the bitterness of that spiteful Test has gone but the puzzle of how more than 50,000 people ever squeezed into the ground remains.

Adelaide Oval has always favoured batsmen rather than bowlers, but Clarrie Grimmett, Bill O'Reilly and Ashley Mallett all had some of their biggest coups there. Grimmett was such a consistent wicket-taker on Adelaide Oval that he finished his career with an incredible 669 wickets for South Australia, twice as many as the next best effort for the State. George Giffen (1887–88 *v* England), Henry Hay (1902–03 *v* Lord Hawke's XI), Len Pascoe (1980–81, for NSW *v* South Australia), Wayne Prior (1975–76 *v* NSW), Donnell Robins (1965–66 *v* NSW), Andrew Sincock (1977–78 *v* India), and Merv Waite (1935–36 *v* MCC) all took hat-tricks on the ground.

Leslie O'Brien Fleetwood-Smith, an expert at imitating magpie calls and in producing unplayable deliveries, had the honour of bowling the finest ball ever seen at Adelaide Oval, however, when he scattered Wally Hammond's stumps at a crucial stage of the Fourth Test against Australia in 1936–37. The ball pitched 18 inches outside the off stump and struck middle and leg stumps, enabling Australia to draw level in the five-Test series after being 0–2 down.

Since the Second World War Adelaide's tradition of mayhem has been continued by the Chappell brothers and more recently by David Hookes and Wayne Phillips. They breed fine cricketers in Adelaide but often they have short fuses. Ian Chappell endured several suspensions by the SACA and to hear him on television discussing Hookes's larrikinism is to realize how knowledgeable he is on the subject.

Hookes remains one of the greatest 'eye' players in cricket, regularly defying coaching manuals to thrash an attack. Nothing more spectacular has been seen at Adelaide than Hookes's century in 43 minutes from 34 deliveries for South Australia against Victoria in 1982–83 – unless it was Hookes's 462-run fourth-wicket stand with Wayne Phillips against Tasmania in 1986–87. They batted for 299 minutes to set a record for any wicket in Australian first-class cricket. Hookes took 336 from 330 balls, with 40 fours and 2 sixes, Phillips 213 from 253 balls with 30 fours and 1 six.

The SACA opened the new Creswell Stand at the start of the 1989–90 Australian summer. This stand has been built to conform with the other buildings on the ground, all of them part of a government heritage register, at a cost of $8.5 million. The Creswell Stand features 34 corporate boxes over two levels, and includes an air-conditioned public restaurant. For the first time since the ground was built, the media will be able to look straight down the wicket, instead of from square leg or point.

Adelaide				
Ref/No	*Season*	*V*	*T*	*Result*
17/1	1884–85	E	1	E-8w
37/2	1891–92	E	3	E-I&230
44/3	1894–95	E	3	A-382
55/4	1897–98	E	3	A-I&13
67/5	1901–02	E	3	A-4w
80/6	1903–04	E	3	A-216
98/7	1907–08	E	3	A-245
113/8	1910–11	SA	3	SA-38
118/9	1911–12	E	3	E-7w
137/10	1920–21	E	3	A-119
160/11	1924–25	E	3	A-11
179/12	1928–29	E	4	E-12
199/13	1930–31	WI	1	A-10w
215/14	1931–32	SA	4	A-10w
222/15	1932–33	E	3	E-338
258/16	1936–37	E	4	A-148
282/17	1946–47	E	4	Draw
293/18	1947–48	I	4	A-I&16
330/19	1950–51	E	4	A-274
346/20	1951–52	WI	3	WI-6w
363/21	1952–53	SA	4	Draw
394/22	1954–55	E	4	E-5w
467/23	1958–59	E	4	A-10w
505/24	1960–61	WI	4	Draw
538/25	1962–63	E	4	Draw
551/26	1963–64	SA	4	SA-10w
600/27	1965–66	E	4	A-I&9
624/28	1967–68	I	1	A-146
645/29	1968–69	WI	4	Draw
678/30	1970–71	E	6	Draw
708/31	1972–73	P	1	A-I&114
730/32	1973–74	NZ	3	A-I&57
754/33	1974–75	E	5	A-163
768/34	1975–76	WI	5	A-190
793/35	1976–77	P	1	Draw
813/36	1977–78	I	5	A-47
838/37	1978–79	E	5	E-205
871/38	1979–80	WI	3	WI-408
895/39	1980–81	I	3	I-59
920/40	1981–82	WI	3	WI-5w
940/41	1982–83	E	3	A-8w
972/42	1983–84	P	3	Draw
999/43	1984–85	WI	3	WI-191
1032/44	1985–86	I	1	Draw
1060/45	1986–87	E	3	Draw
1088/46	1987–88	NZ	2	Draw
1114/47	1988–89	WI	5	Draw

Australia: P 47, W 21, D 12, L 14

Brisbane
EXHIBITION GROUND WOOLLOONGABBA

Queensland cricket found its headquarters in the suburb of Woolloongabba after a long search. Matches involving the State team were played at Eagle Farm, Breakfast Creek, Bowen Bridge Road, the Exhibition Ground and other inferior venues before five hectares of ground were dedicated as the Brisbane Cricket Ground and the Queensland Cricket Association (QCA) found a home.

The QCA, painfully aware that teams visiting Brisbane from the south endured primitive conditions, imported Merri Creek soil from Victoria for the Gabba pitches, and deposited thousands of tons of local soil around the outfield. Grandstands were built of wood, a fence installed to circle the ground, and by 26 November 1897 the ground was ready for its first international match between XIII of Queensland and New South Wales and A.E. Stoddart's touring England team.

Seven of the 13 players who opposed England in this match were from New South Wales, but the player with the best pedigree was Marmaduke Francis Ramsay, an old Harrovian who played for MCC in 1894 and was related to W.G. Grace. Ramsay played most of his cricket in Toowoomba but sent his two sons to Harrow. The English batsmen showed that the Gabba pitch was as good as any in the colonies by scoring 636, Archie MacLaren contributing 181 and the former Cambridge University captain Norman Druce 126. George Hirst (75 not out), John Mason (74) and Prince Ranjitsinhji (67) also got amongst the runs. Tom McKibbin took 5 for 158 with his off-breaks for the locals, who scored 316 for 8 when time ran out on the third day, Syd Gregory scoring 77 and Sam Jones 69.

Test cricket was confined to Sydney, Melbourne

The Gabba in November 1897 during its first international match between XIII of Queensland and New South Wales and Stoddart's England team.

and Adelaide at that time as New South Wales, Victoria and South Australia were the foundation teams when the Sheffield Shield competition began in 1892–93. But when the Australian Board of Control was formed in 1905 South Australia refused to join, arguing that the Board was not truly representative of Australian cricket. The MCC at Lord's accepted Australian captain Joe Darling's advice that the Board did not have the players' support and declined to send a team to Australia in 1906–07. The Board was forced to postpone the tour while it redoubled its efforts to persuade South Australia to join.

Darling remained adamant that unless players had financial control of overseas tours, they would forfeit all their rights by joining the Board. Queensland joined the Board on 22 September 1905, accepting a promise from Board delegates that Brisbane would get a Test when English teams toured Australia. This may have made the Board look more representative but it did not help Queensland cricketers who were denied a place in the Sheffield Shield competition until 1926–27 and did not get a Test in Brisbane until 1928–29.

In its years in the wilderness Queensland cricket suffered immense harm because the QCA simply could not provide enough first-class cricket to satisfy talented Queensland cricketers. Toowoomba-born Jack Cuffe went off to Worcestershire, Alan Marshall, the brilliant all-rounder from Warwick, to Surrey, and Dr Robbie McDonald to Leicestershire. Even Arthur Coningham, the first player chosen from the Queensland side to play for Australia (in 1894–95 at Melbourne), and the first to score a century for Queensland, deserted to play for New South Wales.

The first Queensland-born cricketer chosen to play for Australia (Coningham was born in Melbourne) was 'Ginger' McLaren, the fast-medium bowler who took 1 for 140 in his sole Test in 1912. But the man who really established Queensland's reputation at Test level was Roger Hartigan, who made 48 and 116 on his Test debut in 1907–08 against England, putting on 243 in the second innings with Clem Hill.

After that knock Hartigan found himself the leading advocate for Brisbane's bid to stage a Test. For 20 years Hartigan and his fellow Queensland

Brisbane's first Test in progress on the Exhibition Ground, 1 December 1928.

delegate, stubborn, flamboyant Jack Hutcheon, debated their case at Board of Control meetings. They faced formidable opposition from southern States who, in the days before regular airline travel, were worried about the time and expense involved in playing in Brisbane. Year after year the southern States withheld Queensland's entry into the Sheffield Shield because the QCA could not provide pitches that would last four days.

The breakthrough came in 1926–27, following years of protest meetings in Brisbane, when Queensland was granted Shield status. But instead of staging their first Shield matches at the Gabba, where they had spent a fortune improving facilities, the QCA put the game on at the Exhibition Ground, home of the State's biggest agricultural shows. The Exhibition Ground, a natural amphitheatre, had several thousand more seats than the Gabba.

Queensland's initial Shield match against NSW at the Exhibition Ground proved a thriller, with Queensland captain Leo O'Brien run out for 196 when his side were only 8 runs short of scoring the 400 needed to win. In the return match in Sydney the following week O'Connor made 103 and 143 not out and was carried shoulder-high from the field as Queensland recorded their first Shield win, defeating NSW by five wickets.

Queensland's first Test, 23 years after being promised one by the Board, was held on 30 November 1928 at the Exhibition Ground. This was also Don Bradman's first Test, a match that was a disaster for Australia with Jack Gregory's knee finally giving way and Charles Kelleway going out of Test cricket with food poisoning. Larwood took 6 for 32 in Australia's first innings of 122 and J.C. ('Farmer') White 4 for 7 in Australia's second innings of 66, England wining by 675 runs. Bradman made 223 next time he appeared in a Brisbane Test. Australia won this time at the Exhibition Ground by an innings and 217 runs against the West Indies in 1930–31.

These two Tests proved Brisbane could successfully stage big cricket but they provided unsatisfactory returns for the QCA. Too many spectators got in free by using their agricultural society badges. To ensure bigger returns the QCA moved permanently to the Gabba, which had its introduction to Test cricket on 27 November 1931 with the first of the Australia *v* South Africa matches. Bradman made 226, still the highest Test score in Brisbane, as Australia scored 450. South Africa were caught on a vicious 'sticky' wicket and managed only 170 and 117 in reply. Australia won by an innings and 163 runs.

The Gabba in the decade before the Second World War was a strange cricket venue, noted for the generous use of barbed wire to prevent patrons on the outer ground mixing with members. Facilities were as backward as the thinking of QCA officials under the iron control of president Jack Hutcheon.

Hutcheon was responsible for having the celebrated English Test batsman C.B. Fry barred from the members' stand and the English dressing-room during the 1936–37 England-Australia series on the grounds that he was a journalist. Fry was writing special commentaries on the match for English newspapers. Hutcheon used to force paid officials of the QCA to eat facing the wall in the Gabba dining-room because he did not want them looking out on his guests.

Hutcheon, a QC whose nickname was 'Czar Czar', never learned from his mistakes or the hammering he took from the media. In 1947–48 he was in trouble again when the touring Indian cricketers were denied admission to parts of the Gabba pavilion because of their colour. Then he tried to deny Harold Larwood admission to the ground as a reporter. 'Twenty years too late,' quipped Neville Cardus, mindful of Larwood's role in the Bodyline series in 1932–33.

The Gabba Test in the Bodyline series was, of course, one of cricket's most memorable affairs, with the advantage passing from one team to the other throughout the six days. With England in trouble at 225 for 7 chasing Australia's 340, Eddie Paynter left hospital where he had been confined to bed with tonsillitis to bat for four hours for 83. Later he struck the six which won the match for England and regained the Ashes. Temperatures soared past 100 degrees every day of this epic.

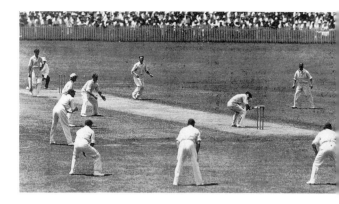

Bill Woodfull at the receiving end of a Larwood bouncer during the Bodyline series of 1932–33.

Bill O'Reilly later wrote that 'Dainty' Ironmonger, who bowled 78 overs in the match, was near collapse after ten overs but pluckily kept going to the end of the day, eyes glazed, unsure of his balance. 'Dainty' was then 50 years old, a heavily built man, $15\frac{1}{2}$ stone, six feet tall, who wore pieces of rubber tubing about six inches wide around each thigh, elastic knee guards, two pairs of socks and boots with soles an inch thick.

When the Australians came off after a day in the fierce tropical heat, O'Reilly and Ironmonger slumped down in their sopping wet gear, unable to get themselves into the showers. Stan McCabe suggested a glass of cold champagne might revive them. Captain Bill Woodfull agreed and sent room attendant Sid Redgrave out for a bottle with instructions to charge it to the Board of Control. Redgrave returned empty-handed, saying that Hutcheon refused to have alcohol in the dressing-room. Woodfull, a parson's son who never drank, was enraged at this and stormed out with Redgrave, returning with a cold bottle.

Some fine cricketers had to put up with Hutcheon and his nonsense. Ron Oxenham, an intense student of the game, bowled his heart out for Queensland from the time he came into the side in 1911–12 but did not get a Test chance until 1928 when he was 38. Consistently impressive displays from Ron and his brother Lionel, F.C. Thompson, Alec Hurwood, Leo O'Connor and Percy Hornibrook made Queensland a hard side to beat. Ron Oxenham died in pain after a car smash at the age of 40 showing visitors to the hospital a new grip he had perfected for his off-break.

Other Gabba favourites in the 1930s were Glen Baker, an all-rounder who was so keen he practised with all six Townsville clubs as a teenager; Geoff Cook, who put on 265 with Bill Brown against New South Wales in 1938–39 in Queensland's highest opening stand; Rex Rogers, a left-hander with forearms so powerful his square cut was known to smash paling fences; and a young wicket-keeper from Bundaberg with a swiftness in stumping that defied the eye, Don Tallon, a bewildering omission from the Australian side that toured England in 1938.

Immediately after the war England toured Australia before she had properly recovered, under the captaincy of Wally Hammond, with the praiseworthy notion that restoring international cricket was more important than the outcome. Hammond was well past his best and the selectors had given him an unbalanced team. Australia had only Bradman, Hassett, Barnes and Brown left from the 1938 side and what should have been a tightly fought series all came undone in the First Test.

Half an hour after rain began to fall at the Gabba the stumps were floating and the entire field was inches under water. In the press-box the rain beat on the galvanized-iron roof like artillery shelling. Australia had scored 645 before the rain, thanks to a 276-run stand by Bradman and Hassett for the third wicket, embellished by a brilliant 79 from Miller and a 95 that was full of lovely strokes

from McCool. Miller completed a superb double by taking 7 for 60 in England's first innings of 141 after the weather cleared. Toshack had 6 for 82 in the second innings of 172. Hammond's last tour never recovered: Australia won that rubber 3–0.

The Gabba's reputation for providing wicked 'sticky' wickets was further enlarged in the following series against India. Bradman, who had taken Toshack out and shown him where to pitch the ball on the gluepot against Hammond's side, had no need to do that when India were caught on a similar pitch. Toshack took 5 for 2 and 6 for 29. Australia won by an innings and 226 runs after Bradman had punished the poor Indians before he was out hit-wicket for 185.

Gabba crowds were captivated in this period by the emergence of a left-handed batsman who seldom hit the ball but relied on deflections, a gum-chewing individualist who made runs with squirts rather than strokes, and, above all, was marvellously impervious to critics and coaches. This was Kenneth Donald ('Slasher') Mackay, who scored a lot of his 23 first-class centuries on the Gabba. Ian Peebles, noted English critic, wrote of him: 'Most of his strokes are largely of his own invention, one particularly fascinating when the half-volley is half cut, half trapped, so that it spurts past cover like an apple pip playfully squeezed from finger to thumb.'

'Slasher' often had as his team-mate in his Gabba endeavours a wonderful humorist named Vincent Norman Raymer, commonly known as 'Mick' or 'Possum', a left-arm bowler of medium-pace spin and a spectacular hitter, who was deaf, the result of an infection picked up in his Pacific Islands war service. When his captain Bill Brown sent out instruction to 'have a go for the light', Raymer did not hear the last three words and swished at every ball, scoring a whirlwind half-century. He once

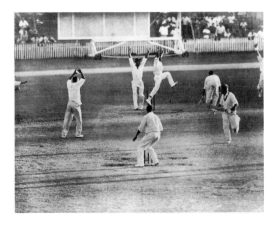

The climax of the tied Test of 1960–61: Ian Meckiff is run out by a throw from West Indian Joe Solomon off the seventh ball of the final over.

clubbed sixes off what he thought were no-balls called by an umpire who was only grunting.

In the days before Queensland entered the Sheffield Shield competition, Victor Trumper hit four sixes and 25 fours in an innings of 207 not out at the Gabba in May 1906. This became the benchmark for big-hitting at the ground. One of Trumper's sixes went into Stanley Street outside the ground. The next player to land a shot in Stanley Street was the English exile J.N. Crawford, who did it for an Australian XI against England in the 1911–12 summer.

The Gabba did not experience anything like this until Cec Pepper hit seven sixes out of the ground in an innings of 81 for NSW against Queensland in November 1939. One of Pepper's blows landed in Vulture Street, two in Stanley Street. Inside a year the Victorian fast bowler Barry Scott took up the challenge and struck a ball into Vulture Street against Queensland.

The mayhem continued at the Gabba after the Second World War. In the 1946–47 England-Australia Test, Keith Miller hit a no-ball from leg-

spinner Doug Wright on to the top of the old members' stand. That was the Test in which Arthur Mailey, confined to the press-box by barbed wire, sent a telegram to the English manager asking for the reason Denis Compton had left the field. Back came the reply within minutes: 'Natural causes.'

Colin McCool and Don Tallon formed a formidable Gabba combination in those years. Lifting a foot to play a McCool spinner was a dangerous exercise with Tallon behind the stumps. McCool was one of a long list of cricketers from the south who went to Queensland to further their Test claims when they could not be certain of a place in sides fielded by their home States. Sam Trimble, born at Lismore in northern NSW, played for NSW Colts but could not make the NSW senior team and he went to Queensland in 1959–60. He had 17 seasons in the Queensland side, appearing in 133 matches for the State, scoring 22 centuries and two double-centuries.

Garry Sobers, during an innings of 196 at the Gabba in January 1963, took advantage of the ground's short boundaries and then lofted John Mackay over the roof of the Leslie Wilson Stand, across Vulture Street into a service station opposite the ground. But probably the most sustained exhibition of big hitting ever seen at the Gabba came in the opening stand of 328 in 1968–69 by Colin Milburn and Derek Chadwick for Western Australia against Queensland. Milburn, an 18-stoner, started quietly, scoring 61 out of 92 by lunch on the first day. After lunch he set about the Queensland bowlers, scoring 181 off 134 balls by tea. He was out in the first over after tea, having hit 38 fours and lofted four sixes out into the street.

The only Queenslander who could match that kind of hitting was burly Peter Burge, who made 24 of his 38 first-class centuries for his State. His retirement left a big gap in the Queensland batting

The Gabba in the 1980s, viewed from the Vulture Street end. Further planned developments include the demolishing of The Hill (bottom left).

up. In 1988 plans were announced to build an international sporting complex with an adjoining top-class hotel at the ground. This will involve tearing down a police station and school, lengthening the ground and encircling it with new stands, relocating the greyhound track, and demolishing The Hill. A new bridge will cross a major road to bring customers into the ground. It will all cost millions of dollars – but that's the way they do things in Queensland.

line-up which officials have since tried to fill by importing players like Greg Chappell and Allan Border from the south. Both have treated Gabba spectators to some wonderful innings.

Strangely, for such a small ground, the Gabba has been very kind to bowlers. Geoff Dymock, whose 309 wickets was a record for Queensland, had some of his best days there. Tom Veivers, Phil Carlson, Malcolm Franke, Carl Rackemann and Jeff Thomson all returned outstanding analyses at the Gabba. But the best figures ever achieved at the ground were in the 1985–86 Test between Australia and New Zealand when Richard Hadlee had 9 for 60 in the first innings and finished the match with 15 for 123. The biggest crowd to attend a match at the Gabba was the 30,598 who turned up on the Saturday of the 1936–37 England-Australia Test. The only other time a Gabba crowd reached 30,000 was in 1954–55 for the Saturday of the England v Australia Test. Since then a greyhound racing track has been laid down inside the fence, reducing the spectator capacity but improving the solvency.

For over a century the Gabba has been a ground where buildings are always coming down or going

Brisbane				
Ref/No	Season	V	T	Result
Exhibition Ground				
176/1	1928–29	E	1	E-675
201/2	1930–31	WI	3	A-I&217
Woolloongabba				
212/3	1931–32	SA	1	A-I&163
223/4	1932–33	E	4	E-6w
255/5	1936–37	E	1	E-322
279/6	1946–47	E	1	A-I&332
290/7	1947–48	I	1	A-I&226
327/8	1950–51	E	1	A-70
344/9	1951–52	WI	1	A-3w
360/10	1952–53	SA	1	A-96
391/11	1954–55	E	1	A-I&154
464/12	1958–59	E	1	A-8w
502/13	1960–61	WI	1	Tied
535/14	1962–63	E	1	Draw
548/15	1963–64	SA	1	Draw
597/16	1965–66	E	1	Draw
626/17	1967–68	I	3	A-39
642/18	1968–69	WI	1	WI-125
674/19	1970–71	E	1	Draw
750/20	1974–75	E	1	A-166
764/21	1975–76	WI	1	A-8w
809/22	1977–78	I	1	A-16
834/23	1978–79	E	1	E-7w
867/24	1979–80	WI	1	Draw
890/25	1980–81	NZ	1	A-10w
910/26	1981–82	P	2	A-10w
939/27	1982–83	E	2	A-7w
971/28	1983–84	P	2	Draw
998/29	1984–85	WI	2	WI-8w
1029/30	1985–86	NZ	1	NZ-I&41
1058/31	1986–87	E	1	E-7w
1087/32	1987–88	NZ	1	A-9w
1110/33	1988–89	WI	1	WI-9w
1132/34	1989–90	SL	1	Draw

Australia: P 34, W 17, D 7, L 9, Tied 1

Hobart

BELLERIVE OVAL

Although it has been the last Australian State to be given a Test match, Tasmania played a valuable pioneering role in the early years of the 19th century when it was known as Van Dieman's Land. Indeed, it had the honour of staging Australia's initial first-class match when Van Dieman's Land played Port Phillip District (Victoria) at Launceston in February 1851.

Despite such early promise, entry into the Sheffield Shield competition was denied Tasmania until the 1977–78 season when they were accepted

on a restricted basis, playing five matches compared with the nine by the other States. Full Shield membership was granted in 1982–83, by which time three Tasmanian grounds – Devonport on the north-west of the island, Launceston and the Tasmanian Cricket Association (TCA) ground in Hobart – had been established as first-class venues.

At the start of the 1988–89 season the Tasmanian Cricket Council gave up the rundown ground on the Domain in Hobart and moved to the Bellerive Oval, home of the Clarence Cricket Club. Bellerive has only had a turf wicket since 1957 and all of the seven grandstands are small buildings, accommodating no more than 4000 of the ground's 15,000 capacity. Up to 9500 can occupy The Hill, a large grassy mound on the eastern side of the ground. The Clarence club has prospered there, with members enjoying superb clubrooms. Clarence has won six of the last eight Hobart district premierships.

The TCC has a 21-year agreement to lease Bellerive from the local council from 1 October to 30 March each summer. The ground is close to the water and most afternoons a cooling southerly springs up to renew bowlers' hopes. By allocating the second of Sri Lanka's two Tests in 1989–90 to Bellerive, the Australian Cricket Board accepted the argument that Test cricket would provide a huge stimulus for a State that has relied heavily on ACB funds. Successful staging of the game at Bellerive gave Tasmanians the chance to stand on their own feet financially, but nobody suggests that Bellerive can match the traditions of the five mainland Test grounds.

Close to the River Derwent, Hobart's Bellerive Oval became the 62nd ground to stage Test cricket.

Hobart				
Ref/No	Season	V	T	Result
1133/1	1989–90	SL	2	A-173

Melbourne

MELBOURNE CRICKET GROUND

Test cricket was born in Melbourne. The staging of the first Test astonished even the most experienced English players, and the ground has gone on surprising players and spectators alike. For this is a place where even the smallest details are carefully attended to, the home of the Melbourne Cricket Club, Australia's most prestigious sporting body whom many would prefer to have administering Australian cricket instead of the Australian Cricket Board.

The club's first ground was at Batman's Hill, on what is now the site of Spencer Street railway station. There on 15 November 1838 five gentlemen drew up a document to form the Melbourne Cricket Club, subscription one guinea. At the time Port Phillip was a small settlement comprised mainly of free settlers who had arrived too late to take up land in Tasmania. Almost naked aborigines roamed everywhere, kangaroos hopped through the long grass, and locals shot ducks that flew off the town's outlying marshes.

Under the presidency of F.A. Powlett, who made the colony's first century and took its first hat-trick, the club spent ten happy years on Batman's Hill. There they played matches between Benedicts and Bachelors, Whiskers and Clean Shaven, and other clubs such as Brighton and the Melbourne Union Cricket Club, and endured the drama of one of its members, Peter Snodgrass, losing a toe in Melbourne's first pistol duel.

In 1848 the Melbourne club moved to a location on the south bank of the Yarra River, between the river and Emerald Hill, the centre of today's suburb of South Melbourne. The first inter-Colonial match on the mainland, Victoria *v* Van Dieman's Land (Tasmania) was played at South Melbourne in March 1852 when the popping of champagne corks drowned conversation after Victoria avenged her defeat in Launceston a year earlier.

After the Melbourne club had spent thousands of pounds draining, grading and fencing the South Yarra ground and erecting a small pavilion, the arrival of Australia's first railway line in September 1854 forced the club to make its third and final move. The railway line from Melbourne to Sandridge (now Port Melbourne) passed right through the middle of the club's South Yarra ground.

As compensation Governor La Trobe offered the Melbourne club the choice of two sites in the Police Paddock. The club chose a plot of ten acres in the paddock, a delightful area full of wattle, wildflowers and thick with timber at the Richmond or outer end. This has remained the site of the Melbourne Cricket Ground since the Melbourne Cricket Club moved there in 1853.

The committee determined from the start to make the MCG the finest ground in the colonies. Migrants poured into Melbourne at the rate of three thousand a week and on Sundays took time off from their labours to promenade in Richmond Park adjoining the MCG. The club invited the band of the 40th Regiment to play at the ground on weekends to entertain the walkers.

The club membership increased by 200 in 1855 thanks to the discovery of gold at Bendigo and Ballarat. To entertain these well-heeled members the club issued a challenge in all Melbourne newspapers offering to play any cricket team in the Australian colonies for £1000. New South Wales accepted the challenge but disdained to play for money, a move *The Argus* applauded. 'The stake is now for the supremacy of local play respectively, and the broader the grounds upon which the contest is placed are decidedly more calculated to produce the better sport,' the paper said.

The truth was that the Sydney cricketers had no chance of raising betting money and only managed the £181 needed to pay for their team's voyage to Melbourne because barrister Richard Driver put in £60 of his own money. Hurt by the implication that they were greedy money-grubbers, the Melburnites argued about the toss, who should bat first, whether different pitches should be used for each innings, and what umpires should wear before the first ball was bowled on 26 March 1856. After Victoria won the toss, the New South Wales captain George Gilbert insisted that convention gave the visiting team the right to choose who should bat first. Gilbert won his point and sent Victoria in to bat.

Both teams fielded without their boots, either barefooted or in stockings, for the MCG had been a grazing pasture for cows and goats in the 1850s and was a dust bowl. Set to score only 16 to win in the final innings, New South Wales lost 5 for 5 to hostile bowling by Gideon Elliott and Frederick Lowe before a few solid blows by Gilbert won the match for New South Wales by three wickets.

For a further six seasons the Melbourne club steadily improved its ground and by 1861 it became clear that club cricket and occasional inter-Colonial matches were not enough to satisfy Melbourne's appetite for cricket. Various schemes were suggested to bring out a team of English cricketers to test the locals' skills, but they all fell through until finally the restaurateurs Spiers & Pond, proprietors of the Cafe de Paris in Bourke Street, sent one of their employees, a Mr Mallam, to England to arrange an English team's visit.

Mallam encountered problems from great batsman George Parr and other English players who claimed his guarantee of £150 a player was inadequate for a trip involving such vast distances. Finally with the help of Surrey's secretary, William

Burrup, Mallam got together a team captained by Heathfield Stephenson. The team travelled to Australia in the six-masted steamship *Great Britain* to find more than 3000 people waiting to greet them on the dock in Melbourne on Christmas Eve 1861.

Each English player was given a white-trimmed hat with a blue ribbon to wear as the team paraded through Melbourne before cheering crowds. Their days began with a champagne breakfast and everywhere they went they were mobbed. They had to be taken out into the bush by Spiers & Pond to practise, the only way they could avoid the crowds.

England's first match in Australia began on New Year's Day 1862 on the Melbourne Cricket Ground. Stephenson tried to have the number of England's opponents reduced from 22 to 15 but eventually agreed to face 18. People flocked in from outlying districts from before dawn. Coaches, waggons, sulkies, drays and men on horseback jammed Melbourne's streets. The Melbourne *Herald* said more than 5000 were present for the start of play, but others considered the crowd much larger.

On a very hot day each English player was given a helmet-style sun hat. They wore specially coloured sashes around their waists and around their hats and these colours were printed against each man's name on the scorecard for spectators to identify him. A new grandstand with accommodation for 6000 had just been completed for the game. Bright marquees rimmed the ground, some of them occupied by publicans who brought in 500 cases of beer for the occasion.

Outside the ground there were shooting galleries, hurdygurdies, fruit and sweet stalls, small boys selling scorecards and sketches of the players. A house painter who took his ladder to the ground did a thriving business selling places in the trees.

William Caffyn ('The Surrey Pet') opened the bowling for England but had to come off because of pains in his arms caused by mosquito bites. George Marshall gave XVIII of Victoria a sound start by scoring 27 but his team were all out for 118, with six ducks. George ('Farmer') Bennett took 7 for 53, George Griffith 7 for 30, and there were three run-outs. Stephenson's XI replied with 305, Caffyn top-scoring with 79. There were seven ducks in the Victorians' second innings of 92, the Englishmen winning by an innings and 96 runs.

More than 45,000 people paid to see the match which finished on the morning of the fourth day but at least as many as that got in free because nobody had any experience of handling such crowds. This was the biggest crowd ever reported for a cricket match anywhere in the world to that time. The takings more than covered Spiers & Pond's outlay for the entire tour.

To fill in the remaining time of the fourth day, Spiers & Pond organized the first balloon ascent in Australia. The balloon was called 'All England' and had portraits of Queen Victoria and the England players painted on the outside. It was aloft for 35 minutes drifting all over Melbourne, before the balloonists, Mr and Mrs Brown, brought it down in Albert Street.

Spiers & Pond made £11,000 profit from the 13-match tour after giving the English players handsome gifts and half the takings from their last match against XXII of Victoria. The Englishmen were offered £1200 to stay a further month but declined because of commitments at home. After the last match the English team each planted an elm tree on the outskirts of the Melbourne ground and some of these flourished to such an extent that Paddy Horan, Australia's first widely read cricketer writer, was able to call his weekly piece in *The Australasian* 'Under the Elms'. Spiers & Pond spent

their profits building a refreshment room at the Old Bishopsgate station in London and similar rooms at other stations. These ventures did well enough for them to build the Criterion Hotel near Piccadilly Circus.

Word quickly spread among cricketers in England about the lavish hospitality provided for the first English team and further tours followed. In 1863–64 George Parr brought out a team. In 1873–74, when W.G. Grace made the first of his two tours to Australia, the East Melbourne, South Melbourne and Melbourne clubs combined to put up £170 per man, plus £1500 for Grace and all expenses for him and his wife. Matches played by these teams fully taxed the accommodation of almost every ground on which they played, but it was the fourth English team led by James Lillywhite in 1876–77 which helped revolutionize cricket as it was known by introducing Test matches.

Lillywhite's team was a powerful outfit comprising seasoned professionals from four counties – Sussex, Yorkshire, Surrey and Nottinghamshire – but they had to struggle from the start against vastly improved Australian sides. A New South Wales XV beat them by two wickets and 13 wickets in the return. Fifteen of Victoria beat them by 31 runs. Encouraged by these successes, New South Wales met the tourists on level terms but had the worst of a drawn match.

Lillywhite felt that his players had done well enough against New South Wales to indicate they could beat Australia's best on level terms and when an All Australia *v* All England match was suggested he agreed to add it to the tour programme. Lillywhite took his players off on a New Zealand tour, leaving John Conway to make all arrangements. Conway, a shrewd Melbourne cricketer who had played against all the English teams going

The MCG groundstaff at work prior to the first of all Tests. On the far boundary can be seen the press and scorers' box and the MCG Members' Stand. The new grandstand, also used for watching Rules football in neighbouring Richmond Park, occupies the right-hand side of the boundary.

back to Stephenson's tour, ignored the Victorian Cricketers' Association and the New South Wales Cricket Association. He virtually selected the All Australia team himself and contacted the players direct. The NSWCA expressed displeasure at this action but could not prevent its players accepting Conway's invitations to play. There were some strange reactions from those chosen for what became the first of all Tests. Edwin Evans, rated Australia's best all-rounder, said he could not play because of his job as an inspector of selections. Fred Spofforth refused to play because his pal Billy Murdoch was not chosen as wicket-keeper. Frank Allan, the left-arm pace bowler chosen to replace Spofforth, preferred to go to the Warrnambool Agricultural Show. Conway stuck to his selection of an Australian team that included only five Australian-born players, including untried wicket-keeper Jack Blackham.

The All England team entered the match on the Melbourne Cricket Ground only a day after a rough voyage from New Zealand, with several players recovering from sea-sickness. Their only specialist wicket-keeper, Ted Pooley, had been left behind in a New Zealand prison after a brawl in a Christchurch pub over a bet. Despite this setback to England, most observers forecast an easy England win and as a result only 1000 spectators turned up for the start on 15 March 1877. In the dressing-room before play began, the Australian players elected Dave Gregory their captain, a surprise considering Victorians outnumbered New South Welshmen in the side.

Gregory won the toss and batted, leaving Charles Bannerman, born in Kent 25 years earlier, to face the first ball in Test cricket from Nottinghamshire's round-armer Alfred Shaw, which he blocked. With his score on 10 Bannerman dollied a simple catch to Tom Armitage but the ball hit Armitage on the stomach before he could get his hands to it. Bannerman went on to play what some have called the finest innings in Test cricket. He was 126 not out at the end of the first day, with Australia 166 for 6, and next day took his score to 165 before George Ulyett split his thumb and he had to retire.

Southerton, whose appearance in this match at 49 years 111 days made him England's oldest-ever Test cricketer, took 3 for 61 from 37 four-ball overs in Australia's innings of 245. Australia's bowling and wicket-keeping reached a very high standard when England batted but sloppy ground fielding enabled England to score 196, 49 behind. Alfred Shaw then improved on the 3 for 51 he had taken in the first innings by capturing 5 for 38 in Australia's second innings of 104. Tom Horan top-scored with 20 for Australia. Set to score 154 to win, England made only 108, giving Australia victory by 45 runs. Bannerman's unbeaten century and Tom Kendall's 7 for 55 in England's second innings had paved the way to Australia's win.

The Sydney *Daily News* in applauding Australia's surprise success said: 'It may console the leaders of the game at Lord's and The Oval that the English race is not disintegrating in a distant land and on turf where the blackfellow hurled his boomerang.' The return match on the MCG a fortnight later was played as a benefit for the English team, since takings at the first match exceeded all Conway's expectations despite the poor first day crowd.

Australia improved their side by replacing the 38-year-old Ned Gregory with Spofforth, and brought in Billy Murdoch for Horan and T.J.D. Kelly for Bransby Beauchamp Cooper, who simply refused to practise. England had only 11 fit players and were still without the unfortunate Pooley. One of the intriguing sidelines to this game was that the MCG had a reversible stand. The seats faced towards the centre for the cricket but could be reversed to look out on to the neighbouring park for Australian Rules football, the club committee believing that footballers would ruin the MCG's surface for cricket.

Grand buildings in a parkland atmosphere provide the backdrop to the first day's play of the Fifth Test of 1903–04.

Australia scored only 122 in their first innings, to which England responded with 261 thanks to solid batting by Greenwood (49), Emmett (48) and Hill (49). Highlights of Australia's second innings of 259 were Charles Bannerman's 30 in 13 minutes and Kelly's eight successive boundaries in his knock of 35. Left to score 122 to win, England got them with the loss of six wickets because of a marvellous innings of 63 by John Selby after Australia had dismissed three England batsmen for 9 runs.

Two summers later Australia beat Lord Harris's England touring team by ten wickets on the MCG, Spofforth taking 6 for 48 and 7 for 62, including

Test cricket's first hat-trick in England's first innings. Spofforth's victims in both innings included F.A. MacKinnon, 35th Chief of the Clan MacKinnon. A riot in Sydney during the match between Lord Harris's team and New South Wales caused cancellation of what would have been the fourth Test between England and Australia.

Although Melbourne had staged the first three Tests, there was no question that in those early days of international cricket England was the stronger, winning 17 of the first 32 Tests to Australia's 11, with 4 drawn. The Melbourne club remained the leader of the game's affairs Down Under, the arbiter on good behaviour of players and spectators alike, and in 1886 the club even sponsored Australia's tour of England, with club secretary Major Ben Wardill as manager.

The Melbourne Cricket Club shrugged off the losses incurred in 1887–88 when two English teams toured Australia simultaneously by inviting Lord Sheffield to bring an English team out in 1891–92. W.G. Grace agreed to captain Lord Sheffield's side. The team played three Tests, the first of them at the MCG, during which Alick Bannerman achieved a stonewalling milestone by batting 435 minutes to score 86 runs (45 and 41).

In the 1890s an attempt to install the Australasian Cricket Council as administrators of all cricket in Australia and New Zealand failed because the Council lacked the support of the leading players and the Melbourne Cricket Club. The Australian Board of Control encountered similar opposition when it was first formed in 1905 and in the early years of the Board some of its members were said to be paranoid about the Melbourne club and the MCG.

Years of feuding ended with the Melbourne club's ground freely available to the Board, which in turn desperately needed the huge gate money cricket attracts at the MCG. A succession of hard-working committees had made the MCG the biggest money-making venue in cricket and apart from Lord's the ground to which membership is most prized.

Australia's highest first-class score, 1107, was made on the MCG by Victoria against New South Wales in 1926–27 when Arthur Mailey took 4 for 362, the highest number of runs hit off a bowler in first-class cricket. Mailey, who said he was always suspicious of periods of accuracy, claimed he was just finding a length when the Victorian innings ended, and added that he would have had better figures if a chap in the crowd had not dropped several catches from his bowling.

The MCG is one of the sternest tests for big-hitters in world cricket, with shots that elsewhere would clear the fence being caught in the outfield, but in that innings of 1107 Jack Ryder hit six sixes, all driven, in a knock of 295. Nothing as spectacular as Ryder's hitting had been seen on the MCG since 6ft 10in, 17-stone George Bonnor struck a ball from England off-spinner Willie Bates 20 yards beyond the MCG into Richmond Paddock in 1881.

At the MCG in 1931–32 Australia bowled out South Africa on a sticky wicket for 36 and 45 to win by an innings and 72 runs. The match aggregate of 234 remains the lowest in all Test cricket. Bert Ironmonger, the Australian left-arm spinner who held the ball on the stubs of two fingers shortened in sawmill accidents, took 5 for 6 and 6 for 18 to finish with 11 wickets for 24 runs for Australia. The world record crowd for a cricket match (350,534 – held until 1980–81) was set at the MCG for the Third Test between England and Australia in 1936–37 when Australia won by 365 runs and

went on to win the rubber 3–2 after losing the first two Tests. The best crowd on any of the six days of that Test was surpassed in February 1961 when 90,800 attended the second day of the Australia v West Indies Test that decided a thrilling series. But even that crowd was well short of the MCG record of 121,696 for the 1970 Australian Rules football grand final.

At a ground that has known many sensations, one of the most debated occurred during the Third Test of the 1954–55 England v Australia series when groundsman Jack House illegally watered the pitch on the rest day Sunday. Big cracks had appeared after a heat wave on Saturday. Former Victorian cricket captain Percy Beames, a crony of House's from their football days, broke the story in *The Age* but both teams agreed to finish the match. England won by 128 runs after the last eight Australian wickets fell for 36 runs in the final innings, Frank Tyson taking 6 for 16 in 51 balls with some of the fastest bowling ever seen on the MCG.

Over the years the Melbourne Cricket Club replaced old stands with bigger stands. Where one-storey wooden buildings once stood, huge three-tiered concrete trays 50 seats deep appeared. The elms disappeared, every shred of greenery went on a ground that is within walking distance of the centre of Melbourne. The Melbourne club's pursuit of unrivalled facilities for vast crowds was matched by the ingenuity of its administrators, who were always several steps ahead of their counterparts at other Australian grounds.

In 1989, the Melbourne Club began demolition and replacement of the MCG's Southern Stand, a $14.2 million venture that will take two years to complete and will increase the ground's seating capacity to 110,000. With standing room added, this will allow the MCG to accommodate more

than 130,000 spectators. The new stand will provide seating for 41,000 and standing room for 6000, plus bars and catering facilities.

Through a trick of acoustics in which the crowd's roar echoed down from the layers of seating, the MCG became a daunting place on which to fail. For those who succeeded, however, there was nothing in cricket like an MCG roar

Top Largely rebuilt in order to play host to the 1956 Olympic Games, the MCG can accommodate vast crowds. The crowd seen here watching Australia play West Indies on Boxing Day 1975 numbered 85,596.

Bottom Melbourne under floodlights for the first time during the opening match of the World Championship of Cricket in February 1985.

of approval. Since Hitler's war, players like Alan ('Froggy') Thomson, a right-arm pace bowler who had the wrong foot forward in his delivery stride, laconic leg-spinner Jimmy Higgs and gawky swing bowler Max Walker all earned regular roars. To say Walker lumbered in to bowl is to bless him with mobility; his action was more shamble than lumber. But the big decibels of the MCG crowd were reserved for Dennis Lillee and Jeff Thomson, frightening propositions running in to bowl off an MCG chant.

At Melbourne in March 1977 they replayed the first of all cricket Tests to celebrate 100 years of Test matches. This joyous reunion, later copied without the same success at Lord's in 1980 and at Sydney in 1988, was the brainchild of former Australian bowler Hans Ebeling, an MCC committeeman whose energies had previously been occupied in developing a wonderful cricket museum at the ground. Ebeling attracted 244 surviving Test cricketers, many of whom thought they had been forgotten, to watch England play Australia. The advantage ebbed and flowed and on the fifth day either side had chances to win, before Australia triumphed by precisely the same margin as 100 years earlier – 45 runs.

The money attracted through MCG turnstiles by crowds eager for more and more cricket has in the past been awesome, and the cashflow at the ground has reached staggering sums since the lights

Melbourne

Ref/No	Season	V	T	Result	Ref/No	Season	V	T	Result
1/1	1876–77	E	1	A-45	178/29	1928–29	E	3	E-3w
2/2			2	E-4w	180/30			5	A-5w
3/3	1878–79	E	–	A-10w	202/31	1930–31	WI	4	A-1&122
5/4	1881–82	E	1	Draw	214/32	1931–32	SA	3	A-169
8/5			4	Draw	216/33			5	A-1&72
10/6	1882–83	E	1	A-9w	221/34	1932–33	E	2	A-111
11/7			2	E-1&27	257/35	1936–37	E	3	A-365
18/8	1884–85	E	2	E-10w	259/36			5	A-1&200
21/9			5	E-1&98	281/37	1946–47	E	3	Draw
35/10	1891–92	E	1	A-54	292/38	1947–48	I	3	A-233
43/11	1894–95	E	2	E-94	294/39			5	A-1&177
46/12			5	E-6w	328/40	1950–51	E	2	A-28
54/13	1897–98	E	2	A-1&55	331/41			5	E-8w
56/14			4	A-8w	347/42	1951–52	WI	4	A-1w
66/15	1901–02	E	2	A-229	361/43	1952–53	SA	2	SA-82
69/16			5	A-32	364/44			5	SA-6w
79/17	1903–04	E	2	E-185	393/45	1954–55	E	3	E-128
82/18			5	A-218	465/46	1958–59	E	2	A-8w
97/19	1907–08	E	2	E-1w	468/47			5	A-9w
99/20			4	A-308	503/48	1960–61	WI	2	A-7w
112/21	1910–11	SA	2	A-89	506/49			5	A-2w
114/22			4	A-530	536/50	1962–63	E	2	E-7w
117/23	1911–12	E	2	E-8w	549/51	1963–64	SA	2	A-8w
119/24			4	E-1&225	570/52	1964–65	P	–	Draw
136/25	1920–21	E	2	A-1&91	598/53	1965–66	E	2	Draw
138/26			4	A-8w	601/54			5	Draw
159/27	1924–25	E	2	A-81	625/55	1967–68	I	2	A-1&4
161/28			4	E-1&29	643/56	1968–69	WI	2	A-1&30
					–	1970–71	E	3	Abandoned

went on in 1985–86. MCG gate money is in fact never far from the thoughts of all Australian cricket administrators. Gate receipts for cricket matches at the ground in 1987–88, a lack-lustre season, were $2.4 million, and in 1988–89 gate receipts reached $2.6 million for cricket.

In those two seasons 30 limited-over matches attracted an average of 54,000 per game or 1,632,000 patrons. Two Test matches in that period were attended by 240,000 people, averaging 24,000 per day. This meant that for both one-day games and Tests Melbourne attendances were more than all the other first-class venues combined.

Ref/No	Season	V	T	Result
677/57			5	Draw
709/58	1972–73	P	2	A-92
728/59	1973–74	NZ	1	A-I&25
752/60	1974–75	E	3	Draw
755/61			6	E-I&4
766/62	1975–76	WI	3	A-8w
769/63			6	A-165
794/64	1976–77	P	2	A-348
803/65	1976–77	E	–	A-45
811/66	1977–78	I	3	I-222
836/67	1978–79	E	3	A-103
849/68	1978–79	P	1	P-71
869/69	1979–80	WI	2	WI-10w
872/70	1979–80	E	3	A-8w
892/71	1980–81	NZ	3	Draw
895/72	1980–81	I	3	I-59
911/73	1981–82	P	3	P-I&82
918/74	1981–82	WI	1	A-58
941/75	1982–83	E	4	E-3
973/76	1983–84	P	4	Draw
1000/77	1984–85	WI	4	Draw
1033/78	1985–86	I	2	Draw
1061/79	1986–87	E	4	E-I&14
1089/80	1987–88	NZ	3	Draw
1112/81	1988–89	WI	3	WI-285

Australia: P 81, W 42, D 13, L 26

1970–71 Test abandoned without a ball being bowled and excluded from the records.

Perth

WESTERN AUSTRALIAN CRICKET ASSOCIATION GROUND

On 9 December 1889 a deputation from the Western Australian Cricket Association met the colony governor, Sir Frederick Broome, and asked him to set aside a plot of land on the foreshores of the Swan River in East Perth that was under water at the time and a nuisance to the city. The association delegates said that with a government loan of £3000 to £4000 at five per cent interest, and with the help of a dredge and prison labour, a cricket ground could be established.

Sir Frederick realized that this would benefit all sports and in one of his last acts before ending his term as governor agreed to the proposal, setting aside 11 hectares of swampland on a 999-year lease. 'I am delighted that in my last official act after a long administration of this colony's government I can serve so good a cause as cricket,' said Sir Frederick.

The association trustees issued debentures, which they personally guaranteed, erected a fence, let a contract to raise the level of the entire ground by two feet, took levels, planted trees, erected a small wooden pavilion, imported Merri Creek soil from Melbourne for the centre wickets, and laid down a bicycle track and some tennis courts. Until that time all cricket in Western Australia had been played on concrete, coconut matting or ill-prepared turf pitches. There was dismay when it was discovered that the government planned to build a sewerage farm next door, but a letter to the colony administrator protesting that this would destroy all the hard work done on the ground resulted in the Board of Health finding another site for the farm.

Cricket had begun in Western Australia with a match over the Easter weekend in 1835 between builders on the new Government House and their

counterparts on the Commissariat Building. No scores survive but the *Perth Gazette & Western Australian Journal* on 13 April 1835 applauded the staging of the match. 'The revival of the sport of our native country in a distant land forms a connection which it should be our pride to encourage,' the paper said.

Cricket clubs sprang up throughout the colony over the next fifty years, with regular matches played in Perth, York, Bunbury, Vasse, Bussel Town (later Bussleton), Toodyay and Fremantle. The rivalry between Perth and Fremantle was particularly keen and often led to ill-feeling. One Fremantle team was farewelled by a volley of stones before they began the coach ride back to Fremantle. Geraldton and Beverley formed cricket clubs in 1866 and in Perth the game was enlivened by the appearance of a team from the 53rd Regiment which included several players who had appeared regularly in England.

Perth newspapers often raised the need for a superior ground on which the colony's best matches could be held. The Bishop of Perth allowed one match to be played on his school wicket because of the shortage of good pitches. By far the best pitches in the State were at Fremantle, the sea port where, in 1869, the officers and crew of HMS *Galatea* played in the presence of HRH the Duke of Edinburgh.

The Western Australian Cricket Association was formed on 22 November 1885 and for four years its member clubs endured a succession of unsatisfactory grounds, often putting money into sites that were quickly taken over by the government for use by public servants. The breakthrough that came with the governor's grant of swampland at

The WACA ground, sited on reclaimed land on the foreshores of the Swan River, soon after it was opened.

East Perth also ushered in years of hard work for the association officials who had to make the site suitable for big matches. The idea of sending a Western Australian team east had to be shelved for a time because every penny was need for the WACA ground.

The first annual return of the association boasted that a water barrel with handles attached had become the association's property. Later reports spoke of the outlay of £15 on cleaning, grubbing and levelling. Test cricket flourished in eastern Australia while in the west cricket officials struggled to secure an adequate supply of water for their ground. In 1887, on the recommendation of Harry Boyle and Dr 'Tup' Scott, the Melbourne Test

players, the Perth Metropolitan Club engaged W.V. Duffy as professional coach for £100 a season. Duffy arrived thinking he had to prepare a team for an eastern tour, only to find the money needed for this had to go instead into developing the WACA.

The first Western Australian team to visit the eastern colonies played seven matches on their trip at the end of the 1892–93 summer. They lost by ten wickets in their first-ever first-class match to South Australia on Adelaide Oval and by an innings and 243 runs to Victoria on the Melbourne Cricket Ground. The team had no preparation for this tour on turf wickets because the WACA was still not ready, and they found the pace of the Adelaide and Melbourne pitches troublesome.

The mayor of Perth, Alexander Forest, officially opened the ground that year and to mark the occasion his daughter, Sylvia, was made the association's first life member. Turf pitches were first used at the WACA in February 1894 and were so successful that the trustees were immediately authorized to spend a further £3000 on improving the ground. Transportation of convicts from England to Western Australia was found to be too expensive and ended in 1868 and for a time the State stagnated. In the 1890s discovery of gold at Coolgardie and Kalgoorlie gave the State the boost it needed, bringing prospectors into the west in large numbers. Harry Brown became the association's first paid secretary in 1896, on a salary of £100 per annum, and tried hard to get eastern State and English teams to Perth. But before the railway to the east was completed the only link between eastern and western Australia was by small coastal ships which took a buffeting crossing the Great Australian Bight. No sane cricketer would make the trip. Gold provided the money to start work on the railway but even when it opened passengers needed days to recover from the long, arduous trip.

South Australia defeated Western Australia by four wickets in April 1899 in the initial try-out of the WACA as a first-class venue. South Australia scored 159 and 235 for 6, Western Australia 100 and 293. One of the best of the Western Australian batsmen in that match was Lloyd Herring, whose 34 in the second innings delighted WACA spectators. Seven years later Herring made 69 (retired hurt) when Fremantle caused a major upset by defeating the South Australian side captained by Jack Lyons by an innings. This match was over in two days and doubt remains over whether it was a first-class fixture. Fremantle made 220 before jockey-sized off-spinner Bobbie Selk, bowling with his shirt-sleeves buttoned, took 6 for 39 and 5 for 50 in the South Australian innings of 76 and 121.

This result created enormous interest in South Australia's match with Western Australia from 27 January 1906 at the WACA. The inexperienced West Australians gave a plucky display of team batting in their first innings of 198. Karl Quist, father of Davis Cup tennis player Adrian Quist, made 47, Ernie Parker, who later won an Australian tennis singles title, scored 30, Tim Howard 34, and Harold Rowe 33. Selk, 5 for 19, and Tom Coyne, 5 for 27, combined to rout South Australia for 54. Western Australia pressed home their advantage by scoring 189 in the second knock, giving them a lead of 333, Lionel Gouly, the North Perth left-hander, scoring 70 not out. Selk then bowled Western Australia to an historic win by taking 7 for 108 in South Australia's second innings of 230. His match bag of 12 for 127 gave his side victory by 103 runs.

The second match was drawn after dogged batting by both teams. Algie Gehrs, a disappointment on Australia's 1905 tour of England, made 100, Fred Hack 152 not out, in South Aus-

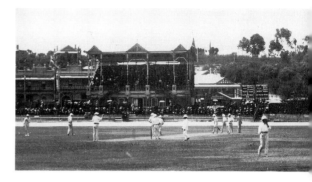

A match at the WACA during the 1901–02 season.

tralia's 451 for 6 declared, Ernie Parker 61 in Western Australia's 234. The third match saw Gehrs at his swashbuckling best, despite lack of support. He made 148 not out in a total of 235 in South Australia's first innings of 235 and 100 not out in the second innings of 259 for 4. This was the first time that a batsman had scored not-out centuries in each innings of a match anywhere in the world. Western Australia made 202 and 252 for 5 to earn a praiseworthy draw. Parker scored 116 in Western Australia's second innings.

Overweight rugby star Harold Evers captained Western Australia when New South Wales made the long train trip to the west for the first time in March 1907. Evers, 22 stone, had gone to the west after playing for New South Wales from 1896–97 to 1901–02. He was a highly astute tactician who had captained New South Wales and a capable right-hand batsman and wicket-keeper. New South Wales won the first match by one wicket after Western Australia had made 307 and 238. The teams moved from WACA to Fremantle for the return match where Western Australia produced another upset in winning by 5 runs, scoring 255 and 185 to 251 and 184.

This remarkable victory was followed the next season by the first appearance of an England team at the WACA when the side captained by A.O. Jones met Western Australia from 26 October 1907. The Essex batsman F.L. Fane began his second Australian tour by scoring 133 in a total of 402. Arthur Christian, the left-arm spinner, took 5 for 132 before a record crowd. Western Australia were dismissed for 152 despite an innings of 60 not out by Tim Hogue, and in their second innings of 116 the 20-year-old John Neville Crawford moved the ball about appreciably.

This was the English players' first encounter with the 'Fremantle Doctor', the cooling south-westerly or southerly breeze which blows across the WACA most afternoons. Meteorologists are not sure of the origins of the name but believe it is related to the Cape Town Doctor, a wind that is said to blow germs and infection away off southern Africa. With the Doctor's assistance Crawford achieved the movement and variation that had enabled him to break into the Surrey team at 17 and win a place in the England XI at 19.

At the end of their tour Jones's team popped into Perth on their way home and gave Western Australia a second match on the WACA. This time the home team played an honourable draw by scoring 256 and 265 for 7 against England's 362 for 7 declared. The North Perth batsman Harold Rowe scored 105, the first century by a Western Australian against England. This match-saving effort came in the second innings after George Gunn had made 122 not out, his fourth century of a tour that he originally planned only to watch. Gunn was on holiday but was co-opted into the team when injuries occurred.

The success of these initial international matches on the WACA and their impressive win the previous season over the powerful NSW team still failed to give Western Australia a regular place on overseas teams' itineraries. Eastern Australian

States found it easier to tour to New Zealand than make the long trek across the Nullabor to Perth. For half a century talented Western Australian players had to move east to prove themselves.

South Australia temporarily relieved Western Australia's isolation by playing three matches in the west in April 1909. Disputes within the Western Australian side forced them to change captains for each match. They did well to get out of it with three draws. Christian took 25 of the 46 South Australian wickets that fell in these matches at 17 runs apiece. Gehrs again showed his liking for the WACA wicket by scoring 113 in the third game. In 1910 a strong Victorian team visited the west, winning the two matches on the WACA and losing the one at Fremantle.

Denied a match against the 1911–12 England team, Western Australia made their second trip east in 1911–12, losing three and drawing two of their five matches. Christian flourished as an all-rounder, scoring a lot of runs and taking 6 for 40 against New South Wales. Algie Gehrs made 119 against them in Adelaide, this time in 50 minutes, the fastest in Australia until David Hookes made a century in 43 minutes on the same Adelaide Oval 70 years later in 1982–83.

A major development for Western Australian cricket came in 1917 with the completion of the railway line linking the State with the eastern States, but the trip remained so gruelling that even fit cricketers required several days to recover. They kept sending teams east whenever they had the funds but it was really not until the advent of regular airline travel after the Second World War that the isolation of Western Australian cricketers ended and they were able to make their remarkable contribution to Australian cricket. Before that happened, Perth was just a pleasant stopover for teams travelling to and from England.

Don Bradman played a big part in Western Australia's admission to the Sheffield Shield competition. The stumbling block had always been the high cost of sending teams from Queensland, New South Wales, Victoria and to a lesser extent South Australia all the way to Perth. In view of the fact that the eastern State teams travelled to Adelaide each year for their game against South Australia, Bradman suggested that Western Australia should offer to pay the cost of extending their trips from Adelaide to Perth.

The Australian Board of Control agreed to admit Western Australia on a restricted basis provided they guaranteed their opposing States the return Adelaide-to-Perth fares. They were admitted on a percentage points basis which provided that they should play four Shield matches compared with seven by the other four States. The cost of reimbursing the other States for their fares was to keep the Western Australian Cricket Association broke for years, although – to their credit – New South Wales never once asked for their money.

Keith Carmody, the former squadron leader and innovative cricketer from the Sydney suburb of Mosman, went to the WACA as the west's Shield coach and in his very first match on the ground in this capacity scored 198 against South Australia. His side's display in winning their first-ever Shield match on the WACA shocked all Australian cricket buffs, even though South Australia had been weakened by the absence of Bradman, Hamence and Dooland on Test duty. Western Australia's 444 proved too many for South Australia who made 109 and 211 to be beaten by an innings and 124 runs. Western Australia proved it was no fluke in their very next match by beating Victoria on the first innings at the WACA, where George Robinson made 134 and Alan Edwards 134.

On their trip east for their other two Shield matches that summer, Western Australia produced a marvellous workhorse in right-arm medium-pace bowler Charlie Puckett, a Perth postman who could bowl for hours in hot sun without losing accuracy. After NSW had beaten them in Sydney, Puckett virtually won the Shield for Western Australia by taking 6 for 48 in Queensland's second innings in Brisbane. This gave Western Australia their third win in their four matches and against all the odds assured them of the Shield at their first attempt.

Overnight the stream of gifted players to the east stopped. No longer had players such as Ernie Bromley to go to Melbourne or Sydney to win Test places. Indeed, good players began migrating to the west where they saw better opportunities playing next to men like Tony Mann, Wally Langdon and Rick Charlesworth than in the east. Ken Meuleman, the Victorian who played in one Test against New Zealand in 1945–46, settled in Perth in 1952. In eight seasons he scored more than 3000 runs for Western Australia, including eight centuries and a superb 234 not out in 1956–57 against South Australia at the WACA. Bob Simpson, Mark O'Neill, and Shaun Graf were among others who went west.

In 1956 Perth mathematics master John Rutherford became the first player chosen for a major overseas tour by Australia and the first to play in a Test. Rutherford earned his selection by scoring four centuries, three of them on the WACA, in the two seasons prior to the English tour. Against MCC, at Lord's, Rutherford and 'Slasher' Mackay got lost after leaving the Australian dressing-room to open the innings. They knew the crowd was waiting but could not find a way to the field, finally jumping the fence 40 yards from the players' gate.

But the player who laid the foundation for Western Australia's extraordinary recent success was Barry Shepherd, a burly figure born at

Donnybrook, who captained the side with the pugnacity of a prize-fighter. He lifted the standard of the fielding, instilled a fierce desire to win in his players, but above all gave them pride in representing their State. He inspired a whole generation of Western Australian cricketers, lifting them to their second Shield win in 1967–68. Since then they have dominated the competition. The great English left-arm bowler Tony Lock carried on the Shepherd build-up between 1967 and 1971 with Western Australia winning 19 of their 33 games under his captaincy. Lock joined the side at 33 when most believed his first-class career was virtually over but he proceeded to take 326 wickets for the State and score 1531 runs. Lock, now a naturalized Australian, took five wickets in an innings 16 times for Western Australia, including eight times on the WACA, and was captain-coach of four Perth clubs.

Lock was fortunate to have in his teams players like Graham McKenzie, Australia's fast bowler in 60 Tests; Ian Brayshaw, a plucky all-rounder who took 10 for 44 at the WACA in 1967–68 in an innings against Victoria; John Inverarity, later to lead Western Australia to four Shield wins and surpass Don Bradman's record for the highest number of runs in Shield cricket.

Lock went out of cricket as two absorbing newcomers were starting to make their names in the Test arena. He called one of them 'Fot', short for 'Flipping Old Tart' – bestowed on Dennis Lillee when he was a gangling youngster lacking in control who sprayed the ball all round the batsmen. The other, Rodney Marsh, became known as 'old Iron Gloves' because initially his wicket-keeping completely lacked grace. Both gave some devastating performances at the WACA, and in combination they were deadly. Few more incredible destructions of a batsman have been seen than

The WACA viewed from one of the lighting towers during the Perth Test of 1986–87.

Lillee's bowling to Vivian Richards when Richards played for Queensland against Western Australia at the WACA in 1976–77. Lillee had the great man back-pedalling with two ferocious bouncers and then scattered his stumps with a ball of fearsome pace.

Test cricket arrived at the WACA on 11 December 1970 after 674 Tests had been played around the world, 204 of them in Australia. The match was drawn after Greg Chappell became the sixth Australian to score a century in his first Test innings and Brian Luckhurst made a century for England in his second Test. More than 85,000 people attended the Test. Gate receipts were almost £50,000. With Australia needing 245 runs to win in 145 minutes, Bill Lawry made only 6 runs in his first 68 minutes.

Four seasons later Doug Walters adopted a different approach when he scored 100 runs between tea and stumps on the second day, taking his score to 103 with a six from the last ball of the day. This enabled Australia to achieve her first win over England at the WACA by nine wickets, with a day and 50 minutes to spare.

Walters's last-ball six was compared with Barry

Shepherd's effort for Western Australia against Queensland in 1961–62 when he hit six sixes over the fence on his way to 207. But the blow that WACA members reckon was the biggest on the ground came from Jeff Thomson, playing for Queensland against Western Australia in 1979–80, when he landed a ball on the framework of the members' bar window.

The WACA at the end of the 1980s was undergoing extensions to grandstand accommodation and improvements to catering facilities. Out in the middle, the wickets laid down by John Maley remain the fastest in Australia, guaranteeing fireworks on the first morning of a Test. From the Prindiville Stand for ground members, opened in 1986 to celebrate the Western Australian Cricket Association's centenary, 5600 people can look down on the cricket knowing that in its short history the WACA has built a tradition for excitement. Around them extensions are going on that will lift the WACA's capacity to 35,000 spectators, 23,000 of them seated. Not bad for a former swamp.

Perth				
Ref/No	Season	V	T	Result
675/1	1970–71	E	2	Draw
751/2	1974–75	E	2	A-9w
765/3	1975–76	WI	2	WI-I&87
810/4	1977–78	I	2	A-2w
835/5	1978–79	E	2	E-166
850/6	1978–79	P	2	A-7w
868/7	1979–80	E	1	A-138
891/8	1980–81	NZ	2	A-8w
909/9	1981–82	P	1	A-286
938/10	1982–83	E	1	Draw
970/11	1983–84	P	1	A-I&9
997/12	1984–85	WI	1	WI-I&112
1031/13	1985–86	NZ	3	NZ-6w
1059/14	1986–87	E	2	Draw
1094/15	1987–88	SL	–	A-I&108
1111/16	1988–89	WI	2	WI-169
1131/17	1989–90	NZ	–	Draw

Australia: P 17, W 8, D 4, L 5

Sydney

SYDNEY CRICKET GROUND (No. 1)

Major cricket in Sydney had moved from pastureland on the Domain to the fully fenced Albert Ground and finally to the Civil and Military Ground at Moore Park when the sixth Test was played between England and Australia. There, on ground originally pegged out for rifle-shooting practice by soldiers from nearby Victoria Barracks, Billy Murdoch led Australia to a five-wicket win from 17 to 21 February 1882.

The field was first known as the Garrison Ground when it was used by 11th North Devonshire Regiment in 1848. The North Devons drilled and practised shooting on the land in front of their barracks, and in the 1850s flattened and graded the area at the southern end of their shooting range for a cricket field. Matches between teams of soldiers were played there in 1853 but the first match for which scores still exist was between the Garrison Club and the Royal Victoria Club on 16 February 1854. Set to score 18 to win in the final innings, the Royal Victorians collapsed for 16, making Privates Harefield and Tester, who bowled out the opposition, the toast of the barracks.

Lieutenant-Colonel John Richardson, the British-born commander of the Sydney garrison, was a keen cricketer and polo player, and when he affiliated his cricketers with the East Sydney Cricket Club he began to refer to the ground as the Civil and Military Ground. This upset the Albert Cricket Club, who complained that the soldiers' cricket field should be freely available to all clubs. The government responded by appointing the first trustees, Richard Driver, W. W. Stephen and Phillip Sheridan, to run the ground in 1877 and as soon as Richardson took his troops to fight in the Sudan the trustees named it the 'Association Ground'.

Sydney Cricket Ground in the 1880s, with The Hill – not yet fully banked – on the left.

The initial matches there were not greeted enthusiastically by critics. The *Sydney Morning Herald* said the ground was too far from the centre of Sydney to attract reasonable crowds. But this attitude changed dramatically when the swampy area in front of the ground known as Moore Park was filled in and Sydneysiders were presented with a delightful walk into the ground.

Driver, president of the New South Wales Cricket Association, was a Mason, but he formed a formidable combination with Sheridan, a practising Catholic, in building a famous ground. The few soldiers who were left at Victoria Barracks made an unsuccessful attempt to regain control of the ground and then in a scramble by Carlingford, Redfern, Fitzroy and the Albert cricket clubs to play there, Sheridan and Driver persuaded the government to let the association administer the ground. They argued that as the colony's cricket authority, with several hundred pounds in the bank, the association was best suited to improve the ground.

They had made big progress by the time of the first Test, dismissing the association's commitment to the Albert Ground, and developing the Associ-ation Ground with regular inter-State fixtures and matches against touring English sides. They had overcome the problems created by the famous riot of the 1878–79 season when spectators invaded the ground and England's captain Lord Harris was struck across the shoulders by one of the mob protesting against an umpiring decision. They had executed a master stroke by appointing Ned Gregory, the first man to make a Test duck, curator of the ground and giving him a cottage next to the ground in which to install his family. The Gregory family's association with the ground lasted for 60 years.

Gregory had the ground in fine shape for Sydney's first Test. Although both England and Australia were weakened by injuries, the bowling and batting on both sides ensured a fine contest and the fielding was described as the best ever seen in Sydney. England were dismissed for 133 in the first innings after Joey Palmer took 7 for 68. Murdoch kept wicket, allowing Australia's normal 'keeper, Jack Blackham, to distinguish himself with

England batting on the opening day of the 1897–98 Ashes series. On the far side of the ground the Smokers' Stand (later replaced by the Sheridan Stand) has risen since the photograph on page 45 was taken.

some brilliant stops at mid-off. Australia were 86 for 1 at stumps, but were all out next day for 197, a lead of 64.

England's chances revived with a splendid second innings opening stand of 122 in which Murdoch twice missed stumping Ulyett. With England back in the lead, Blackham replaced Murdoch behind the stumps. The partnership was broken with England 58 runs in front. Fine bowling by Tom Garrett and Palmer swung the game again and from 156 for 4 England were all out for 232. Australia were 35 for 2 after three days, chasing 169 to win. Determined batting next morning gave Australia victory as Alfred Shaw tried seven bowlers. None of them matched Palmer, Garrett and Evans and Australia won by five wickets. Palmer set a record by bowling unchanged with Evans in England's first innings, sending down 58 overs. He then bowled 66 overs in England's second knock.

The tension of this first Test, the euphoria created when two evenly matched teams struggle for supremacy with the players' pride and national prestige at stake, has frequently been repeated on the Sydney ground. There was no architectural plan behind the creation of the ground but somehow it has inherited from that first Test a sense of the big occasion. Famous players appearing at the ground for the first time have often told me that when they walked out on the field they had an uncanny feeling that something historic was about to happen.

Ned Gregory had a lot to do with creating this atmosphere. Born in Sydney in May 1839, he had been a professional cricketer from his early days. From his experiences as a professional with Bathurst, New South Wales and in the first Test, he was regarded as a genuine first-class player who knew what cricketers wanted. He was once reported to have hit the great pace bowler Fred Spofforth out of the attack. He was in the running for the first Australian team to tour England in 1878 but missed out.

The only buildings on the ground when first-class cricket began there were in the shape of a long warehouse later known as the Brewongle Stand, aboriginal for watering hole, and a small pavilion where the Members' Stand now stands. First improvements were to build two large, sloping mounds opposite these buildings called The Hill and the Paddington Hill. In 1881–82 Billy Murdoch drew the first huge roars from The Hill by scoring 321 for New South Wales against Victoria, an incredible knock given the prevailing conditions. Three years later the present Members' Stand was opened with an annual membership fee of two guineas. In 1895, the Bob Stand, a barn with a galvanized-iron roof built on the slope separating the Paddington Hill from The Hill, opened, taking its name from its admission price.

A fortnight before the Victoria v New South Wales match in 1895–96 Phil Sheridan went to Ned Gregory and asked him to build a new scoreboard for the match. Uninhibited by union working conditions, Gregory thrilled at the challenge because he believed after studying photographs of scoreboards in England and other Australian cities that they were all inadequate. The board that was ready for the big match became one of the wonders of cricket.

Gregory's board sat on top of a refreshment booth that served oysters as big as saucers for ninepence a dozen. The board was 25 yards wide and 12 yards high and was operated by two men turning rollers bearing numbers on strips of calico. They painted players' names on planks that hung on the board and simply ran the numbers up alongside the names. The first time the board was used Victoria beat New South Wales by four wickets.

Ned Gregory was a proud man when his son Syd, born in the family cottage at the ground, had his name hung on the scoreboard. Syd made the first of his seven English tours in 1890 at the age of 20. He played 58 Tests for Australia, a record that lasted until Ray Lindwall passed it 40 years

after Syd's last Test. He played the innings of his life in front of his father at Sydney in December 1894, by scoring 201, the first double-century in an Australian Test, helping Australia to a first innings score of 586. England replied with 325 to be 261 behind, but still won the match by 10 runs. This thrilling match had many heroes, the drama lasting until the sixth day when Australia – 113 for 2 overnight, chasing 177 to win – lost their last eight wickets for 54 runs on a sodden pitch.

Ned Gregory's brother Dave, who captained Australia in the first ever Test at Melbourne and led the first white Australian team to England, was made an honorary member of the ground in 1887, and sustained the New South Wales Cricket Association's strong links with the ground as association secretary. Dave was an important man in the New South Wales government as Paymaster of the Treasury and the trustees could not have had a better friend when funds were needed to improve the ground.

The Ladies' Stand was opened in 1896 on the same day as a new concrete cycling track which circled the inside of the ground. One of the carpenters who built the form work for the track before the concrete was poured was George Bradman, the son of an English migrant to Australia from an area on the borders of Cambridgeshire and Suffolk formed by the villages of Horseneath and Haverhill. Cycling at that time was a threat to cricket, attracting large crowds to the cricket ground for match races between Australians and champion American bike riders.

The man most responsible for converting the Association Ground into the Sydney Cricket Ground and attracting world attention to the place was Phil Sheridan, a dedicated cricket fan. Sheridan was a sunny natured Irishman who migrated to Australia in 1849 at the age of 15. He formed the

Sydney Cricket Club and was that club's delegate to the association when he was appointed a trustee and then secretary to the SCG. Sheridan worked tirelessly to improve the ground until his death in 1910, the year after the stand named in his honour was opened.

When Lord Sheffield brought the twelfth England team to Australia in 1891–92 under the captaincy of W. G. Grace, a body known as the Australasian Cricket Council controlled the sport there. The Council lacked direction, had no money, and completely failed to persuade leading players a national administration was needed. Despite the Council's mismanagement, the tour was a huge success, mainly because of the tremendous public eagerness to see Grace in action. At the end of the tour Lord Sheffield sent a cheque for £150 back to Ben Wardill, secretary of the Melbourne Cricket Club, as an expression of his delight over the way Australians had treated his team.

Wardill realized cricketers would get no benefit from the money if he passed the cheque on to the Council, so he sent it to his friend Phil Sheridan for safekeeping. Sheridan hung on to it until the Council, after rejecting a proposal to split the money between the three strongest States, decided to spend it on a trophy to be known as The Sheffield Shield for competition between the States. Sheridan applauded this move and immediately handed over the £150 to the Council. It turned out the only positive move the Council ever made, for it disbanded in 1898.

South Australia were not considered strong enough to join New South Wales and Victoria in this competition until they met New South Wales on the SCG in January 1892, in only the third match between these colonies. New South Wales had won both the previous encounters so easily that South Australia were given little chance, but they shocked the SCG crowd by winning by an innings and 53 runs. Dismissed for 215 on the first day, New South Wales could not contain the batting of Jack Lyons (145) and George Giffen (120) who added 234 for the second wicket. Leading by 115 on the first innings, South Australia then dismissed New South Wales for 62, Giffen taking 5 for 28 and Fred Jarvis 5 for 33. It was one of the biggest upsets ever on the SCG and assured South Australia of a place in the Shield.

By the time Australia became a nation with Federation of the colonies in 1900, Victor Trumper had emerged as the player who continually delighted SCG patrons. Trumper practised daily at the SCG nets as a teenager and in his adult years his artistry was at its best on this ground. To see him go out to bat partnered by Reggie Duff at the start of a match filled the ground with an expectant air of thrills to come. His 101 out of a total of 137 in 57 minutes, on a pitch favouring bowlers, for New South Wales against Victoria in 1905–06 always has rated as one of the great innings on the SCG. But it was little ahead of his 166 in the Fifth Test against England on the ground in 1907–08 when great bowlers Sydney Barnes, Wilfred Rhodes and Len Braund could not contain him.

The SCG scoreboard was rebuilt and moved further south and higher up The Hill in 1904 and in 1909 the Sheridan Stand replaced a small structure known as the Smoker's Stand. Sheridan died the following year at 77, with The Hill already famous as the place where workers assessed the cricket. Patsy Hendren made himself a great favourite when the 1920–21 England side visited Australia by jumping the fence at the fall of a wicket and sharing a beer with spectators on The Hill while waiting for the incoming batsman.

George Bradman, the Bowral carpenter, brought his son Don to watch the Fifth Test of that series.

A section of the crowd gathered on The Hill watch the opening overs of the Second Test against England on 13 December 1936.

That night going home in the train after watching Charlie Macartney set up an Australian win with a swashbuckling knock of 170 young Don confessed that all he wanted to do in life was to bat on the same ground as Macartney. The young Bradman set about achieving his ambition by reeling off a series of prodigious scores in bush cricket.

Through the 1920s The Hill was ruled by an English-born spectator named Stephen Harold Gascoigne, whose witty, knowledgeable comments reverberated around the ground, adding to the crowd's pleasure. Yabba, as he was known, lived by hawking rabbits from a cart he wheeled through the back streets of south Sydney. In the days before television and crowd larrikinism, this open-hearted, fleshy man would set up camp looking down on the pitch from around mid-on.

Bill Ponsford was one of Yabba's heroes from the time he made 110 in both innings for Victoria *v* New South Wales on the SCG in 1923–24, and Stan McCabe's masterly 187 not out in the First Test of the Bodyline series in 1932–33 found Yabba

in sparkling form. Yabba captured the acrimony of that dramatic rubber when he spotted England's enigmatic captain Douglas Jardine brushing his face. 'You leave our flies alone, Jardine,' he hollered.

In the 20 years from 1928 to 1948 Don Bradman attracted crowds to Australian cricket grounds of such proportions that many of the grandstands which now decorate our grounds were built with the money he attracted. Bradman scored a century at a rate slightly better than every third time he batted. If he was not at lunch, you could look out from the SCG and watch the hordes of people streaming across Moore Park to see the great man bat. When he moved to live in Adelaide, the NSWCA suffered a grievous financial blow.

In Bradman's time as Australia's captain work began on a huge stand next to the Members' Stand.

The first stage was opened in 1935 and called the Noble Stand. The second stage, opened in 1973, became the Bradman Stand. It was on the SCG that Bradman made his highest score, 452 not out, in 1928–29, in a Sheffield Shield match for New South Wales against Queensland, a performance which in 1989 remained the highest first-class score on grass anywhere in the world.

On the SCG in 1955–56 New South Wales captain Keith Miller threw the ball to Alan Davidson to open the bowling against South Australia. Davidson stepped out his run, but before he could bowl the breeze with which Miller always liked to operate blew across and ruffled Miller's long hair. Miller called for the ball, took 7 for 12, and had South Australia out for 27. Davidson did not get a bowl.

Miller, Davidson, Arthur Morris, Richie Benaud, Brian Booth and Doug Walters all experienced the joy of having the SCG as their home ground. Benaud, with 266 wickets, took over as New South Wales's highest wicket-taker from Bill O'Reilly. Booth surpassed Alan Kippax's appearance record with 93 matches for the State. Walters became the first player for whom fans made a banner on the Sydney Hill, 'The Doug Walters Stand'. But none of them could have anticipated the changes that came to the ground because of the Packer-inspired World Series Cricket revolt against traditional authority in 1978.

World Series Cricket introduced cricket under floodlights, coloured clothing, white balls, microphones in the stumps and other innovations that often converted the SCG into a bullring or, as the 1984 *Wisden* said, created 'an atmosphere more like a Coliseum than a cricket ground'. Architecturally, WSC also ruined the SCG, bringing with it obscene floodlight towers that completely destroyed the harmony of the place, an error that was later com-

In the 12 years which separate these photographs, a massive rebuilding programme at the SCG has included the erection of lighting pylons; the virtual removal of The Hill; and the replacement of the Sheridan and Brewongle stands by the new Brewongle stand.

pounded with the erection of a horror of an electronic scoreboard.

To accommodate Packer's matches the New South Wales government amended the Sydney Sports Ground and Cricket Ground Act in the middle of the night. This removed the association's legal right to give the staging of its matches at the ground priority. A new Sydney Cricket Ground Trust was appointed simultaneously with the new legislation becoming law, with those who had opposed WSC omitted.

Under the settlement that ended three seasons of WSC, Packer's promotional arm, PBL Marketing, was given the job of promoting all cricket. PBL consistently failed to do this, promoting only those matches featured on Packer's TV network and ignoring the famous Sheffield Shield competition. The sale of the Packer TV stations in 1987 to Perth magnate Alan Bond gave cricket lovers fresh hope that this would change.

In 1988 only a small part of The Hill remained and it was dominated by the space-age scoreboard that provides little of the information Ned Gregory's board offered. The rest of the ground is circled by new concrete stands studded with private boxes leased for large sums to business houses. The old magic remains inside the fence, however, although wind currents and backgrounds have changed. Inside the gate the SCG remains a wonderful place to play cricket. You face the front to enjoy it without looking around.

Sydney

Ref/No	Season	V	T	Result	Ref/No	Season	V	T	Result
6/1	1881–82	E	2	A-5w	329/39	1950–51	E	3	A-I&13
7/2			3	A-6w	345/40	1951–52	WI	2	A-7w
12/3	1882–83	E	3	E-69	348/41			5	A-202
13/4			4	A-4w	362/42	1952–53	SA	3	A-I&38
19/5	1884–85	E	3	A-6	392/43	1954–55	E	2	E-38
20/6			4	A-8w	395/44			5	Draw
25/7	1886–87	E	1	E-13	466/45	1958–59	E	3	Draw
26/8			2	E-71	504/46	1960–61	WI	3	WI-222
27/9	1887–88	E	–	E-126	537/47	1962–63	E	3	A-8w
36/10	1891–92	E	2	A-72	539/48			5	Draw
42/11	1894–94	E	1	E-10	550/49	1963–64	SA	3	Draw
45/12			4	A-I&147	552/50			5	Draw
53/13	1897–98	E	1	E-9w	599/51	1965–66	E	3	E-I&93
57/14			5	A-6w	627/52	1967–68	I	4	A-144
65/15	1901–02	E	1	E-I&124	644/53	1968–69	WI	3	A-10w
68/16			4	A-7w	646/54			5	A-382
78/17	1903–04	E	1	E-5w	676/55	1970–71	E	4	E-299
81/18			4	E-157	679/56			7	E-62
96/19	1907–08	E	1	A-2w	710/57	1972–73	P	3	A-52
100/20			5	A-49	729/58	1973–74	NZ	2	Draw
111/21	1910–11	SA	1	A-I&114	753/59	1974–75	E	4	A-171
115/22			5	A-7w	767/60	1975–76	WI	4	A-7w
116/23	1911–12	E	1	A-146	795/61	1976–77	P	3	P-8w
120/24			5	E-70	812/62	1977–78	I	4	I-I&2
135/25	1920–21	E	1	A-377	837/63	1978–79	E	4	E-93
139/26			5	A-9w	839/64			6	E-9w
158/27	1924–25	E	1	A-193	870/65	1979–80	E	2	A-6w
162/28			5	A-307	893/66	1980–81	I	1	A-I&4
177/29	1928–29	E	2	E-8w	919/67	1981–82	WI	2	Draw
200/30	1930–31	WI	2	A-I&172	942/68	1982–83	E	5	Draw
203/31			5	WI-30	974/69	1983–84	P	5	A-10w
213/32	1931–32	SA	2	A-I&155	1001/70	1984–85	WI	5	A-I&55
220/33	1932–33	E	1	E-10w	1030/71	1985–86	NZ	2	A-4w
224/34			5	E-8w	1034/72	1985–86	I	3	Draw
256/35	1936–37	E	2	E-I&22	1062/73	1986–87	E	5	A-55
280/36	1946–47	E	2	A-I&33	1090/74	1987–88	E	–	Draw
283/37			5	A-5w	1113/75	1988–89	WI	4	A-7w
291/38	1947–48	I	2	Draw	Australia: P 75, W 40, D 11, L 24				

Lord's pavilion, an image as familiar as the game itself and 100 years old in 1990 – seen here during the 1988 Test Match against West Indies.

②

England

MARCUS WILLIAMS

While interntional cricket has mushroomed in recent years the list of Test grounds in England has remained unchanged since 1902. This is not to be interpreted as a statement of retrogression, rather that those great centres of the game – Lord's and the Oval (London), Old Trafford (Manchester), Trent Bridge (Nottingham), Headingley (Leeds), Edgbaston (Birmingham) – established themselves from the earliest days of international cricket and have developed with the times to maintain their positions of primacy. Only one other ground, Bramall Lane (Sheffield), has joined the elite, albeit for a single Test, but that original home of Yorkshire closed its doors to cricket in 1973.

Though Lord's is the acknowledged home of world cricket and the oldest of the major grounds in the country, seniority in terms of Test matches rests south of the River Thames at the Kennington Oval. It was there that England faced Australia on 6–8 September 1880. England won by five wickets, but two years later Australia turned the tables at the same ground when the 'Demon' Spofforth took 14 wickets for 90 runs to bowl them to victory by 7 runs. It was this result, the first defeat of England's full strength on home soil, that gave rise to the renowned 'Ashes' obituary notice which appeared in the following Saturday's issue of the *Sporting Times*.

On the Australians' next visit in 1884 Test matches were staged at Old Trafford and Lord's, in addition to the Oval, and in 1899 those grounds were joined by Trent Bridge and Headingley in a series now extended to five matches. The line-up was completed in 1902, when Edgbaston was awarded the first Test in place of Trent Bridge and Bramall Lane replaced Headingley.

England did not entertain new Test match opponents until 1907, when South Africa played a three-match series, the opening encounter of which was at Lord's and established a precedent whereby all countries, as the family of cricket has expanded, have subsequently played their first Test match in England at headquarters, viz. West Indies (1928), New Zealand (1931), India (1932), Pakistan (1954) and Sri Lanka (1984).

Much has changed in cricket, as in the world, since 1899, but that very first five-match series established a pattern for major tours (i.e. Australia and, from 1924, South Africa) that was to endure for more than half a century: the opening Test at Trent Bridge or Edgbaston, the second always at Lord's, the third and fourth at Headingley and Old Trafford (or vice versa), and the final match often providing a memorable climax to the summer at the Oval. The re-establishment of Edgbaston on the Test match circuit in 1957 necessitated a reorganization and the subsequent introduction of shared tours, of regular one-day internationals in 1972, and the Prudential World Cup competitions of 1975, 1979 and 1983 served further to change the face of the English season. However, a legacy of the old pattern remains in that the second Test of the summer is almost invariably at Lord's and the final one at the Oval.

Birmingham
EDGBASTON

Edgbaston is very much the junior among the current English Test grounds. It was awarded its first game in 1902, staged only three more up to 1929 and then disappeared from the scene until 1957. By then extensive development had transformed it into a stadium to rival any in the country, extensively equipped with stands, banqueting suites and car parks; and though the folk of Birmingham have not always been noted for their support for cricket, Edgbaston has remained firmly on the provincial Test match rota. It has also had more than its fair share of incident and is by some way England's most successful ground.

Warwickshire County Cricket Club was founded by William Ansell in 1882 and after examining several possible sites for their home ground they chose a meadow of rough grazing land in Edgbaston Road on the Calthorpe estate, some two miles from the city centre – country then, strictly residential now. They got it at 'a fair and reasonable rental, without harrowing conditions'. Among other work required to get the ground ready for play a stream which ran along the west side had first to be drained, so the opening match on the ground, a draw against MCC, did not take place until 1886; later that season the Australians paid their first visit to Edgbaston. Warwickshire, who had through Ansell's vehement lobbying advanced to first-class status in 1894, were admitted to the county championship in the following year and Ansell's persuasive powers secured them their first Test in 1902 in preference to Trent Bridge.

The event put a severe strain on the club's administration, although the cricket – so far as the weather permitted – was nothing short of sensational. Preparations to accommodate a larger crowd than ever before began in earnest several months before the game: committees were formed and met frequently; help was sought from, among others, Aston Villa FC; new stands were built and thousands of seats brought to the ground; 60 gatemen were hired, and as many police, and 200 catering staff; 90 pressmen had to be housed. All this had to be organized by a clerical staff consisting solely of the secretary, R.V. Ryder, who had neither telephone nor typewriter.

On the opening day, 29 May, England ran up a formidable score on an excellent pitch thanks mainly to Tyldesley's splendid 138 and after rain had delayed the resumption until after lunch the next day Lockwood and Rhodes, number 11 in a side regarded as perhaps the strongest in batting ever fielded by England, extended their last-wicket stand to 81 before MacLaren declared at 376. Then, in well under an hour and a half Australia were routed for 36, their lowest total in Test cricket. The pitch was wet and the light bad, but not sufficiently so, it was said, to warrant a collapse of such proportions. Credit was due, however, to the magnificent bowling of the great Yorkshire all-rounders, Rhodes, who took 7 for 17, and Hirst; the Warwickshire wicket-keeper, Lilley, had three victims and only the peerless Trumper, who batted 70 minutes for 18, offered lasting resistance. Rhodes's performance was particularly galling for the home club, for they could not afford to take him on to the staff four years earlier and he joined his native Yorkshire.

Following on, Australia reached 8 for no wicket by the close but were then saved by 12 hours' continuous rain, so that by nine o'clock on the last morning the ground was flooded (no Brumbrella in those days, of course, to cover most of the playing area). Not unreasonably the committee paid off half the gatemen and released half the

police, but the players and umpires waited patiently, a sizable crowd – it was a Saturday – assembled outside and at two o'clock a hot sun came out. The crowd eventually stormed the gates and, as Ryder put it, 'To save our skins we started play at 5.20 on a swamp.' Australia ended at 46 for two and the match was drawn, but the cost to Edgbaston of its first Test was high: the club received only £750 as its share-out from the series and at the end of a very wet season had to make a public appeal for £3000 to put its finances straight.

Edgbaston had its next taste of Test cricket in 1909, when another left-arm combination, Hirst and Blythe, took all 20 Australian wickets and England, thanks to an undefeated 62 by Hobbs on his debut (after a first-innings duck), won by 10 wickets. Edgbaston was excluded from the 1912 Triangular Tournament, despite there being nine matches, and the next Test there was not until 1924. Again, however, the happenings were remarkable, although a half-crown (12$\frac{1}{2}$p) admission charge meant that there were not many people there to witness them. England rattled up 438, Hobbs and Sutcliffe together in a Test for the first time putting on 136 for the first wicket, and then South Africa, on a blameless pitch, were shot out by Gilligan, captaining England for the first time, and Tate for 30 in just 48 minutes. The same bowlers took all

the wickets second time round as England won by an innings. The 1929 South Africans held their own in a drawn match on an easy-paced pitch.

That ended Edgbaston's first chapter as a Test ground and so began a long period in exile. The problem was that whenever Edgbaston had a Test it was at the expense of Trent Bridge, where the facilities and crowds were far better. The fact that Edgbaston was able to sell only £800 worth of tickets in advance for the 1929 match was the final blow and Warwickshire cricket temporarily fell into the doldrums – to revive, ironically during the Second World War.

Despite some enemy action (a bomb destroyed the old wooden indoor cricket school) and the occupation of the pavilion by the National Fire Service *Wisden* reported in 1942 that Edgbaston was kept in excellent order. A Birmingham Festival week, inaugurated by Councillor R.I. Scorer, was staged there for the last four years of the war, with such a response from the public that a record crowd of 14,000 which attended one Sunday held up traffic and proved more than the turnstiles could cope with. Members' subscriptions enabled a reserve

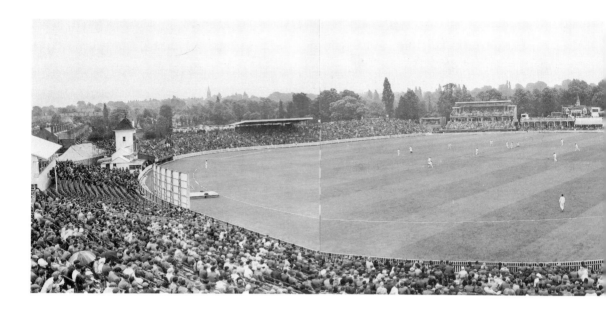

The Australians batting during the Edgbaston Test of 1961. Extensive improvements to the ground in the mid-1950s helped to establish Edgbaston as one of the best equipped Test venues in England.

fund to be built up towards post-war renovations and by the end of the war plans were already under way to make Edgbaston suitable again as a Test match ground. The full scheme was estimated to cost £200,000, but an initial appeal for £50,000 met with such a good response that the club were able to buy six acres of land adjoining the pavilion to make a total of nearly 20 acres on the whole site. A further three were added in the 1960s with the acquisition of college playing fields across the River Rea on the east side.

By the time Test cricket returned to Edgbaston in 1957 the ground had been transformed at a cost of nearly £500,000. The cindered banks on the popular sides had been replaced with concrete terracing; seats with comfortable backrests had supplanted the splintery, single-plank benches which made wriggling a danger. The Birmingham public

responded by turning out in unprecedented numbers, 32,000 on the Saturday (gates closed) and 64,698 in all, producing receipts of £29,496, and they were rewarded with a match which featured one of the most famous recoveries in Test history. It looked like a repeat of the 1950 tour. with Ramadhin bowling England out for 186, West Indies piling up 474 and having England on the run at 113 for 3 in their second innings. However, May and Cowdrey batted for the next day and a half, adding 411 in England's highest stand for any wicket, and in the end West Indies were clinging on at 72 for 7 when stumps were drawn. In the second innings Ramadhin bowled 98 overs (a Test record) and took only two wickets; his threat to England was never the same again.

It was the Warwickshire County Cricket Supporters' Association, founded in 1953, which played a major part in the redevelopment of the ground thanks to its now legendary football pools scheme, which by the early 1970s had over 300,000 members and 7000 agents. Its first big project was a new indoor school, followed by the trans-

England gained their only win of a losing series against West Indies, thanks largely to Trueman's 12 wickets, the best in an Edgbaston Test. There was continued confirmation of Edgbaston as England's favourite ground when New Zealand were defeated by nine wickets in 1965 – apart from a commendable recovery by the visitors, the match is best remembered for the hot drinks which were brought on to the field on a desperately cold second day – and then it became eight wins in 12 Tests when India were overcome in three days in 1967 on a pitch which turned from early on.

A rain-affected match against Australia in 1968 was drawn after Cowdrey had fittingly celebrated his 100th Test with a century and he also made his last home Test appearance at Edgbaston when England returned there in 1971. Their unbeaten record was saved by the rain after Pakistan's mammoth 608 for 7 declared, founded on Zaheer Abbas's 274 in his first Test in England. A draw against West Indies in 1973 brought controversy when umpire Fagg refused to stand for an over after dissent shown by the West Indies captain, Kanhai, when Boycott was given not out. Kanhai,

formation of the terracing which covered the majority of the ground into the West Bank and Hill Bank extensions on the popular side; the Pavilion (East Wing); Press Box Stand at the opposite, city end; and the Pavilion (West Wing) including, fittingly, the William Ansell Stand. The association also built up a capital fund to ensure the future of the club and Edgbaston, and in 1981 paid for the Brumbrella, the huge motorized cover which can protect much of the playing area. Many other cricket clubs and organizations, including MCC, the Cricket Council and the Test and County Cricket Board, have had cause to be grateful for the support of the Supporters' Association.

Edgbaston now enjoyed regular Test cricket. New Zealand and South Africa were comfortably beaten in the next three years and then 1961 saw the return of the Australians for the first time since 1909. England trailed by 321 on first innings, but Dexter and Subba Row saved the game on a pitch which became slower as the game went on. Pakistan were beaten by an innings with more than a day and a half to spare in 1962 and the next year

The Brumbrella, one of many gifts to Warwickshire from its Supporters' Association.

incidentally, who played for Warwickshire with great success for 10 seasons, figured in a world-record second-wicket partnership at Edgbaston in 1974 with Jameson against Gloucestershire, a sign of the splendid batting pitches of that era.

Not long before the 1974 Test against India, whom England crushed by an innings after David Lloyd's double-century, a small memorial was established in the perimeter wall to S.F. Barnes, arguably the greatest bowler of all time. It houses his ashes, which rest at Edgbaston at the request of his family; the spot chosen is at or near the point where he entered the ground in 1894 to play his first match for the county. It should be pointed out that he is not to be identified with the other S. Barnes, Dr Stanley, a former club president after whom a stand is named at the north-east corner of the ground.

England's Birmingham bubble finally burst in 1975 in the ground's 17th Test. Denness flouted Edgbaston convention by putting the opposition in and after Australia had scored 359 a thunderstorm gave Lillee, Thomson and Walker ideal conditions in which to avenge 1902. In 1978 England returned to winning Edgbaston ways with an innings win over Pakistan, Old's seven-wicket return including four wickets in five balls in the first sponsored Test match in England. Controversy again erupted when a bouncer from Warwickshire's Willis struck the nightwatchman Iqbal Qasim in the face. England won by an innings again the following year against India after amassing the highest total in Edgbaston Tests – 633 for 5 declared, to which Gower contributed an unbeaten 200.

Edgbaston during the 1981 Test: a general view of the ground, and part of the crowd which surged on to the field to celebrate England's snatched win over Australia after Botham's 5 for 1 off 28 balls.

The Edgbaston match of 1981 was as remarkable as any of that memorable series. Three modest totals on a dry, unreliable pitch left Australia needing 151 to win and they passed 100 with only four wickets down. To no avail. Botham, reluctant at first to bowl but eventually steaming in with much of his old zest, took 5 for 1 in an astonishing 28-ball spell from the Press Box Stand end and England won yet another victory at Edgbaston by 29 runs. The uncertainty of the batsmen was highlighted by the fact that it was the first Test since 1935 not to contain a half-century.

England won again in 1982, a straightforward affair against Pakistan, but even Edgbaston was not exempt from defeat in 1984, the year West Indies completed their 'blackwash'. Their batsmen amassed 606 and the bowlers did the rest as England lost by an innings and 180 runs. It was a particularly unhappy Test debut for Andy Lloyd on his home ground, who was struck on the temple and did not play again that season. England overcame Australia the following year after Gower scored his second double-century at the ground and Ellison took 10 wickets. At a crucial stage of Australia's second innings Phillips was given out after hitting a ball from Edmonds hard on to the instep of Lamb at silly point and the ball rebounded into Gower's hands. Australian opinion held that the batsman should have had the benefit of the doubt; the umpires were in no doubt that the catch was legitimate.

A stoppage for bad light and rain in the final session left the 1986 match tantalisingly poised, with India 62 runs short of a target of 236 and five wickets in hand on a pitch helpful to bowlers. Edgbaston 1987 produced another memorable finish: after four fairly tedious days the match burst into life on the last afternoon and eventually England had to score 124 in 18 overs. With a little more composure they might have got closer than 109 for 7 but it was a thrilling conclusion to an otherwise mundane encounter – and one that happily passed off more peacefully than the one-day international earlier the same season in which disgraceful scenes culminated in one spectator having his throat cut by flying glass.

At the end of 1988 the Warwickshire club announced an ambitious programme for further development at the ground. A new stand was built at the city end, necessitating the removal of an Edgbaston landmark, the Thwaite scoreboard (named, like the main gates, after a former benefactor and president). A replica, at least, was erected above and behind the new structure in time for the following summer's Test against Australia

in which rain enabled an increasingly beleagured England to emerge with a draw. More significantly, though, in the longer term a new pavilion was planned, subject to members' approval, at an estimated cost of £4 million. Since it has always seemed strange that a ground so otherwise well-appointed as Edgbaston should still have such an insignificant pavilion amid its other edifices – a squat, two-storey building, albeit comfortably equipped and housing in its club room a fine collection of Warwickshire memorabilia – many thought this change long overdue. As the chairman stated that the ultimate objective was to establish Edgbaston as an automatic Test venue, there is no question that William Ansell would have supported the scheme to the hilt.

Birmingham				
Ref/No	*Season*	*V*	*T*	*Result*
70/1	1902	A	1	Draw
101/2	1909	A	1	E-10w
153/3	1924	SA	1	E-I&18
181/4	1929	SA	1	Draw
439/5	1957	WI	1	Draw
454/6	1958	NZ	1	E-205
492/7	1960	SA	1	E-100
507/8	1961	A	1	Draw
530/9	1962	P	1	E-I&24
545/10	1963	WI	3	E-217
591/11	1965	NZ	1	E-9w
620/12	1967	I	3	E-132
639/13	1968	A	3	Draw
687/14	1971	P	1	Draw
726/15	1973	WI	2	Draw
741/16	1974	I	3	E-I&78
760/17	1975	A	1	A-I&85
825/18	1978	P	1	E-I&57
851/19	1979	I	1	E-I&83
906/20	1981	A	4	E-29
931/21	1982	P	1	E-113
989/22	1984	WI	1	WI-I&180
1021/23	1985	A	5	E-I&118
1048/24	1986	I	3	Draw
1078/25	1987	P	4	Draw
1123/26	1989	A	3	Draw

England: P 26, W 14, D 10, L 2

Leeds

HEADINGLEY

It seems anomalous that Yorkshire, traditionally if not always in practice the stronghold of English cricket, should not have a home of its own. True the Headingley ground in Leeds houses the offices of the Yorkshire County Cricket Club and is regarded as the county's headquarters; but the owners, and Yorkshire's landlords, are the Leeds Cricket, Football and Athletic Co. Ltd. To use the words of the county's secretary: Yorkshire owns not a blade of grass or a plank of wood. Moreover, Leeds itself was, in the early days of Yorkshire cricket, secondary in importance to Sheffield, although by the time Test cricket came to be allocated to Yorkshire, in 1899, Leeds had claimed superiority and has retained that position ever since – with one exception: the 1902 Test against Australia was awarded to Bramall Lane, Sheffield.

In contrast to industrial Bramall Lane, the surroundings of Headingley in north-west Leeds are much different: suburban, and utilitarian rather than handsome. The ground is also shared with football, the rugby league code, although unlike Bramall Lane the football pitch is separate, at the back of the solid main stand, whose bulk tends to dominate the cricket ground in the absence of an eye-catching pavilion. The ground gives, too, the impression of an open-air arena rather than a stadium, with its broad, open terraces to the north and west, although plans are afoot to transform it. They include the addition of a third floor to the main stand, to provide seating, dining and exhibition areas, and a new roof to cover not only all the seats in that stand but also most of the popular western terracing. With hospitality boxes and tiered seating already established above the Winter Shed (previously the indoor cricket school) at the northern, Kirkstall Lane end, and the stately line of poplars reputedly planted to prevent free viewing from the adjacent houses, Headingley should ultimately resemble the leading modern sports complex that it hopes to become – and a setting to match the many mighty deeds it has witnessed.

Formerly part of the Cardigan estates, the ground was acquired by the Leeds CFAC in January 1889 and first used for cricket in 1890. Yorkshire fixtures were soon established there and the first Test match was not too long in coming. When, following an initiative from the Yorkshire captain and president, Lord Hawke, it was decided to play five Test matches in an English series for the first time in 1899, Headingley was chosen to stage the match awarded to Yorkshire on account of its amenities and accessibility from the city centre. Astonishingly, and much to the consternation of the home crowd, England left out Rhodes even though rain on the night before the match had produced conditions ideal for his left-arm spin, but there were two Yorkshiremen in the side, Brown and Jackson. Hearne, of Middlesex, performed a hat-trick in Australia's second innings, but rain prevented play on the final day.

The aristocratic Jackson, born at nearby Chapel Allerton and son of a Cabinet member whom he followed into Parliament, was England's captain when the Australians returned after the Sheffield interlude for their next Test at Headingley in 1905 and his undefeated 144 was his highest score in Tests. Although the match was drawn, this was very much Jackson's year; not only did he lead England to a 2–0 win in the series to retain the Ashes, he also finished top of the batting and bowling averages.

Headingley saw a remarkable, low-scoring match in 1907, on a gluepot of a pitch and amid heavy showers. The scores – England 76 and 162,

South Africa 110 and 75 – indicate the treacherous batting conditions, but do not tell of Blythe's tormenting left-arm spin (8 for 59 in the first innings and 7 for 40 in the second, still the best match figures in a Leeds Test) and Fry's tenacity as he compiled the only half-century of the match and defied the googly quartet of Vogler, Schwarz, Faulkner and White. No wonder Fry described it as 'the game of a lifetime', though according to *Wisden* 'A less satisfactory test game has seldom been played'!

England's batsmen struggled too on their next visit to Headingley and collapsed in their second innings for 87, their lowest total at the ground. Barnes and Rhodes shared 13 Australian wickets, but they were outshone by the ebullient Macartney, who at this stage of his career was a destructive slow left-armer as well as a budding batting talent, which he was to reveal to the Leeds public when Australia returned after the First World War: in 1921 he scored 115 and in 1926 made 151, 112 of them before lunch on the first day – a harbinger of Bradman.

That match in 1921 was perhaps England's most trying of a traumatic summer, which saw them lose the series 3–0 and call on 30 players in the process – a total not approached until 1988. Their catalogue of woe began within an hour of the start, Tennyson, the new captain of a side with seven changes,

A general view of Headingley during the 1985 Test. The Winter Shed is to the left of the sightscreen.

splitting his left hand stopping a hard hit from Macartney. Then came an even more devastating blow: Hobbs, who had missed the first two games of the series because of a torn muscle, was stricken with appendicitis during the first afternoon and put out of cricket for the rest of the season. As if that was not enough, Brown, the wicket-keeper, needed a runner in the second innings and Douglas was unable to field on the final day because his wife was ill. It was little surprise then that England were trounced by 219 runs, their eighth successive defeat by the old enemy. English pride was assuaged by the captain, whose performance would have warranted an heroic couplet or two from his grandfather, as he flailed away one-handed against the fearsome pace of Gregory and McDonald to score 63 in the first innings and 36 in the second. Tennyson's acclaim was matched only by that for the Australian wicket-keeper, Carter. The reason? A son of Halifax, he was the only Yorkshire-born player in the match.

At Headingley in 1926 it seemed as though England were in for another tousing. Carr had put Australia in, a rare occurrence in Test cricket until

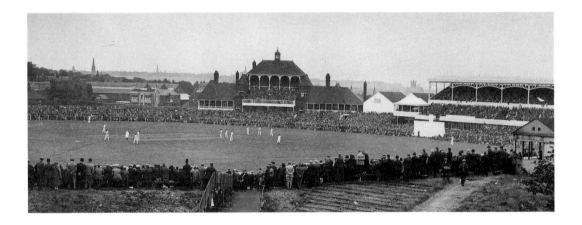

Looking towards the packed Members' pavilion – now
much altered – during the 1926 Test.

modern times, and though Bardsley fell to the first
ball of the match, Carr himself dropped Macartney
from the fifth. The little man took full advantage
of his good fortune, racing to his hundred out of
131 in 103 minutes, and Australia reached 494.
England collapsed to 182 for 8 against the leg-spin
of Mailey and Grimmett, but a resolute 76 by the
Yorkshire fast bowler, Macaulay, and a dominant
opening partnership in the follow-on by Hobbs
and Sutcliffe secured a draw.

There was another hundred before lunch in
Headingley's next Test, by Owen-Smith, of South
Africa, in 1929, and another the following year,
though it was but the prelude to a remarkable era
straddling the Second World War in which Don
Bradman (963 runs in six Test innings) took
Headingley by storm and Yorkshiremen treated
him like one of their own, bestowing on an outsider
the unique honour of life membership of the county
club and, he said, the most stirring public acclaim
of his career. He was fortunate to be playing at
Headingley in an era when it had earned a reputation for superb batting pitches and if this has not

always been the case in recent years, it should be
remembered that prevailing conditions have often
included an atmosphere heavily conducive to
swing, making for low-scoring games.

In a nutshell Bradman's Test match achievements at Headingley were: 334 in 1930 against an
attack opened by Larwood and Tate; 304 in 1934;
a mere 103 and 16 in 1938; and in 1948, on his last
tour, 33 and then an undefeated 173 as Australia,
set 404 for victory in 344 minutes, got home for
the loss of only three wickets in one of the most
remarkable Test wins of all time. No wonder that
Bradman, even in the days before television,
acquired a superstardom attained even now by very
few – sportsmen or others.

The first Bradman innings at Headingley was
the most famous of them and though he did not in
fact score a hundred runs in each session of play (it
was 105 before lunch, 115 in the afternoon and 89
after tea), he did achieve the still extant Test record
of 309 runs in a day; the highest individual Test
score to date; the fastest Test double-century (214
minutes); and he passed 1000 runs in only his
seventh Test match – all this at the age of 21 years
and 318 days. The innings, which began at an
unpromising 2 for 1, contained 46 fours, and the
Falstaffian figure of Dick Tyldesley, the Lancashire

leg-spinner, chased many of them down the hill from mid-on with the ball always tantalisingly just out of reach. One could sympathize with his desire at the end of the first day to get back to Manchester where he could put his 'poomps' on and his feet up. Australia eventually totalled 566, Tate ending with a commendable 5 for 124, and forced England to follow on 175 behind despite a commanding century by Hammond. Bad light and a thunderstorm came to England's rescue.

As Tyldesley and many fast bowlers have discovered to the cost of their run-ups, there is a marked slope on the ground towards the football stand, and the overall speed of the outfield lends credence to the impression – illusory one is told – from the boundary that the square is a plateau from which the outfield falls away to all sides. To the fielder despairingly chasing the ball that stand must present a forbidding sight and when Bradman returned for his second instalment, it had taken on a new aspect, for on Good Friday 1932 the old one had been burnt down. Its replacement, built at a cost of £20,000 by the Airey company (whose chairman was also chairman of Leeds CFAC), appears even more overpowering than photographs show its predecessor, though it has since been adapted to accommodate broadcasting boxes and the Leeds Taverners Club.

In the 1934 Test Grimmett and O'Reilly spun out England for exactly 200 on the first day, but England hit back when Bowes, on his home ground, claimed three wickets for 39 before the close. Bowes also bowled Bradman ... but by then he had made 309, shared a fourth-wicket partnership of 388 with Ponsford and put Australia in a dominant position despite no other batsman scoring more than 27. The total of 584 is still the record for a Leeds Test and would probably have won the match had not rain again intervened.

The return of 21-year-old Don Bradman after his remarkable triple-century at Headingley in 1930.

It was beyond the powers even of Bradman to manage a treble of triple-centuries when Australia were back in 1938, but, batting in poor light, he did contribute a masterly 103 in his first innings of a low-scoring match towards an Australian victory by five wickets which retained the Ashes. The key factor, however, was O'Reilly's leg-spin which exploited the conditions to claim ten wickets.

A few charity games were staged at Headingley during the Second World War, when Yorkshire folk mourned the death in a prisoner of war camp of their great left-arm spinner, Verity (all ten Nottinghamshire wickets for 10 runs at Headingley in 1932 was the statistical peak of many great feats); but they had the consolation of their beloved Hutton's recovery from an arm broken in the gym. Surprisingly it was not until 1947 that he made his first Test appearance on home territory, but they flocked to Headingley to see him; nor were they disappointed. Thirty-one thousand were present on the first day to see South Africa bowled out for 175 and in the final hour Hutton and his famous Lancastrian partner, Washbrook, safely put

'The crowd within and the crowd without' – Jack Hickes's
classic view of the 1948 Headingley Test.

completed. An England victory was eventually a
formality and fittingly, perhaps inevitably, Hutton
made the winning hit, a six to square leg.

It was Bradman again the following year when
the powerful 1948 Australians achieved one of the
greatest Test wins of all time in front of more huge
attendances – 158,000 over the five days, a record
for a match in England. They saw a record number
of runs too, the aggregate of 1723 (for 31 wickets)
also being a record for this country. England batted
first on a perfect pitch and amassed 496 thanks to
hundreds from Washbrook and Edrich, Australia,
led by Harvey's 112 in his first Test against
England, replied formidably to finish only 38 runs
behind, but by the start of the final day England
led by 400 with two wickets in hand. Yardley
batted on briefly in the morning to get the heavy
roller on an already turning pitch and left Australia
344 minutes to score 404. Against a weak spin
attack lacking a leg-spinner and profiting from
missed chances, Morris and Bradman shared a
second-wicket partnership of 301 and Australia
gained an historic victory with a quarter of an hour
to spare, Bradman, by now almost an adopted son
of Yorkshire, was accorded an ovation he described
as the most moving he received anywhere in his
glittering career.

Headingley's tradition of featherbed pitches continued in the next few Test matches, the 1951
match against South Africa being notable for May's
hundred on his Test debut, another hundred by
Hutton and Eric Rowan's 236, the highest by a
South African against England, as well as an attendance of 116,000 over four days (the last was washed
out). The match the following year, against India,
was memorable for two Yorkshiremen: Hutton
was appointed England's first regular professional
captain and Trueman, bursting on to the scene in
his first Test, hastened him to a winning start by

on 53. On the second day, despite a storm flooding
the ground an hour before play, the gates were
closed on a crowd of 35,000 inside and several
thousand outside; many of the lucky ones in the
ground were exposed to the elements for Headingley has always been short of covered accommodation. The start was delayed, but the openers
completed a stand of 141 before Washbrook was
bowled for 75. Hutton, however, moved on com-
mandingly, his every run cheered – and spectators
several times strayed over the boundaries, forcing
the umpires to halt play – until the century was

taking three wickets in eight balls at the start of India's second innings (seven in all in the match) as they lost four wickets for no runs in a start unparalleled in Test history. It was hard to ignore the irony in Hutton's appointment, for it was a famous Yorkshireman of a previous generation, Lord Hawke, who had said: 'Pray God no professional shall ever captain England' – though in the light of what Hawke did for professional cricketers in terms of winter payments and other benefits, the latter part of this often misunderstood quote should be added: 'When the day comes when we shall have no more amateurs captaining England it will be a thousand pities.'

Hutton was still captain when Australia returned to Headingley in 1953 and England, after being behind for much of the game, managed finally to stall Australia's attempt to score 177 runs in 115 minutes to win, Bailey, having batted at his most adhesively for more than four hours, then came on from the Kirkstall Lane end when Australia required 66 in three quarters of an hour and fired the ball down the leg side with a packed field to halt the batsmen in their tracks. Attendances were again enormous, with the gates locked on 35,000 on the Saturday and Monday.

In 1955 South Africa achieved their only win in eight appearances at Headingley. Recovering from 98 for 7 on the first day, they scored 500 in their second innings and were then bowled to a 224-run victory by Tayfield and Goddard. Even Bailey, batting two hours for 8 runs, could not save England. This match marked the 48th and last appearance as a Test umpire of Frank Chester, the Worcestershire batsman whose highly promising career was ended by the loss of an arm in the First World War. Accommodation at the ground had been increased, so that a new record of 36,000 was set on the Monday.

The extraordinary start to India's second innings in the 1952 Test when Trueman – on his Test debut – took three wickets in his first eight balls.

At the eleventh attempt England finally scored a win over Australia at Headingley in 1956 – and in no uncertain manner. May, now captain, scored a century in a total of 325 and then his Surrey colleagues, Laker and Lock, shared 18 wickets as Australia were bowled out for 143 and 140 on a pitch which favoured spin from the second day. However, the most remarkable feature of the match was the return of Washbrook, aged 41, a selector and absent from international cricket for five years. His recall had been roundly condemned and he came to the wicket with England tottering at 17 for 3. However, his fellow-selectors – Washbrook had left the meeting when his name was discussed – were utterly vindicated as he and May added 187. The only misprint in this storybook return was that Washbrook was out on the second morning 2 runs short of his hundred. Never has a Lancastrian been greeted as warmly at Headingley as when Washbrook returned to the pavilion.

That match was the beginning of a long run of crushing English successes at Headingley, the next five Tests all being won within three days' actual playing time and four of them by an innings. Loader's hat-trick, the first by an Englishman in a home Test for 57 years, accounted for West Indies in 1957; hundreds by Milton, England's last double (cricket and association football) international, on his debut and 19 wickets shared again by Laker and Lock overwhelmed New Zealand in 1958; and Trueman claimed 11 Australian wickets for 88 in 1961, including a devastating spell of 5 for 0 in 24 balls. It was magnificent fast bowling but the pitch was widely criticized, John Arlott, as ever, had the words: '. . . peculiar, pie-bald, chemical-ridden and shifting'.

Shifts of another kind were soon afoot. Building development in Leeds city centre meant that Yorkshire CCC, who, remarkably, still had their offices there, finally moved out to Headingley at the end of their centenary year, 1963. They were accommodated, together with new dressing-rooms, in a singularly unattractive building square to the wicket on the east side of the ground. Notwithstanding traditional rivalries, Lancashire marked the event by presenting a clock for the new offices. To make way for this building, usually known as the players' pavilion, the old winter practice shed was demolished and a new one later erected at the north end (itself superseded in 1988 by a much grander indoor school, located just outside the ground). Near the players' pavilion is a bowling green, which, together with the old cycling track surrounding the boundary, helps to explain the 'Athletic' part of the landlords' name.

Newcomers to Headingley may be surprised that the ground also has a members' pavilion, which stands at the south-east corner beside the football stand. Originally it looked like a traditional pavilion, being modelled on the one at Trent Bridge and featuring a high centre and capacious balcony plus wings with tiled gables and chimney stacks; but the central part has now gone, replaced by a plain balcony and, above, glass-fronted boxes, which house the scorers, press and official guests.

West Indies brought England's successful run to an end in 1963 with a 221-run victory, to which Sobers contributed a century, a fifty and some important wickets, and the next year a splendid 160 by Burge helped Australia to soothe their wounds from the last tour as they completed a seven-wicket victory which retained the Ashes. Against New Zealand in 1965 John Edrich evoked memories of Bradman when he scored 310 not out, England's first triple-century since Huttin in 1938 and containing a record number of boundaries in a Test innings (five sixes and 52 fours). Edrich shared a second-wicket stand of 369 with Cowdrey (163) and was on the field throughout the match, which England won by an innings.

Sobers made an even more telling contribution when West Indies returned in 1966. He scored 174, his third century of that series, and then claimed eight wickets for 80 as England went down by an innings. In a remarkable match the following year India followed on 386 runs behind, but taking the lead from their captain, the Nawab of Pataudi, they amassed 510 second time around and captured four wickets before England got home. The main contribution to England's enormous first innings total of 550 for 4 declared was Boycott's undefeated 246, but it occupied more than $9\frac{1}{2}$ hours and cost him his place in the next Test. The furore in Yorkshire was nothing compared to the arguments over Boycott that were to cleave the county in the years ahead.

Yorkshire crowds, as already mentioned, are not renowned for their impartiality, and pity the cricketer who incurs their wrath. There was never one who did so more than the Essex batsman, Fletcher, then aged 24, who made his debut against

Australia at Headingley in 1968. It was Fletcher's 'crime' to be preferred to Yorkshire's Sharpe for this match and he compounded his felony by being placed in Sharpe's usual position at first slip and then failing to hold three horribly difficult chances; the crowd, of course, felt that Sharpe, an expert slip-fielder, would not have missed them and they made their opinions known. In such an atmosphere it was little surprise that the unfortunate Fletcher was dismissed for a duck in his first Test innings, though he redeemed himself somewhat in the second innings.

That Test was also Illingworth's last at Headingley before his move to Leicestershire – he marked the occasion with six second-innings wickets – and in no cricketer's case has a change of environment proved more efficacious: Illingworth turned from solid county all-rounder into one of England's most successful captains almost overnight. He was welcomed back to Headingley the very next year in his new role and he went on to lead England to four successive Test wins there, local knowledge serving him well. He began with a close-fought 30-run win over West Indies and followed in 1971 with a 25-run win against Pakistan which featured a century for Boycott and the then slowest day's Test cricket in England, 159 runs, though this time it was Pakistan and not Boycott who were responsible. In 1972 Australia were no match for an attack of Underwood (10 for 82) and *fusarium,* which made still more treacherous a pitch that took spin from the first morning. England, winners by nine wickets, had retained the Ashes soon after five o'clock on the third day of the match. The fast bowlers, bolstered by a fine hundred from Boycott (completing his set against all the Test-playing countries) dominated the next year's match against New Zealand on a green pitch in another innings win.

The 1975 Test, against Australia, will forever be associated not with a cricketer but with a convicted criminal, George Davies, campaigners on whose behalf vandalised the pitch beyond repair in the small hours of the final day. The match was splendidly poised, with Australia at 220 for 3 needing another 225 to win, but as it happened, rain set in around noon and would almost certainly have ensured a stalemate anyway.

Headingley spectators were compensated the following summer by a superb match against West Indies, who were just beginning their long domination of world cricket. They amassed 437 for 9 on the first day with a riot of attacking strokes, but thanks to Greig and Knott, both of whom scored 116, England finished only 63 in arrears. Good bowling, particularly by Willis, eventually left them needing 260 to win and they went down gallantly by 55 runs, with the captain, Greig, scoring an undefeated 76.

The next year, 1977, was the Queen's Silver Jubilee and national celebrations were matched by some special sporting happenings; a royal horse won one of the major classic races; an Englishwoman won a Wimbledon singles title; and Geoffrey Boycott, whom some Yorkshiremen apparently placed on a higher pedestal even than royalty, chose the Headingley Test to score his 100th first-class hundred, the first man to do so in a Test match. The on-drive off Greg Chappell and the arms raised in salute as the ball sped downhill to the boundary for the 100th run are imprinted indelibly on the memory from a myriad television replays and the roar that erupted from the crowd must have been heard all over Leeds. It was almost an anti-climax when England won by an innings and 85 runs on the fourth day, a triumph crystallized by Randall's joyous cartwheel after he had taken the final catch. A particularly nostalgic

Geoffrey Boycott with Herbert Sutcliffe and Sir Leonard Hutton after becoming the third Yorkshire batsman to score a hundred hundreds.

moment at this match was provided by the meeting of Boycott with the other two great Yorkshiremen to score a hundred hundreds, Sutcliffe and Hutton. Sadly, Sutcliffe died early the following year but his great deeds have been commemorated at Headingley since 1965 by ornamental gates next to the main entrance in St Michael's Lane.

Rain destroyed the next three Tests at Headingley, with more than eight days' playing time wiped out, but all that could be forgotten in 1981 when the ground witnessed one of the greatest of all Test matches. It had begun straightforwardly, almost pedestrianly, with Australia declaring at 401 for 9 (Botham 6 for 95) late on the second day. England, led by the recalled Brearley, stuttered in their reply to 174 all out and when, following on, they lost

Gooch for a duck before the end of the third day, the bookmakers offered 500–1 against an England win. Their judgement appeared fully vindicated on Monday afternoon when the new electronic scoreboard showed England at 135 for 7, undermined by the skilled fast bowling of Lillee and Alderman. The rest of the match has passed into English folklore and Australian horror comics. Botham, wielding his heavy bat like a mediaeval warrior, tore into the attack with a mixture of devastating and improbable strokes and with heroic support from Dilley, Old and Willis carried England to 356 on the final morning. Botham himself remained undefeated with 149, having reached 100 off only 87 balls. Even so, Australia remained favourites, requiring only 130 to win, and at 56 for 1 the outcome seemed a formality.

The switching of Willis to bowl downhill from the Kirkstall Lane end brought another dramatic change and not long after lunch Australia had plummeted to 75 for 8. Lillee and Bright gave proceedings a final twist by adding 35 for the ninth wicket, but Willis, with the performance of a lifetime, eventually claimed them both and his return of 8 for 43 had brought England victory by 18 runs. It was only the second time in Test history that a team had won after following on (England at Sydney in 1894–95 were the first). The match – and indeed the rest of the series – seized the imagination of even the non-cricketing public and it was small surprise that, eight years after the event, a collector was prepared to pay nearly £1,300 for an auction lot containing the ball with which Willis destroyed the Australians on that day.

Australia were beaten on their next visit in 1985,

Opposite page **Bob Willis, hero of the hour, races off the field after England's win over Australia in 1981.**

an excellent match highlighted by Robinson's 175 and another all-round exhibition from Botham, but the years either side established Headingley as the only ground on which England have lost to all the major Test playing countries. New Zealand achieved their first win on English soil there in 1983; India were victorious at Headingley in 1986, a crushing win by 279 runs as they outplayed England in every department on a rapidly deteriorating pitch; and Pakistan, largely through the brilliant bowling of their captain, Imran Khan, triumphed by an innings in 1987. West Indies, meanwhile, recorded crushing wins in 1984 – Marshall batting one-handed with echoes of Tennyson on the same ground in 1921 and then claiming seven wickets in the second innings – and in 1988, in Gower's 100th Test match, to bring their tally at Headingley to five wins in eight matches, as England took their place among the also-rans of Test cricket. The following year Gower, reinstated as captain, put Australia in and the gamble came badly unstuck as the pattern for the series was set. They amassed 601 for 7, led by centuries from Taylor and Waugh, and then the old hands, Alderman and Lawson, bowled England to defeat by 210 runs.

Leeds				
Ref/No	Season	V	T	Result
62/1	1899	A	3	Draw
85/2	1905	A	3	Draw
94/3	1907	A	2	E-53
103/4	1909	A	3	A-126
	1912 Triangular Tournament			
124/5		EvSA	2	E-174
142/6	1921	A	3	A-219
155/7	1924	SA	3	E-9w
165/8	1926	A	3	Draw
183/9	1929	SA	3	E-5w
196/10	1930	A	3	Draw
236/11	1934	A	4	Draw
244/12	1935	SA	3	Draw
265/13	1938	A	4	A-5w
288/14	1947	SA	4	E-10w
302/15	1948	A	4	A-7w
314/16	1949	NZ	1	Draw
337/17	1951	SA	4	Draw
351/18	1952	I	1	E-7w
375/19	1953	A	4	Draw
411/20	1955	SA	4	SA-224
427/21	1956	A	3	E-I&42
442/22	1957	WI	4	E-I&5
456/23	1958	NZ	3	E-I&71
476/24	1959	I	3	E-I&173
509/25	1961	A	3	E-8w
532/26	1962	P	3	E-I&117
546/27	1963	WI	4	WI-221
563/28	1964	A	3	A-7w
593/29	1965	NZ	3	E-I&187
608/30	1966	WI	4	WI-I&55
618/31	1967	I	1	E-6w
640/32	1968	A	4	Draw
655/33	1969	WI	3	E-30
689/34	1971	P	3	E-25
701/35	1972	A	4	E-9w
724/36	1973	NZ	3	E-I&1
742/37	1974	P	1	Draw
762/38	1975	A	3	Draw
780/39	1976	WI	4	WI-55
807/40	1977	A	4	E-I&85
827/41	1978	P	3	Draw
853/42	1979	I	3	Draw
884/43	1980	WI	5	Draw
905/44	1981	A	3	E-18
933/45	1982	P	3	E-3w
958/46	1983	NZ	2	NZ-5w
991/47	1984	WI	3	WI-8w
1017/48	1985	A	1	E-5w
1047/49	1986	I	2	I-279
1077/50	1987	P	3	P-I&18
1101/51	1988	WI	4	WI-10w
1121/52	1989	A	1	A-210

England: P 52, W 22, D 15, L 15

London
LORD'S CRICKET GROUND

Lord's may not be the most handsome cricket ground in the world, nor by a long way is it the largest in terms of capacity or playing area; but, set in affluent St John's Wood not far from the West End of London, it is indubitably the most famous ground, acknowledged as such at home and overseas. For no cricketer is there a greater thrill than to play at Lord's, nowhere that he is keener to succeed; for no visiting player is any game more important than the Lord's Test. The very names of Lord's and its owners, MCC, are synonymous with cricket; the Father Time weathervane atop the Grand Stand is an instantly recognizable symbol of the game itself.

It is important to establish at the outset a few small but often confused facts about Lord's. First, the name of the ground comes not from aristocratic connections – though it is true that members of that class featured prominently among the membership in the early years – but from its founder, a Yorkshire-born entrepreneur called Thomas Lord (hence the apostrophe). Second, the ground is owned by the Marylebone Cricket Club (universally known by its initials, MCC), not by Middlesex County Cricket Club, who as tenants play most of their home matches there and have their headquarters there but have no say in its running. Third, MCC no longer controls English cricket. It is a private members' club, with an all-male membership of some 18,000 (and a waiting-list of 8000 eager for the chance to wear the famous buttercup and marigold – or as some have it, tomato and custard – tie) which in 1968 ceded all those rights apart from responsibility for the laws of cricket and an administrative role in the International Cricket Conference.

There are other misconceptions about Lord's and though long outdated, like other misconceptions, they stick; one of the most popular concerns retired colonels swigging pink gins in the Long Room, the huge, glass-fronted room in the grand red-brick, Victorian pavilion. To put the record straight the number of military men, active or retired, in an increasingly broad-based membership is minuscule; drinking (and eating) in the pavilion is confined to the outdoor seating areas and the bars.

At all events, the present Lord's is the third ground to bear the name. The first was opened in 1787 about a mile away on seven acres leased from the Portman Estate, where Dorset Square now stands to the north of Marylebone Road. Middlesex beat Essex in the first match by 93 runs and, as well as pigeon-shooting, athletics and a balloon ascent, the ground had already staged the first Eton *v* Harrow (1805) and Gentlemen *v* Players (1806) matches when a rise in rent caused Lord to move operations. Foreseeing that a move would become necessary, he had rented two fields at North Bank in autumn 1808 and for two seasons ran two grounds; but North Bank was not popular and had anyway to be abandoned in 1813 because of the cutting of the Regent's Canal. So Lord upped his original turf again a couple of hundred yards further north – it survived virtually intact on the square until relaying was undertaken in 1972 – and established his ground at the present site. In the first recorded match MCC beat Hertfordshire by an innings and 27 runs on 22 June 1814.

The setting of Lord's at this time was pretty rural but the aspect changed with the building of St John's Wood Church and houses in the area; this was matched on the new ground by the building of a pavilion, tavern and several smaller buildings and the enclosure of the site with a high fence. In 1825

Thomas Lord's association with the ground ended; now nearly 70, he alarmed club members by unveiling plans to build seven pairs of houses at the south-west corner of the ground, which would have severely reduced the playing area. That Lord's did not now pass into oblivion was due to William Ward, an outstanding cricketer (he scored 278 for MCC *v* Norfolk in 1820, a remarkable score on the unprepared pitches of those days), a director of the Bank of England and latterly an MP, who wrote out a cheque for £5000 to buy out the remaining years of Thomas Lord's lease. Lord himself eventually retired to West Meon in Hampshire, where he died in 1832. Colin Cowdrey, president of MCC in its bicentenary year of 1987, visited Lord's grave as the initial public act of that year, thereby indicating that no grudges are held against Thomas Lord for his final (failed) speculation.

In that same year of 1825 the largely wooden pavilion on the ground was burnt down, with the sad loss of club records, scorebooks and 'a very valuable wine-cellar ... belonging to the gentlemen of the various clubs who frequently play in the

Thomas Lord (left), founder of Lord's, and James H. Dark, proprietor from 1836 to 1864.

ground'. The attending fire crews, who numbered more than 20 from all over London, were hampered by the lack of water. Ward worked quickly to have a new pavilion ready in time for the next season and the one after that, 1827, saw Lord's host the first match between Oxford and Cambridge.

In 1835 Ward was granted a lease on the ground for the next 59 years and this he transferred to James H. Dark, a man who had been associated with Lord's since the age of ten as a ball boy in the Dorset Square days. Such was his influence that the ground was referred to in some quarters as Dark's and though it never supplanted Lord's the name of Dark can be seen to this day over the sweet shop which nestles at the rear of the Mound Stand. During Dark's tenancy the appearance of the ground was much enhanced by a garden, 400 trees around the periphery and the redecoration of the pavilion, followed shortly afterwards by the laying of a bowling green at the west side and a real tennis court.

The year 1837 marked not only Queen Victoria's accession but also the jubilee of Lord's, which was celebrated with a match between North (with Box of Sussex and Cobbett of Surrey) and South. Highest score in the match was the South's 70 which secured victory by five wickets, the Lord's pitches then – and for many years afterwards – being notoriously rough. It was not until 1864, the 50th anniversary of Thomas Lord's decampment to St John's Wood, that David Jordan was engaged as the first full-time groundsman; in earlier days the grass was cropped by sheep brought in shortly before a match was due to be played. It is also a feature of the playing area that, to this day, there is a slope of some $6\frac{1}{2}$ feet from the north side (now occupied by the Grand Stand) to the Tavern, which in modern times has sometimes caused problems in keeping the playing area properly protected.

That year of 1864 saw too the beginning of MCC's renowned collection of cricketing art and memorabilia, part of which is now on public display in the Memorial Gallery at the rear of the pavilion and more in the pavilion itself on view restricted to members and their guests. The 1860s also brought another period of crisis for Lord's: the Eyre Estate put up the lease at auction and, with the club short-sightedly deciding not to bid despite the urgings of Dark and others, it was bought for £7000 by Isaac Moses. MCC's failure to bid proved costly for when six years later they acquired the freehold, it cost them over £18,000. William Nicholson, later to be president, advanced the money at five per cent.

MCC celebrated the fact that the ground was now finally their own with the erection of the first Grand Stand on the north side and hereon began a process of development. The following winter a tavern was built to replace the one put up by Thomas Lord and right up to the present day there has been steady replacement and refurbishment of existing structures.

Major matches at Lord's at this period were the All England XI *v* United All England XI, Gentlemen *v* Players, North *v* South, Oxford *v* Cambridge and Eton *v* Harrow, but the year 1868 presaged the international encounters that were to grace Lord's and all the other Test match grounds with the visit of the first overseas side to England, the Australian Aboriginals. The match, variously described in the 1869 *Wisden* as MCC *v* The Australians, Gentlemen of MCC *v* Aboriginal Blacks and MCC *v* Aboriginals was won by an MCC side containing an Earl (Coventry), a Lieutenant-Colonel (Bathurst), a Viscount (Downe) and the club secretary, R.A. Fitzgerald, by 55 runs, but the Aboriginals additionally entertained the spectators with their customary display of boomerang throw-

ing and one of their number, Dick-a-Dick, used a club to ward off cricket balls thrown at him from 15 to 20 yards. The club he used with almost 100 per cent success during the tour can still be seen in the Memorial Gallery at Lord's.

By the time the next, all-white Australian team came in 1878 Lord's was developing into more of a cricketing centre, with turnstiles installed and Middlesex having begun their long association. If the visit of the Aboriginals had been a novelty, the presence of this latter side proved nothing short of sensational: the Australians (41 and 12 for 1) beat a strong MCC side (33 and 19) including Grace, Hornby, Shaw and Morley, by nine wickets in only $4\frac{1}{2}$ hours' playing time on 27 May on a decidedly sticky pitch. That evening London was ablaze with news of the victory, the cricketing reputation of Australia was established forever, and Lord's has perhaps never recovered from the shock, for it has down the years become, by a long way, England's least and Australia's most successful Test match ground in this country. Although England won four of the first six encounters there between 1884 and 1896, in a total of 29 matches up to the end of the 1989 season England have had only one further victory – in 1934 – whereas Australia have achieved 11 wins in all.

As recorded in the appropriate sections of this book, the Oval and Old Trafford had already staged Test matches and England and Australia had met a total of 14 times in both countries when Lord's entered the lists in July 1884. England won this inaugural match by an innings and 5 runs, Steel's magnificent 148 giving them a first-innings lead of 150 and then Ulyett's 7 for 36 completing Australia's discomfiture. An interesting footnote is that Murdoch, the Australian captain, fielded substitute for England when Grace hurt a finger and took the catch which ended a last-wicket stand of 69.

This match established Lord's as a Test match ground and every touring team since then has played there. All newcomers to Test cricket have made their English debut at Lord's and with both countries in double tours (begun in 1965) being awarded a game there, it has numerically far outstripped all other English grounds. Since the turn of the century the Lord's Test has been established almost invariably in June as the second of the summer and as part of the London social scene, the Saturday being the best attended day and another day frequently being the occasion for a visit by the sovereign and presentation of the teams. The timing in the context of a Test series, however, means that although Lord's has witnessed many notable occasions, the number of truly memorable Test matches is smaller compared to the transpontine ground at the Oval. It has the advantage of usually hosting the last match of the summer, on which the outcome of the rubber often hangs.

Back, however, to 1886, when England recorded another innings win thanks to a masterly 164 by Shrewsbury on a rain-affected pitch and then 11 wickets by the slow left-arm Briggs. The end of this season, which had also brought the first visit to England of an Indian side, the Parsees, saw the introduction of a new scoreboard, which updated the batsmen's scores as the runs were made, and fittingly the first run recorded was scored by W.G.

Looking towards the old Grand Stand (opened in 1865 and replaced in the 1920s) during the Eton and Harrow match of 1895.

Grace. The following year Lord's and MCC celebrated their centenary with a match against England and the purchase for £18,500 of the $3\frac{1}{2}$ acres of Henderson's Nursery to the east of the ground; famous then for its pineapples and tulips, this 'Nursery End' is now renowned as a practice area and forcing ground for promising young cricketers.

In 1888 Australia won a Lord's Test for the first time in a match which produced only 291 runs from four completed innings. Twenty-seven wickets fell in just over three hours' playing time on the second day on a gluepot of a pitch, with Ferris and 'Terror' Turner claiming all but two of England's wickets. As threatening as the Australian pair were to England's batsmen, so in that year was yet another scheme to the future of Lord's: the Great Central Railway promoted a Bill to take over the ground and run their line through it, but pressure from cricketers and non-cricketers saw this scandalous part of the Bill thrown out and Lord's, for the last time, saw off a planners' threat to its existence. (When another railway, the Manchester and Sheffield, sought rights to tunnel under the Nursery ground three years later, MCC from a position of strength acquired the Clergy Orphan School in exchange, giving them valuable extra property at the corner of the ground; part of it is still in use as the Lord's Shop.) The future secured and all its debts cleared, MCC pressed ahead with the building of a new pavilion to replace the old structure, which, though extended several times during its existence, was now totally inadequate for a membership which had grown to over 3000. Sir Spencer Ponsonby-Fane laid the foundation-stone on 17 September 1889 and the imposing building, one at last worthy of its setting, was ready less than eight months later in time for the club's AGM. The architect was F.T. Verity and the cost, inclusive of furniture and fittings, was £21,000. There have been several internal refits since then but the exterior of the building is substantially unchanged, apart from the addition of a press box at the north end, which became offices for the club secretariat after the press were rehoused in the newly built Warner Stand in 1958. Incidentally, the old pavilion was reassembled on the Ranfold estate in Slinfold, Sussex, where it survived, latterly as a gardening shed, until the early 1980s.

The 1890 Test began with a flurry of scoring by the Australian opener, Lyons, who reached 50 in only 36 minutes but ended in a seven-wicket victory for England; the match was also notable for the fact that it was the first Test without a bye, a tribute to the wicket-keepers, two of the best, Blackham and McGregor. Shrewsbury scored another hundred in the 1893 match, which was cut short by rain, but there was further success for England in 1896, by six wickets, that year also seeing MCC take revenge on the Australians for the trouncing of 1878 by dismissing them for only 18 in their first innings. A record crowd of nearly 30,000 crammed into the ground on the opening day of the Test match two weeks later and saw the formidable

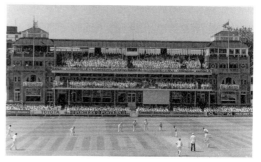

The old pavilion (top), as it appeared in 1889, and its successor, photographed here in 1989 and largely unchanged since its completion in 1890.

Surrey pair of Richardson and Lohmann skittle Australia for a mere 53 on a perfect pitch. *Wisden* complained that the playing area was 'seriously encroached upon' and that there was 'an absence of the quiet and decorum usually characteristic of Lord's'. Australia fared better second time around thanks to a partnership of 221 between George Trott and Syd Gregory, but England finally got home by six wickets.

The size of that crowd called for and produced an improvement in public accommodation at Lord's. The tennis and racket courts were demolished (and moved to the rear of the pavilion) and replaced for the 1899 season by the Mound Stand, in which the press were accommodated opposite the pavilion for five years from 1901 until the box was demolished in a storm and they were moved to the

pavilion. Alongside the old Tavern a building housing seven boxes and providing seating for 400 members and friends was erected.

For that 1899 Test W.G., a few weeks from his 51st birthday, was dropped from the England side and Australia, with an undefeated 135 from the emerging Trumper, scored a decisive ten-wicket victory. Jones, the Australian fast bowler whose fame rests on his reputedly having slipped one of his quickest balls through Grace's beard, took ten wickets in the match. Later that season, in the second game between the Australians and MCC, Albert Trott produced the most famous hit at Lord's, when he drove Noble over the comparatively new pavilion. Trott was himself an Australian who settled in England and had a distinguished career with Middlesex as well as playing twice for England and three times for his native country. Trott's feat has never been repeated although Mann (Middlesex) in the 1920s, Carr (Nottinghamshire) in the 1930s, and in more recent times Llewellyn (Glamorgan) and Hughes (Australia) have reached the top deck.

Rain restricted the 1902 Test to 105 minutes and severely disrupted the next two, including South Africa's debut in 1907, when the visitors made a gallant effort to avoid a heavy defeat. Vogler, one

Promenading during the luncheon interval at the 1898 University match. The Tavern, demolished in the 1960s, can be seen on the far side of the ground.

of the noted quartet of googly bowlers, claimed seven wickets. Australia were again dominant in 1909, by nine wickets, against a strange-looking England side: 'Never in the history of Test Matches in England has there been such blundering in the selection of an England eleven,' *Wisden* thundered. That year saw the founding of the Imperial Cricket Conference, which at that time contained only three countries: England, Australia and South Africa. After some wrangling they sanctioned a Triangular Tournament in 1912, which until the World Cup of 1975 was the only cricket competition to involve more than two countries. It was ruined by a particularly wet summer, but of the three matches at Lord's over 35,000 paid for admission to England and Australia, with the Prince of Wales present on the third day, and King George V himself visited the ground during the match between Australia and South Africa.

The centenary of the ground on its present site was commemorated in 1914 with matches between the MCC side which had toured South Africa the previous winter and a Rest of England XI and, a

J. W. H. T. Douglas (in pads) and C. B. Fry being presented to George V by Lord Hawke at the Lord's centenary match in 1914. Prince Albert (with cane) and the Prince of Wales are also in the party.

little strangely, one between the Army and the Navy. The main match was reasonably well attended and again had royal guests, the two captains, Fry and Douglas, being presented to the King in full view of the crowd. During the First World War, while the club's collection of pictures was removed from the pavilion to Petworth as 'a security against hostile aircraft attacks', Lord's made its contribution to the war effort: the ground was put at the disposal of the War Office and used for training and cricket, while in the pavilion the MCC staff and one or two members and their friends made thousands of hay nets for horses.

Lord's has been the venue for several other sports, including hockey and lacrosse (a proposal in 1937 that Harlequins should play rugby there never came to fruition) and in 1916, following an 1874 precedent, a baseball match was played between Canadians and London Americans on behalf of Canadian war widows and orphans; Princess Louise, sister of the King, watched the game

from the pavilion. It is another part of Lord's myth that women are not permitted in the pavilion during playing hours; this is not entirely true for secretaries, catering staff and the one time curator, Diana Rait-Kerr, not to mention the Queen, have been seen within its precincts, even if none may actually watch play from the seats. However, there is photographic evidence of women actually spectating from the front seats of the pavilion in July 1918 during one of the charity matches between an England XI and the Dominions, when King George was again present; wartime presumably brought a relaxation of the usual rules. One of them was identified as Lady Eleanor Byng in *The Times* early in 1989, at the same time as the topic was being given new life when MCC conducted a straw poll among members to gauge whether they would be in favour of women being allowed to spectate from the pavilion or even to become members – though with candidates at the end of the waiting-list at that time subject to a wait of at least 30 years it was more a matter for the next generation. Voting showed a sizable majority of MCC members to be, if not misogynists, at least jealous of their male preserves.

Test cricket resumed in 1921 after a nine-year hiatus and England, suffering amid a long period of Australian domination, were undone by the pace of Gregory and McDonald in the Lord's match and went down by eight wickets despite Woolley's brave innings of 95 and 93. MCC's arrangements for handling the large crowds attracted to the match – particularly the refusal of admission to disabled soldiers – drew widespread criticism and even led to *The Cricketer*, then a fledgling of only eight issues, being withdrawn temporarily from sale at the ground. England crushed South Africa in 1924, losing only two wickets on the way to an innings victory; they also established a Test record

The resumption of Test cricket in 1921 after a nine-year hiatus drew huge crowds to Lord's for the Second Test between England and Australia.

by piling up 500 runs on the second day, Hobbs (211), Sutcliffe (122) and Woolley (134 not out) being the major contributors. There were also runs aplenty, though no outright result, in 1926 when Bardsley, at the age of 43, carried his bat for 193 in Australia's first innings; Macartney made an undefeated 133 in the second; while Hobbs and Hendren responded with hundreds for England. Patsy Hendren, a Lord's favourite for over 30 years, remains surprisingly the only Middlesex batsman to score a hundred on his home ground in a Test against Australia.

MCC members were now able to enter the ground through the Grace Gates, a famous Lord's landmark fronting St John's Wood Road and erected in 1922 (not 1923 as often published) in memory of the most famous cricketer of all time at a cost of £2268. The inscription, a subject of much debate, was finally settled on as:

TO THE
MEMORY OF
WILLIAM GILBERT
GRACE
THE GREAT CRICKETER
1848–1915
THESE GATES WERE
ERECTED BY THE MCC
AND OTHER FRIENDS
AND ADMIRERS

Steps had by now been taken to improve the accommodation for spectators, with the erection of the Grand Stand on the north side of the ground. Though this stand accommodates the Father Time weathervane (not incidentally part of the original plans but a gift from Sir Herbert Baker, the architect of both the stand and the Grace Gates) and houses boxes, the scorers and, below, the Lord's printing press, its design was found to be lacking when it was discovered that from some of the seats considerable parts of the playing area could not be seen. Nor did the new stand quell all complaints about the arrangements for big matches, for there was still criticism about the 1926 Test from disgruntled spectators who failed to find a place among the 72,976 admitted during the three days.

This period between the Wars also saw the gradual expansion of the family of Test-cricketing nations and each in turn made their English bow at Lord's. West Indies lost by an innings in 1928; New Zealand, by scoring 469 for 9 declared in their second innings, earned an honourable draw in 1931 after Ames (137) and Allen (122) had set a still extant world record of 246 for England's eighth wicket; and in 1932 India, after promising well by removing Holmes, Sutcliffe and Woolley for only

19 runs on the first morning, eventually succumbed by 158 runs. South Africa, though visitors to England since 1907, might be said to have come of age in 1935 when they won for the first time in England. The Greek, Xenophon Balaskas, spun his leg-breaks to telling effect and finished with 9 for 103 in the match. It was incidentally in this summer that the square at Lord's was infested by leatherjackets, the larvae of the daddy-long-legs. Much of the grass was killed off and the ground assumed a 'dustbowl' appearance that was eventually remedied with the help of the Oval groundsman, 'Bosser' Martin, whose son, Austin, was subsequently appointed to the same post at Lord's.

Test matches against Australia, however, remained the true contests and the encounters of the Thirties – during which MCC celebrated its 150th birthday with two matches, North v South and MCC Australian XI v Rest of England, in 1937 – are among the most memorable between the old foes at Lord's. In 1930 Bradman, on his first visit, played what he regarded as the best innings of his career, 254, ended only by an astonishing one-handed catch by the England captain, Percy Chapman, at extra cover. Neither before nor since in Bradman's own opinion did he attain such near-perfection in his batting, and none who were lucky enough to witness it would disagree. It followed an outstanding 173 from Duleepsinhji, who thus emulated his uncle, Ranji, by scoring a hundred in his first Test against Australia, as England's first innings produced a highly respectable 425; but Australia, led by Bradman and Woodfull's 155, responded with a gargantuan 729 for 6 declared, which is still the highest total in any match at Lord's and proved too large for the Tavern scoreboard. England's second innings of 375 (Chapman 121) left Australia needing only 72 to win and they got home by seven wickets.

R.101 passing over Lord's during the 1930 Test, when Bradman scored an almost faultless 254.

It was a bowler, the fondly remembered Yorkshire spinner Verity, who stole the show in the Australian match of 1934 (the year of the laying of the Lord Harris garden and of the building of Q, now the Allen, Stand alongside the pavilion). Verity's magnificent performance brought England their first win in the series at Lord's since 1896 and, still more remarkably, the last to date. With outstanding control of length, line and spin, Verity exploited a pitch dampened by weekend rain to take 14 wickets for 80 on the third day (15 for 104 in the match) and bowl England to an innings victory as Australia, 192 for 2 at the start of play, subsided to 284 and then 118 all out. No Englishman produced such bowling in a Test match again until another Yorkshireman, Laker, at Old Trafford in 1956. Brown, the Australian opener who had made a century before the pitch turned spiteful, carried his bat for 206 in the 1938 match and Bradman followed with an unbeaten 102 in the second innings, but the real feature of a high-scoring draw was Hammond's 240, which many rated as the finest of his many great innings: 'more handsome cricket could not be imagined' was how Cardus described it in *The Manchester Guardian*. It was a real captain's innings too, for England had lost their first three wickets for 31.

As the clouds of the Second World War gathered ever darker, the last Lord's Test before the conflagration was graced by two centuries from Headley, the black Bradman (West Indians prefer to call Bradman the white Headley), and one each from Hutton and the successor to Hendren as a favourite son of Lord's, Compton. Lord's, its treasures hidden in the country, was requisitioned by the RAF during the war, but under the influence of Sir Pelham Warner (acting secretary for the period and later honoured for services to Lord's by having named after him the new stand to the north of the pavilion) much cricket was played. The ground also escaped quite lightly from German bombs, although the roof of the tennis court and part of the outfield suffered some damage and Father Time became a victim of his own side when he was dragged from his perch on the Grand Stand by the cable of a stray barrage balloon.

A few wartime incidents on the field bear repeating. The unfortunate Andrew Ducat, formerly of Surrey and England, collapsed and died at the wicket in a match between the Surrey and Sussex Home Guards in 1942 (*Wisden*, following 'official' MCC records, has the entry: Pte. A. Ducat not out 29). During Army *v* RAF in 1944 the descent of a flying bomb caused the players to throw themselves flat on the ground; Lord's shuddered as the bomb went off, in nearby Regent's Park – as it did nearly 40 years later when a military band was attacked by Irish bombers in the same location – but the players dusted themselves off and Captain Jack Robertson (Army, Middlesex and latterly England) hooked the second ball for six. It was a dramatic enough gesture, though not surprisingly popular mythology has it that Robertson's blow came from the very next ball after the resumption of play!

However, the best remembered cricket of the war, which gave many a youngster his first introduction to the international game, was provided by the Victory Test matches of 1945, which proved an ever greater attraction as the summer wore on: Australia won the first at Lord's, watched by 67,000 people over the three days, off the fourth ball of the last over; 84,000 were present at the next, which the Australians won more comfortably; and 93,000 turned up for the last which ended in a high-scoring draw. To crown the season, at the end of August the Dominions, led by Constantine, beat England by 45 runs in a match of 1241 runs described by *Wisden* as 'one of the finest ... ever seen'. There were centuries from Hammond (in each innings), Donnelly and Miller, the last named's including a six which landed on the roof of the old broadcasting box above the England dressing-room. Miller, a typically forthright Australian, came in future years to revise his original impression of Lord's as 'a crummy little ground'.

The resumption of Test cricket with the visit of India in 1946 was greeted with enthusiasm, gates closed before lunch on the first two days and a Royal visit. England's victory, by ten wickets, owed much to Alec Bedser's 11 wickets on his Test debut and Hardstaff's double-hundred. The following season, 1947, was dominated by the achievements of the Middlesex twins, Compton and Edrich, whose run-scoring in that glorious, incomparable post-war summer broke all records: Compton 3816 (18 centuries) and Edrich 3518 (12). City offices, so it is said, suddenly emptied as word spread that the pair were batting at Lord's. This is not the place to document their deeds for county, but when they appeared for country at Lord's against South Africa spectators were not to be disappointed; they shared a a third-wicket partnership of 370, then a world Test record, and took

Compton and Edrich in their golden summer, batting against South Africa at Lord's in 1947.

a combined total of seven wickets and four catches as England completed victory by ten wickets. Melville's fourth successive Test hundred for South Africa and Wright's ten wickets for England were overshadowed.

The 1948 Australians, arguably their strongest side ever, demolished England at Lord's, and even though Bradman scored a mere 38 and 89 and Miller was unable to bowl because of a bad back, they still got home by a monumental 409 runs. England, already one down in the series and set a mere 596 to win, crumbled against the speed of Lindwall and Johnston and spin of Toshack. The following year's high-scoring draw against New Zealand was highlighted by hundreds from the Middlesex pair, Compton and Robertson, and a double-hundred from the graceful New Zealander, Donnelly. The England captain, Mann, caused a minor stir by declaring on the first day, which was not then allowed in Test matches.

The next year, 1950, was the one in which West Indian cricket truly established itself and the celebrations began, fittingly, at headquarters. Only at Eton *v* Harrow matches would the old ground have witnessed such scenes of uninhibited joy as greeted England's trouncing by 326 runs, West Indies' first Test victory in this country and the prelude to a

3–1 win in the series. It gave birth to the *Victory Test Match Calypso* more familiarly known by its opening line, 'Cricket, Lovely Cricket'. The victory owed most to the mesmeric spin bowling of 'those little pals of mine', Ramadhin and Valentine, whose respective figures in only their second Test match make prodigious reading: 115–70–152–11 and 116–75–127–7 – not to mention their ages of 21 and 20. With centuries from Rae and Walcott and sizable contributions from the other two Ws, Worrell and Weekes, the West Indian victory was wrapped up amid singing and dancing.

England recovered ground with victories over South Africa and India, Godfrey Evans in the latter match failing by 2 runs to complete a hundred before lunch and Mankad, on loan from the Lancashire League, scoring 56 runs and bowling 97 overs for the losers. The next year, 1953, produced one of the most memorable Tests at Lord's, when Watson and Bailey saved England from apparently certain defeat by Australia. Requiring 343 to win, England had slipped to 73 for 4; but these two yeomen bristled defiance and with a fifth-wicket stand of

163, stretching from before lunch until well after tea, ensured their place in the history books. The match also goes down as producing the record attendance for a Test at Lord's, 137,915, and the receipts of £57,716, though paltry by modern standards (the 1989 Lord's Test produced more than £1.1 million) were then a record for any cricket match.

The year of 1953 also saw two significant additions to the Lord's landscape: the Coronation Gardens, now the bustling scene of lunchtime picnics during the ground's big occasions, were laid at the rear of A Stand (single-storey predecessor to the Warner Stand) and the Memorial Gallery was opened in the old rackets court at the rear of the pavilion by the Duke of Edinburgh in memory of the cricketers of all lands who died in two world wars. The gallery displays many of the most famous items from the MCC collection of cricketana, most notably the Ashes, and is a particularly popular resort during breaks in play.

There were plenty of those when Pakistan made her bow at Lord's in 1954, play not beginning until 3.45 on the fourth day and being followed by a clatter of wickets. Statham's 7 for 39, his best Test figures, overcame South Africa the next year and Australia continued their remarkable record at Lord's in 1956 with a 185-run victory in an otherwise losing summer. Miller claimed ten wickets. Australia won also on their next visit in 1961 amid complaints about balls rising sharply from a 'ridge' at the Nursery End of the pitch. It was, some said, the path of an old drain; others, more sceptical, attributed it to the imagination of certain batsmen. Whatever the case, the channel was subsequently dug up and relaid, though this did not prevent mutterings about ridges reemerging whenever a ball misbehaved at that end.

Against other countries at this period England

reigned supreme at headquarters and all five were beaten by wide margins, three of the games – New Zealand (1958), India (1959) and Pakistan (1962) – being completed before the end of the third day. The Test against South Africa in 1960, which did at least go into a fourth day, was notable for the bizarre events surrounding the visiting bowler, Griffin: he created two bits of history in England's first innings by performing the first hat-trick in a Test match at Lord's and by becoming the first bowler to be called for throwing in a Test match in England. He was called 11 times in all during the match and to compound his misery was again called, when an exhibition match was staged because of the early finish, first for throwing and then, the final insult, for failing to notify the umpire of his change of action when he switched to underarm! This was necessary to complete an over which ultimately contained 11 balls. The unfortunate Griffin, whose right elbow had been left crooked as a result of a schoolboy accident, did not bowl again on the tour and never again played for his country. The Lord's Test of 1963 had one of the most dramatic finishes of all time. With two balls remaining, England requiring 6 runs for victory and West Indies one wicket, Colin Cowdrey walked to the wicket, his left arm, fractured by a ball from Hall earlier in the day, in plaster and all results possible. If it had been *Boy's Own Paper*, Cowdrey would doubtless have played the first ball defensively and then cracked the last, from the world's then fastest bowler, with his good arm into the crowd and been carried shoulder-high from the field. In reality, Cowdrey was able to take sanctuary at the non-striker's end while Allen kept out the last two balls and those watching at the ground and on television (other programmes were shelved as the cameras stayed with the game) unleashed a collective sigh of relief as the tension broke. The game had had other heroes, not least Close, who was battered about the body as he charged the fast bowlers in an innings of 70 which made possible an England win; Hall, who bowled unchanged on the rain-shortened final day in a splendid display of stamina; and Dexter, whose driving in England's first innings drew rapturous approval from even the sternest critics.

That summer was a watershed in the history of cricket and Lord's, as the seat of government, was deeply involved. The amateur-professional distinction had just been removed from the game, so for the last time in 1962 Gentlemen met Players in a fixture inaugurated at Lord's 156 years previously. In 1963 county cricket staged its first knockout competition, an idea mooted at least three times since 1873 but never adopted until now the game's parlous finances demanded it, with accompanying sponsorship; a full house at Lord's witnessed the first final for the Gillette Cup between Sussex, expertly led by Dexter, and Worcestershire, and so the pattern for the future of top-level cricket was set. More 'instant' cricket in the form of Sunday League, one-day internationals and the Benson & Hedges Cup were instituted by 1972 and a World Cup in 1975. Lord's was the natural home for the cup finals and with very few exceptions the occasions were memorable for capacity crowds and exciting, if technically imperfect, cricket.

There were changes too in the running of the game: in 1965 the Imperial Cricket Conference, founded by England, Australia and South Africa in 1909, reflected world political shifts and the spread of the game by changing its first name to International and admitting Fiji and the United States as the first of more than a score of associate and affiliate members. In 1968, though many are even now ignorant of the fact, MCC ceded its role

as the game's governing body in England to the newly formed Cricket Council and by 1979 it had handed over also control of overseas tours to the Test and County Cricket Board. MCC now reverted to its position as a private members' club, albeit with a public persona and with its sole worldwide responsibility the Laws of Cricket – and a guiding hand in the development of the game, reflected in its most concrete form in the Indoor Cricket School, opened on the Nursery ground in 1977.

The appearance of Lord's, too, had altered fundamentally with the disappearance of the old Tavern, a legendary retreat of many devotees, and the quaintly rambling adjacent stands and clock tower; they were replaced in 1968 by the rather more prosaic new Tavern Stand, which housed boxes and a larger number of spectators, while a new tavern and restaurant were built on the far side of the Grace Gates. A bar was installed at the foot of the new stand, where the old Tavern had stood, and while the facility of drinking – and barracking – in that area remained for more than a decade, the sad increase in boorish behaviour eventually led 20 years later to the establishment of a permanent stand on the concourse. Some

Lord's in 1967, the old Tavern having been knocked down and the new Tavern Stand under construction.

lamented the passing of the old custom, most welcomed the improvement in behaviour. Many more lamented the gradual passing of the facility for spectators to sit on the grass at big matches; it too became the victim of ill manners, in the form of pitch invasions which threatened the safety of players and umpires.

The 1960s reorganization also saw an alteration to the pattern of tours to England. The 1963 West Indians had proved such an attraction that the folly of their next visit not being scheduled for another eight years was soon realized. Thus the ICC revamped their plans and in 1965 was begun the twin tour for all countries except Australia (and latterly West Indies, who were immediately seen as an effective counter-attraction to football's World Cup held in England in the summer of 1966 and invited back then). It was, of course, obligatory that all overseas visitors should have a Test at Lord's, with the result that over the next 24 seasons headquarters staged as many as 36 Tests – not to mention all the other big occasions. It is a tribute to the attraction of the venue that almost always the Lord's Test remains the best attended in a series, even if so often it seems bedevilled by rain. This also accounts in large part for the high proportion of draws (nearly 60 per cent) in this period.

Thus, while the stupendous fielding of Bland for South Africa in 1965; the match-saving partnership of the cousins, Sobers and Holford, for West Indies in 1966, and the hundred on Test debut by the Yorkshireman, Hampshire, against West Indies in 1969 merit mention from the early part of the period, it is the games which ended decisively that stand out. The 1972 match, which produced another Australian win at Lord's, will forever be remembered as Massie's match. In 60 overs of astonishing swing bowling the unassuming Western Australian, on his Test debut, claimed

16 wickets for 137 as England's batsmen were mesmerized by the ball moving prodigiously under low cloud cover. They are the best figures in a Lord's Test and only two bowlers, Laker and Barnes, have taken more in any Test. While none who witnessed the performance would claim it was a fluke, Massie played only five more Tests, in which he took 15 wickets and never again posed a potent threat.

New Zealand finally laid the ghost of that awful match in 1958, in which they were shot out for 47 and 74, by amassing 551 for 9 with three centuries in the first of the Lord's Tests of 1973 and England were even more firmly on the receiving end later the same summer when West Indies ran up 652 for 8 (Sobers 150 not out, the last of his 26 Test hundreds, and Kanhai 157). All five England bowlers used conceded more than 100 runs and the batsmen fared little better as England were routed by an innings and 226 runs. A bomb scare on the Saturday afternoon caused the stands to be cleared and while many spectators, following police advice to leave the ground, took the opportunity of a stroll in Regent's Park, some adjourned to the middle of the playing area.

Frustrated spectators waiting at the Grace Gates for play to resume after the 1973 bomb scare.

It was England's turn to hand out punishment the following year when they overcame India by an innings and 285 runs in a match which remarkably produced England's highest total ever at Lord's (629) and the lowest total in all Tests there, India's second innings 42, in which they were routed by Arnold and Old in ideal swing bowling conditions. The second match of the summer at Lord's produced controversy when rain seeped under the covers over the weekend, a problem exacerbated by the slope from Grand Stand to Tavern. Pakistan had to contend with Underwood, the world's best bowler on a damp pitch, and he evoked memories of Verity 40 years previously when he followed his first-innings 5 for 20 with 8 for 51, including a spell of 6 for 2 in 51 balls. Rain on the final day, however, saved Pakistan from defeat and England from an embarrassing victory.

Following the hugely successful first World Cup of 1975, in which West Indies defeated Australia by 17 runs in a match which held spectators enthralled for the best part of ten hours, the Australians stayed on for a Test series. The Lord's match produced a high-scoring draw, perhaps more readily recalled for the streaker who hurdled the stumps before being escorted from the field by embarrassed police than for Edrich's 175 or Edwards's 99 or even Lillee's highest career score of 73 not out. The next Australian Test, two years later, was celebrated as a Jubilee match to commemorate 25 years of the Queen's reign and it produced the then record receipts for a match in England of £220,384. It was also the first Test in charge for Brearley, a Middlesex stalwart, whose intellectual abilities helped him to become one of England's most successful captains. So to 1978 and Botham, a former Lord's groundstaff boy, marked his first Test at the ground in typical style with a century off only 108 balls and then the best Test

figures at the ground, 8 for 34, in Pakistan's second innings as England achieved a resounding win. In the second game of the year Botham claimed 11 wickets as New Zealand, all out for 67 in their second innings, succumbed by seven wickets.

There followed a sequence of rain-affected draws, including the ill-fated Centenary Test against Australia in 1980. Events on the field were overshadowed by an unpleasant incident on the Saturday afternoon in which the umpires were harangued by a group of members as they returned from their fifth inspection of the pitch and one of them, Constant, was assaulted – or at least grabbed by the tie in the ensuing melee on the pavilion steps. The cause of the problem was the delay in starting play, despite excellent drying conditions, because of dampness on two old pitches and if any good came from the incident it is that at Lord's now, perhaps more than at any other English ground, there is an awareness among the officials, reflected in the urgency and devotions of the groundstaff, of the need to provide spectators with play at every opportunity. On no occasion was this better demonstrated than during the enormously successful Bicentenary match between MCC and the Rest of the World in 1987 when play continued on the Saturday amid thunder and lightning: the efforts of the players were universally appreciated.

Willis began his reign as England captain with nine wickets in the defeat of India in 1982, but while he was suffering from a stiff neck later in the summer, his stand-in, Gower, was on the receiving end of Pakistan's first success at Lord's. A double-century by Mohsin Khan and six wickets by his opening partner, Mudassar Nazar, were key factors. Gower restored himself with a hundred the following year in a comfortable win over New Zealand, who remain the only one of the senior Test countries not to have won at Lord's after

India finally triumphed there in 1986 under the inspiring leadership of Kapil Dev. England, meanwhile, had suffered a traumatic defeat in 1984 by West Indies, who scored an astonishing 344 for 1 in the fourth innings, to which Greenidge contributed a masterly, undefeated 214. It was quite a way to mark the centenary year of Test cricket at Lord's, which also saw a first visit from the newest Test nation, Sri Lanka; they surprised many, not least their opponents, by the high level of their play in a high-scoring draw. Lord's continued to be a happy hunting ground for Australia as they won for the only time in the 1985 series by four wickets with their captain, Border, giving a stupendous lead with a total of 237 runs for once out. As the decade approached its finish West Indies emphasized their dominance over England with another big win in 1988, but the home country could gain some small solace from a seven-wicket victory over Sri Lanka at the end of that summer to bring to an end an unprecedented sequence of 18 matches without a win. The respite was short-lived for the next year Australia, inspired by a second masterly unbeaten century from Waugh and strong seam and swing bowling, reaffirmed their liking for headquarters with a six-wicket win.

In conclusion it is perhaps fitting to turn the clock back to the bicentenary celebrations of 1987, which epitomize the way MCC are trying to blend cherished traditions with an awareness of the modern world. The club prepared a wide-ranging programme, highlighted for the public by an auction of cricketing items from the club's reserve collection, which raised more than £320,000 amid frenzied bidding, and a marvellous match between 22 of the world's best players, which revealed many of the game's apparently forgotten virtues: the highest level of skills portrayed in an atmosphere of the keenest com-

Views of and from the splendidly original New Mound Stand during the MCC Bicentenary match.

petition but without the petulance and meanness of spirit which seems to dominate so much of modern international cricket. The match, alas deprived of its final day by rain, offered so many memories, but perhaps the most abiding will be the technical perfection achieved by Gavaskar, the Indian opening batsman and leading run-maker in Test cricket, and the sustained hostility of the West Indian, Marshall, on a pitch on which the groundsman, too, appeared to have perfected his art.

The bicentenary year was also marked by the opening of the dramatically refurbished New Mound Stand, at a cost of more than £5 million. Initially criticized for its canopied roof and stark appearance when empty, it came to be accepted as a welcome addition to the ground, notably when full on big match days and bedecked with flags. Its debenture seats and hospitality boxes – and the marquees at Pavilion and Nursery Ends for the great occasions – were a sure sign that MCC had succumbed to the blandishments of corporate sponsorship, the concomitant of major sporting events in the 1980s. The installation of a computerized scoreboard on the Tavern side, soon to be matched on the Grand Stand, and the Compton and Edrich stands at the Nursery End, were more evidence of MCC's intention to give the home of cricket facilities to match its status.

Lord's Cricket Ground

Ref/No	Season	V	T	Result	Ref/No	Season	V	T	Result
15/1	1884	A	2	E-I&5	493/44	1960	SA	2	E-I&73
23/2	1886	A	2	E-I&106	508/45	1961	A	2	A-5w
28/3	1888	A	1	A-61	531/46	1962	P	2	E-9w
33/4	1890	A	1	E-7w	544/47	1963	WI	2	Draw
39/5	1893	A	1	Draw	562/48	1964	A	2	Draw
50/6	1896	A	1	E-6w	592/49	1965	NZ	2	E-7w
61/7	1899	A	2	A-10w	594/50	1965	SA	1	Draw
71/8	1902	A	2	Draw	606/51	1966	WI	2	Draw
84/9	1905	A	2	Draw	619/52	1967	I	2	E-I&124
93/10	1907	A	1	Draw	621/53	1967	P	1	Draw
102/11	1909	A	2	A-9w	638/54	1968	A	2	Draw
	1912 Triangular Tournament				654/55	1969	WI	2	Draw
122/12		EvSA	1	E-I&62	656/56	1969	NZ	1	E-230
123/13		EvA	1	Draw	688/57	1971	P	2	Draw
125/14		AvSA	2	A-10w	690/58	1971	I	1	Draw
141/15	1921	A	2	A-8w	699/59	1972	A	2	A-8w
154/16	1924	SA	2	E-I&18	723/60	1973	NZ	2	Draw
164/17	1926	A	2	Draw	727/61	1973	WI	3	WI-I&226
173/18	1928	WI	1	E-I&58	740/62	1974	I	2	E-I&285
182/19	1929	SA	2	Draw	743/63	1974	P	2	Draw
195/20	1930	A	2	A-7w	761/64	1975	A	2	Draw
209/21	1931	NZ	1	Draw	778/65	1976	WI	2	Draw
219/22	1932	I	–	E-158	804/66	1977	A	1	Draw
227/23	1933	WI	1	E-I&27	826/67	1978	P	2	E-I&120
234/24	1934	A	2	E-I&38	830/68	1978	NZ	3	E-7w
243/25	1935	SA	2	SA-157	852/69	1979	I	2	Draw
252/26	1936	I	1	E-9w	881/70	1980	WI	2	Draw
260/27	1937	NZ	1	Draw	885/71	1980	A	–	Draw
264/28	1938	A	2	Draw	904/72	1981	A	2	Draw
272/29	1939	WI	1	E-8w	928/73	1982	I	1	E-7w
276/30	1946	I	1	E-10w	932/74	1982	P	2	P-10w
286/31	1947	SA	2	E-10w	959/75	1983	NZ	3	E-127
300/32	1948	A	2	A-409	990/76	1984	WI	2	WI-9w
315/33	1949	NZ	2	Draw	994/77	1984	SL	–	Draw
324/34	1950	WI	2	WI-326	1018/78	1985	A	2	A-4w
335/35	1951	SA	2	E-10w	1046/79	1986	I	1	I-5w
352/36	1952	I	2	E-8w	1049/80	1986	NZ	1	Draw
373/37	1953	A	2	Draw	1076/81	1987	P	2	Draw
387/38	1954	P	1	Draw	1099/82	1988	WI	2	WI-134
409/39	1955	SA	2	E-71	1103/83	1988	SL	–	E-7w
426/40	1956	A	2	A-185	1122/84	1989	A	2	A-6w
440/41	1957	WI	2	E-I&36					
455/42	1958	NZ	2	E-I&148					
475/43	1959	I	2	E-8w	England: P 83, W 31, D 34, L 18				

London
THE OVAL

For all the pre-eminence of Lord's, the Oval is in fact England's senior Test match ground. It staged the first two Tests, against Australia, in 1880 and 1882, and it was a further two years before Lord's, as south Londoners might claim, got in on the act. With the constant bustle of traffic on the busy Harleyford Road, which lies on its western side, and its unfashionable setting the Oval has been described as 'a cricket ground of the workaday world'. The difference between it and Lord's is admirably summed up by the notice in the Oval pavilion which asks spectators not to remove their shirts; Lord's insists that users of the pavilion wear jackets and ties. However, while the Oval can claim no aesthetic qualities, its adjacent gasholders and many memorable matches have secured its niche in the hearts of cricket followers. As the traditional venue for the last Test match of a summer, the Oval has been the scene of many fond farewells, while its high standard of pitches frequently makes for notable contests.

The site of the Oval was previously a market garden, covering ten acres in Kennington 'commonly known as the Oval' because of its shape. The land was leased in 1844 by the Montpelier CC, who were about to lose their ground in nearby Walworth to the developers. Then, as now, the Oval and much of the surrounding land was owned by the Duchy of Cornwall, who had granted a 99-year lease on the land to the Otter family in 1835. The first match at the Oval took place in July 1845 between Montpelier and Clapton and the first with Surrey interest between Gentlemen and Players of the county a few weeks later. The ground, which was surrounded at this time by a hedge, was laid out with 10,000 turves imported from Tooting Common and by the end of the year Surrey County Cricket Club was established, with headquarters at the Oval and with the Hon Frederick Ponsonby (later Lord Bessborough) as vice-president and to be a devoted guiding hand for half a century.

On 25 and 26 June 1846 Surrey beat Kent by ten wickets in the first county match at the Oval and though they followed with other successes in an albeit meagre programme of fixtures, financial difficulties – the persistent bugbears of county cricket – soon beset the club. Lord Bessborough and five others paid £12 each to become life members and thus offset a deficit of £70 on the accounts in 1849. The respite was only temporary and Mr W. Houghton, president of the old Montpelier club and now proprietor of the Oval, put on athletic events and poultry shows in addition to cricket in an effort to raise cash.

The club's lack of financial success and these 'alien' events were not lost on the landlords, the Duchy of Cornwall, and in 1851 their solicitor inaugurated steps which would have turned the Oval over to the builders. Intervention which saved the ground came from an unlikely source: Albert, the Prince Consort, whose German origins would have taught him little of cricket but whose marriage to the Queen of England had seen him take up invitations to become patron of the Brighton and Sussex Royal CC in 1840 and of MCC in 1843; he watched his first match at Lord's in 1846. In 1851 Albert was acting as regent to the young Duke of Cornwall (afterwards Edward VII) and he, happily, blocked the moves. The threat, however, had been real and Surrey took an option on another ground in Brixton.

The matter was finally and fully resolved in 1855 when the lease and management of the Oval were put in the hands of the Surrey club. By the end of the decade Surrey – led by such early stalwarts as

Caffyn, Lockyer, Stephenson and Julius Caesar (no Roman emperor, but a hard-hitting batsman from Godalming) – were carrying almost all before them on the field. A new pavilion was built in 1858, housing a large clubroom and rather smaller dressing-rooms behind, and in 1861, when the club's membership had reached almost a thousand and income had quadrupled in six years, a scoreboard was introduced. Contemporary accounts described it in somewhat different terms: a 'newly built and invented house on rollers with figures for telegraphing on each side'.

This new-fangled device was well exercised in 1866 when W.G. Grace, aged 18, amassed an undefeated 224 for England against Surrey – and on the final day of the match he was excused to go to Crystal Palace and run in a 440 yards hurdles race, which, of course, he won. International cricket, in the persons of the Australian Aborigines, came to England for the first time in 1868 and the Oval staged three of their matches, including the opening encounter of the tour, which Surrey won by an innings and 7 runs, and the last (played remarkably late on 15–17 October), which they also won by nine wickets. The first match caused great interest and 20,000 spectators attended two days of cricket and a third of sports, producing receipts of just over £600. The popular and regional press were loud in their acclaim: 'decidedly the event of the century' the *Sheffield Telegraph* proclaimed; but *The Times* was less impressed by the cricket: 'second-rate character of the bowling' and 'batting … sadly wanting in power', although it suggested that some defects might be overcome by practice against good players during the tour.

Charles W. Alcock, who was to have a great influence on English sport as well as on the Oval, was appointed Surrey's first full-time paid secretary in 1872. Alcock was also secretary of the Football Association and it was largely through him that the FA Cup final (1872–92) and several football (1873–89) and rugby union (1872–79) internationals were played at the Oval. The games – as those played by Corinthian-Casuals and Australian Rules footballers in more recent times and by a charity pop concert in 1971 – did little for the condition of the outfield, but the out-of-season revenue assisted with improvements to the ground, which included a secretary's office and improved refreshment bar, and by the time the first (white) Australian team came in 1878 two additional dressing-rooms had been added to the pavilion and terraced banks had been erected to offer spectators an improved view of play.

Alcock had again played a major part in getting the Australians to the Oval and after their pivotal victory over MCC in a single day at Lord's there was unprecedented demand to see their meeting with Surrey a week later. Around 17,000 people turned up on the first day (and 10,000 on the second), with only a handful of policemen and club stewards to manage them. The turnstiles could not cope and gaps were opened in the fence to allow additional access; as the size of the crowd grew, so they encroached more and more on the playing area, until it was reported to be only half its usual size. The Australians won the match by five wickets, Spofforth and Surrey's Barratt each taking 11 wickets, and the same bowlers also dominated the match at the Oval in September, when the Australians defeated the Players by 8 runs; Spofforth took 12 wickets and Barratt 11, including all 10 for 43 in the first innings. Attendance for this match totalled some 22,000, though the ground authorities were prepared for the tumult, and they were even better ready to handle the still larger numbers which attended the first Test match in England two years later.

England v Australia at the Oval in 1882, the Test which gave rise to 'the Ashes'.

This historic match was organized rather late in the day, primarily because by the time the Australians made their arrangements for the tour all the major fixtures for the season in England had been planned. They were reduced to advertising for opponents and again it was the initiative of Alcock which brought the match to the Oval on 6–8 September 1880. A strong side was assembled under the leadership of Lord Harris and appropriately W.G. Grace scored England's first Test century, 152, out of a total of 420. Australia, whose attack had lacked the 'Demon' Spofforth because of a finger injury, collapsed to 149 all out but recovered sufficiently to score 327 second time around, Murdoch surpassing Grace with an undefeated 153, and then recover some pride by taking five English wickets before the meagre target of 57 was reached. More than 40,000 people paid for admission on the first two days and their accommodation in the ground was eased by the extension of the banking with earth made available when a stream at the southern end of the ground was piped underground.

Australia's next Test at the Oval was one of the most sensational of all time and destroyed any illusions, were any still nurtured, of English invin-

cibility on home cricket fields (Australia had already won four of the seven Tests played down under). England started well, shooting Australia out for 63 on a damp pitch by mid-afternoon, but they too were all out by the end of the day, undone by Spofforth's 7 for 46, though with a total of 101 they had secured a precious lead of 38. The pitch played more easily the following morning and, thanks to a dashing 55 from Massie, Australia reached 122. 'Boys, this thing can be done,' Spofforth is supposed to have said in the dressing-room before England began their attempt to score 85 to win – and done it was, by a mere 7 runs. Spofforth, on a pitch which suited him to perfection, bowled magnificently to increase his tally for the match to 14 for 90 and though England passed 50 with only two wickets down, they lost W.G. for 32 and the pressure told on the rest. According to oft-repeated accounts the tension of the occasion also proved too great for a clergyman, who was alleged to have gnawed through his umbrella handle, and another spectator, who was said to have dropped dead; but these stories, colourful as they are, may be apocryphal.

England's defeat gave rise to the famous black-bordered notice in the following Saturday's issue of the weekly *Sporting Times*:

In Affectionate Remembrance

OF

ENGLISH CRICKET,

WHICH DIED AT THE OVAL

ON

29th AUGUST, 1882,

Deeply lamented by a large circle of sorrowing

friends and acquaintances.

R.I.P.

N.B. – The body will be cremated and the

Ashes taken to Australia

These Ashes, of course, acquired material form the following winter when some Australian ladies burnt a stump or bail and put the remains in a small urn which they presented to the English captain, Ivo Bligh, thereafter to be an object, and often a bone, of contention between the two countries.

The revenue generated by another large gathering of nearly 40,000 enabled further improvements to be made to the ground. The stand to the west of the pavilion was given a roof and another covered stand was built, and in 1890 another dressing-room was added to the pavilion, with the luxury of a bath, followed by a press box and better accommodation for the scorers. In 1896 Surrey renewed their lease with the Duchy of Cornwall for a further 31 years at £750 a year. The lease obliged the club to build a new pavilion and tavern, with at least £10,000 to be spent on this task. As it was, almost four times as much was expended and the pavilion assumed the appearance it has, more or less, to this day. Those who have noticed a marked similarity to the pavilion at Old Trafford

will not be surprised that the two structures had the same architect, Thomas Muirhead.

Australia, meanwhile, made two-yearly and then three-yearly visits to England up to the end of the century, by when the number of Test matches had increased to five and the last encounter of the series became established at the Oval. In 1884 Murdoch confirmed his liking for the ground with the first double-century in Test cricket during an innings in which all England players bowled and the Hon. Alfred Lyttelton produced his famous spell of lobs which claimed four wickets while Grace took his place behind the stumps. Surrey's Read scored a hundred for England going in at number ten and two years later Read scored 94, when another fine Surrey player, Lohmann, captured 12 wickets in the first of five successive victories for England at the Oval. The one in 1888 was achieved with a team containing five Surrey men (in those days Test sides were selected by the host club's committee; a selection panel was not appointed until 1899); that in 1890, by two wickets, with the help of an over-throw; and that of 1893 with Lockwood, another Surrey great, a key bowler. On a wet pitch in 1896 Australia were shot out for 44 in their second innings, but they ended a long, unhappy sequence at the Oval in 1899 by securing a draw despite following on against England's mammoth total of 576, to which Jackson and Surrey's Hayward contributed hundreds, and Lockwood's seven wickets in their first innings.

The first Test of the new century at the Oval, in 1902 (incidentally the first year that women were eligible for membership of Surrey CCC), produced an epic encounter which would feature high on the list of all time great matches – otherwise known as Jessop's match. Australia, with one of their strongest sides, had already retained the Ashes with an epic three-run victory in the previous Test at

Old Trafford and took a grip on this match by scoring 324 on the first day. Rain during the night made for much changed batting conditions on the next day and England, undermined by Trumble who bowled unchanged throughout the match, avoided the follow-on by only 9 runs. Lockwood, however, bowled Australia out for 121 and England needed 263 to win with most of the day to get them. In no time at all England were 48 for 5 and the match looked over; but Jessop, the famed Gloucestershire hitter, joined Jackson in the stand which turned the tables. Jessop started shakily but after lunch launched an assault the like of which was not seen from an England batsman until Botham bludgeoned the Australians' successors of 1981. He reached 50 in 43 minutes and his second 50 took only another 28 minutes as the previously triumphant Trumble and Saunders were dispatched to all quarters. Jessop was eventually caught, rather tamely, at short leg for 104, and on his departure England still required 66 with only three wickets left. Most now rested on the great Yorkshire allrounder, Hirst, and when he was joined for the last wicket by his county colleague and another cricketing immortal, Rhodes, 15 runs were wanted. Even if neither of them actually uttered the fabled words 'We'll get 'em in singles', get them they did, mainly in singles, and England were home by the narrowest possible margin.

The Oval had to wait a while for its next memorable Test match, as a string of generally highscoring draws followed on the excellent pitches prepared by Sam Apted. South Africa made their first appearance in 1907 and then Bardsley took advantage to score a century in each innings for Australia, the first time this had been achieved in Test cricket, in 1909. It was this year, incidentally, which saw the death of Albert Craig, 'The Surrey Poet', a familiar figure at the Oval where he pur-

Albert Craig, the Surrey poet, at the Oval.

veyed penny rhymes on the players and other cricketing topics with sharp wit. 'Oh, take these things away!' a spectator once dismissively told him. 'I beg your pardon, sir,' Craig replied. 'These are not for you, only for people who can read.'

Rain, in which Craig used to be particularly valued as a source of entertainment, gave bowlers the upper hand in the Oval's two matches of the 1912 Triangular Tournament, in which Surrey's most famous cricketer, Hobbs, made his first Test appearances on his home ground. The match against South Africa was over before lunch on the second day, when Barnes was nigh unplayable as he took 8 for 29, still the best Test figures at the ground. Test cricket did not resume after the First World War until 1921 and that year's match was rendered meaningless on the final day when the Australian captain, Armstrong, withdrew to the deep field and left the team to run on automatic pilot. In one of Test cricket's more notorious episodes Armstrong picked up and read a stray newspaper. Years later he offered an explanation: 'I wanted to see who we were playing against' – an allusion to the fact that England used a record number of 30 players in the series.

The ensuing winter saw extensive development at the Oval: the West Stand was almost doubled in size and a new enclosure was built at the Vauxhall (or, as R.C. Robertson-Glasgow preferred it, the House of Commons) End, to be joined by another three years later as crowds flocked to watch the attractive cricket produced by Surrey under the captaincy of Fender, the best captain England never had. The refreshment facilities were also expanded and when the Australians next came, in 1926, the East Stand had given way to a grander structure.

That year's Test match was another of the Oval's memorable occasions. England had beaten Australia only once since the Great War, but now the sides came into the final match of the series with all to play for; the previous four games had been drawn and this one was to be played to a finish. Chapman, aged 25, was appointed captain and Rhodes, who had won his first Test cap before Chapman was born, was recalled at the age of 48. Australia took a first-innings lead of 22 but then Hobbs and Sutcliffe, the illustrious opening pair, each made hundreds with superb batting on a rain-affected pitch and England eventually totalled 436. Further rain had fallen and Australia, watched by the Prime Minister, Mr Baldwin, and several members of the Cabinet, collapsed to 125 all out; Rhodes was the most successful bowler with 4 for 44. The crowd, part of a total gathering of nearly 103,000, exploded on to the ground in joy that England had finally beaten the old enemy by 289 runs and the heroes were acclaimed in the now time-honoured tradition in front of the pavilion.

West Indies' first Test at the Oval came in 1928, when Hobbs made another hundred, and Sutcliffe scored one in each innings against South Africa the next year. Australia were back in 1930 and their innings victory which regained the Ashes by two matches to one was overshadowed in many, particularly Surrey, eyes by the fact that this was Hobbs's last Test. He scored 47 in England's first

innings of 405 (Sutcliffe 161) but then Bradman, as a climax to his first barnstorming tour of England (his aggregate for the series of 974 remains unsurpassed), amassed 232 and Ponsford 110 as Australia piled up 695. When Hobbs came out to bat late on the fourth day, the crowd applauded him all the way to the wicket and then Woodfull led the Australians in three moving cheers. As with Bradman at the Oval 18 years later, there was to be no great swansong: when Hobbs had made only 9, he played on. His total of 5410 runs and 15 centuries, then records, have long been surpassed, but his total against Australia of 3636 runs (average 54.26) with 12 centuries still stands. Hobbs has an undisputed place at the top of cricket's panoply and his achievements for Surrey and England were literally enshrined in concrete at his home ground in 1934 with the opening of the Hobbs Gates, sited at the main entrance in the new wall which replaced the old fence around the ground.

H. D. G. Leveson Gower, President of Surrey, about to declare open the Hobbs Gates – 'in honour of a great Surrey and England cricketer' – in 1934.

New Zealand lost by an innings on their first Test at the Oval in 1931, as did West Indies in 1933, even though England's side lacked a Surrey player at the Oval for the first time. There was none again in 1934, when Australia inflicted on England one of her heaviest defeats, by 562 runs. Again the series hung on this final match, again Australia regained the Ashes (to keep them until another famous Oval occasion 19 years thence) and again Bradman (244) and Ponsford (266) gorged themselves in a batsmen's paradise. Their second-wicket partnership of 451 is still a Test record for any wicket, though since equalled, and it laid the foundation for a total of 701, after which England were never in contention. It was a sad end for another great player, Woolley, who had been recalled at the age of 47, scored 4 and 0, and conceded 37 byes when he kept wicket after Ames's injury.

After a losing debut by India at the Oval in 1936 and a meeting the following year between the women of England and Australia in a match whose quality surprised many a male critic, England's men extracted a full measure of revenge for their trouncing four years earlier when they demolished Australia in 1938, although fate, in the shape of injuries which prevented Bradman and Fingleton from batting, took a large hand. This match was, of course, immortalized by Hutton's 364, then a Test record and greeted by the crowd with a chorus of 'For He's a Jolly Good Fellow'. In a masterly display of concentration he batted in all for 13 hours 17 minutes and became a national hero. There were other huge contributions to England's stratospheric total of 903 for 7 declared, which has never been beaten in Test cricket: Leyland made the small matter of 187 and Hardstaff 169 not out – after which an utterly demoralized Australia were skittled for 201 and 123 to make the margin of

Top **An aerial view of the Oval in 1938.**

Bottom **'Bosser' Martin posing with his heavy roller in front of England's highest Test score, which also included Hutton's heroic 364.**

victory an innings and 579 runs, another Test record. It is said that 'Bosser' Martin, the legendary Oval groundsman who had here produced the ultimate in perfect pitches with his famous heavy roller and layers of Surrey loam, took it as a personal affront that England did not go on to score 1000. Hammond, however, took pity on a stricken foe and declared.

The clouds of war were fast gathering over Europe when England met West Indies at the Oval in August 1939 and the centuries of Hutton, Hammond and the hard-hitting Kenneth Weekes, plus final glimpses of Headley and Constantine left cricket followers at least with fond memories before the conflagration that began ten days after the match ended. The Oval had a bad war. It was requisitioned as a prisoner of war camp and engulfed in concrete posts (sunk into the turf), barbed wire and weeds – but owing to a change of plan it never received a single prisoner – and, to make matters worse, the pavilion and stands suffered heavily in two separate air raids during the Blitz. An appeal to raise £100,000 to carry out major reconstruction was launched in August 1945 to coincide with Surrey's centenary, and was begun with a donation of £100 from the club's patron, King George VI. The landlords had agreed an extension of the lease to 1984 and expressed the wish that the ground should be used for other recreational purposes in the off season, though it supported the club's rejection of overtures from greyhound race promoters. The fund, pitched rather high in austere times, ultimately realized £22,000 and permitted much necessary rebuilding, although plans for a double deck stand on the gasholder side never materialized. The 'ancient lights' of the houses overlooking the ground, whose occupiers are afforded a splendid free view of play, have always had to be taken into account.

It took a remarkable effort by the new grounds-man, Bert Lock, and the ground authorities to get the Oval back into service for the first post-war season of 1946. If somewhat scarred, it was able to stage a Test match against India as well as a fondly remembered Veterans' match (Old England *v* Surrey) which featured, among others, the pre-war giants, Fender, Tate, Hendren and Woolley, and

was attended by the King. The 1947 match against South Africa was full of runs – 1477 – as the visitors, for whom Mitchell made a century in each innings finished only 28 runs short of scoring 451 for victory with three wickets in hand.

The following year was Bradman's final Test match and, as foreshadowed above, the great man failed. The reception from the crowd as he came out to bat and the cheers led by the England captain, Yardley, affected him so deeply that he was bowled, second ball, by a googly from Hollies. No matter that he was acclaimed all the way back to the pavilion, a mere 4 runs would have brought his Test aggregate to 7000 and his average to 100. As with Hobbs in 1930, Bradman's retirement over-shadowed another crushing Australian win, their fourth of the summer. England were demolished by Lindwall for 52, Australia replied with 389 (Morris 196) and England, despite Hutton's resist-ance, collapsed again for 188.

Hutton displayed his liking for the Oval again in 1949, with 206 against New Zealand, and in 1950, carrying his bat for 202 against West Indies, for whom Ramadhin and Valentine shared 14 wickets to complete an innings victory and crown their first series win in England. Hutton was also in the headlines at the Oval in 1951, when he became the only man in Test history to be given out obstructing the field. A turning ball ballooned up from the top edge and in fending it instinctively with his bat away from the wicket he prevented the wicket-keeper from making a catch. The match, a low-scoring affair on a pitch far removed from the usual Oval batting paradise, was won by England by four wickets, with Laker's ten wickets on his home ground, supported by Bedser's five, a key factor. Hutton, now captain, scored 86 in a rain-ruined match against India in 1952 and the following year marked his greatest triumph in a home series – and another unforgettable Oval event – with the return of the Ashes after 19 years and the first win in a home series against Australia for 27 years. As on that earlier occasion, stories of long all-night queues outside the ground kept some spectators away, but there were still over 26,000 present on the first day and 115,000 over the four that the match lasted. England had taken a 31-run advantage on first innings, Hutton himself scoring 82, and then the Surrey spin twins, Laker and Lock, whipped Australia out for 162. It was left to the renowned Middlesex pair, Compton and Edrich, to see England home by eight wickets amid scenes of joy not witnessed since 1926.

At the Oval in 1954 Pakistan achieved the unique distinction of winning a Test in their first series in England, Fazal Mahmood claiming 12 wickets for 99 on a wet pitch to secure victory by 24 runs; but England won another low-scoring match in 1955

The England team (on balcony on right of pavilion) being acclaimed by the huge Oval crowd after regaining the Ashes in 1953.

against South Africa thanks to decisive contributions from three Surrey men, May, Laker and Lock. Surrey were now in the midst of their unequalled run of seven successive county championships and the spinners' roles were decisive both for county and country. In 1956, a match which saw Compton recalled and scoring 94, Laker had seven wickets in the Oval Test to extend his tally for that remarkable series to 46 – and he took all ten Australian wickets in an innings for Surrey – and then Laker and Lock shared 16 wickets as West Indies were skittled for 89 and 86 on a dusty pitch in 1957; the visiting captain, Goddard, is said to have asked for a Hoover rather than a roller.

Against India at the Oval in 1959 England won by an innings to win a series 5–0 for the first and only time, but the Oval regained its reputation as a high-scoring ground over the next few years. Subba Row, later to be an energetic figure in Surrey's administration, ended his Test career there in 1961 with a century against Australia. The next Australian Test, in 1964, was memorable for Trueman becoming the first bowler to capture 300 Test wickets and for the first Test hundred of another Yorkshire scion, Boycott. In 1965 rain, as it had done on the South Africans' previous visit to the Oval five years earlier, intervened at a crucial stage. as England were making good progress towards a formidable winning target of 399 in the last match between the countries. The following year Close, as captain, and Murray, as wicket-keeper/batsman, made unforgettable returns in an innings win against an otherwise rampant West Indies. England's last three wickets added 361 runs, Higgs and Snow making 128 for the tenth, only two runs short of the English Test record. The lower orders were again to the fore in 1967, as Asif Iqbal and Intikhab Alam (later a Surrey player) put up a world Test record of 190 for the ninth wicket in a losing cause; Barrington, a favourite son of Surrey, scored his only Test hundred at the Oval in this match, becoming the first to complete a set at the six current Test grounds.

By now there existed revolutionary plans for the redevelopment of the Oval, including initially the erection of shops and several hundred flats at the Vauxhall end and later a hotel or office block, together with a new pavilion, but the most dramatic change from a cricketing viewpoint was a reduction by almost half of the enormous playing area, which would become a circle within the Oval with a maximum boundary of 75 yards. However, after nearly a decade involving many revisions the plans were finally shelved, much to the relief of many Oval stalwarts. The arena remains intact and the square alone is as wide as many a compact club cricket ground.

Meanwhile, the Test match of 1968 provided another classic finish. Underwood, never more importantly living up to his nickname 'Deadly', bowled England to victory over Australia with only five minutes to spare. This tells only party of the drama, for a freak storm at lunchtime on the final day flooded the ground with half the Australian side out; however, the sun came out and

Underwood strikes again and Australia's last wicket falls in England's classic win at the Oval in 1968.

Herculean efforts by the groundstaff and volunteers from the crowd, armed with brooms and blankets, enabled play to restart at 4.45 with the pitch and surrounding areas liberally spread with sawdust. Australia's resistance was finally broken 70 minutes later when Underwood, with every fielder within ten yards of the bat, trapped Inverarity leg-before. His final spell produced four wickets in 27 balls and he finished with 7 for 50; this writer well remembers listening to the closing stages on a Maltese beach and, even at that distance, the tension and excitement were scarcely less intense.

Underwood claimed 12 wickets in England's win over New Zealand in 1969, but that was their last success at the Oval until they defeated the same opponents nine years later. The intervening period was marked in 1971 by India's first victory in England and in 1973 by the Oval, for the first time in 80 years (though it has happened several times since) not staging the last Test of the summer. It was Chandrasekhar's whippy leg-spin, which skittled England for 101 in their second innings, and then steady Indian batting which ended a record run of 26 Tests without defeat and was the first in 20 matches as captain for Illingworth; this time too it was the visitors' supporters who raced across the Oval turf to salute their heroes.

The Chappell brothers, Ian and Greg, scored hundreds in 1972 when Australia won the first Test in England to contain six days' play and there were shades of the Oval pitches of old in the Pakistan Test of 1974 when 1038 runs were scored for the loss only 13 wickets, Zaheer Abbas making 240 and Amiss 183. There were even more runs in 1975 when England saved the match against Australia by scoring 538 after following on and yet more again the next year (1507) when brilliant fast bowling on an easy-paced pitch by Holding, whose matchwinning figures of 14 for 149 are a West

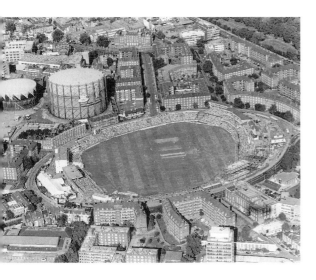

An aerial view of the Oval – or, for some 15 years to come, the Foster's Oval – during the final Test of the 1989 Ashes series, with work already underway on the redevelopment of the West Stand.

Indian Test record, stole the limelight from Richards's 291 and Amiss's 203.

Another monumental innings, Gavaskar's 221, almost brought India a remarkable victory in 1979 when they finished only 9 runs short of a target of 438 with two wickets left at the start of a run of drawn matches, which included the first sixth Test of a series in England when Australia visited in 1981 and a double-century off only 220 balls by Botham in 1982. The sequence was broken by another win over New Zealand in 1983, but the following year England were thrashed by West Indies, who completed a 5–0 'blackwash' in the series. They were the first visiting side to achieve this in England and the event was greeted by a large number of their countrymen, who have in recent years turned Kennington Oval into a recognizable substitute for Kensington Oval, Barbados, by their boisterous presence. A small consolation for England was that Botham in this match became

the first player to complete the Test match double of 3000 runs and 300 wickets.

The return of the Australians in 1985 brought another more typical Oval scene as England, after big hundreds from Gooch and Gower, completed an innings win in four days and a 3–1 victory in the series to make sure the Ashes were regained. Several thousand spectators duly assembled in front of the pavilion to acclaim both sides. A rain-ruined match against New Zealand in 1986 was enlivened by Botham's return after suspension: he took a wicket with his first ball, another with his sixth to become the leading wicket-taker in Test cricket, and then cracked fifty off 32 balls, including 24 off one over. A more subdued Botham (51 in over four hours) and his captain, Gatting, saved England against Pakistan the following year after the visitors had amassed their highest score, 708, to which Javed Miandad contributed 260. Botham's 3 for 217 represented the most runs ever conceded by an England bowler in a Test match and Abdul Qadir, with ten wickets in the match, happily proved that the art of leg-spin bowling was not yet dead. In 1988 things could be deemed 'business as usual' as West Indies completed another dominant win, at that stage their 14th in 15 Tests against England.

The Oval had by now undergone a facelift as the club persisted with efforts to bring the famous old ground up to date. A new perimeter wall was built to replace the 1934 one which was no longer perpendicular; the main entrance at the pavilion end was redesigned, necessitating a repositioning of the Hobbs Gates; and more important to the appearance of the ground the executive suite and 19 boxes which are the prerequisite of modern sport were installed in revamped Tavern and Mound stands adjoining the pavilion on the gas-holder side. This involved moving the scorers and press away from their long-standing homes, the press being given a rough ride in a temporary box on the Harleyford Road side during the 1984 West Indies Test and subsequently being accommodated during Test matches in a permanent looking temporary structure at the Vauxhall end. Plans reemerged for the refurbishment of that end of the ground, including an indoor cricket school, but were eventually replaced by a scheme for the major development of the West Stand on the other side of the pavilion. Some £4 million was required for this but when the amount raised by public appeal fell well short, the ground's soul was sold to an Australian brewery and the Foster's Oval, for the next 15 years anyway, was born. Appropriately its first Test match visitors were the 1989 Australians, who dominated play but fell short of their ambition to win a series in England by 5–0.

The Oval

Ref/No	Season	V	T	Result	Ref/No	Season	V	T	Result
4/1	1880	A	–	E-5w	390/38	1954	P	4	P-24
9/2	1882	A	–	A-7	412/39	1955	SA	5	E-92
16/3	1884	A	3	Draw	429/40	1956	A	5	Draw
24/4	1886	A	3	E-I&217	443/41	1957	WI	5	E-I&237
29/5	1888	A	2	E-I&137	458/42	1958	NZ	5	Draw
34/6	1890	A	2	E-2w	478/43	1959	I	5	E-I&27
40/7	1893	A	2	E-I&43	496/44	1960	SA	5	Draw
52/8	1896	A	3	E-66	511/45	1961	A	5	Draw
64/9	1899	A	5	Draw	534/46	1962	P	5	E-10w
74/10	1902	A	5	E-1w	547/47	1963	WI	5	WI-8w
87/11	1905	A	5	Draw	565/48	1964	A	5	Draw
95/12	1907	SA	3	Draw	596/49	1965	SA	3	Draw
105/13	1909	A	5	Draw	609/50	1966	WI	5	E-I&34
	1912 Triangular Tournament				623/51	1967	P	3	E-8w
128/14		EvSA	3	E-10w	641/52	1968	A	5	E-226
129/15		EvA	3	E-244	658/53	1969	NZ	3	E-8w
144/16	1921	A	5	Draw	692/54	1971	I	3	I-4w
157/17	1924	SA	5	Draw	702/55	1972	A	5	A-5w
167/18	1926	A	5	E-289	725/56	1973	WI	1	WI-158
175/19	1928	WI	3	E-I&71	744/57	1974	P	3	Draw
185/20	1929	SA	5	Draw	763/58	1975	A	4	Draw
198/21	1930	A	5	A-I&39	781/59	1976	WI	5	WI-231
210/22	1931	NZ	2	E-I&26	808/60	1977	A	5	Draw
229/23	1933	WI	3	E-I&17	828/61	1978	NZ	1	E-7w
237/24	1934	A	5	A-562	854/62	1979	I	4	Draw
246/25	1935	SA	5	Draw	883/63	1980	WI	4	Draw
254/26	1936	I	3	E-9w	908/64	1981	A	6	Draw
262/27	1937	NZ	3	Draw	930/65	1982	I	3	Draw
266/28	1938	A	5	E-I&579	957/66	1983	NZ	1	E-189
274/29	1939	WI	3	Draw	993/67	1984	WI	5	WI-172
278/30	1946	I	3	Draw	1022/68	1985	A	6	E-I&94
289/31	1947	SA	5	Draw	1051/69	1986	NZ	3	Draw
303/32	1948	A	5	A-I&149	1079/70	1987	P	5	Draw
317/33	1949	NZ	4	Draw	1102/71	1988	WI	5	WI-8w
326/34	1950	WI	4	WI-I&56	1126/72	1989	A	6	Draw
338/35	1951	SA	5	E-4w					
354/36	1952	I	4	Draw					
376/37	1953	A	5	E-8w	England: P 72, W 28, D 31, L 13				

Manchester

OLD TRAFFORD

It is obligatory when talking of Manchester and its cricket to mention the weather. It has been a topic ever since the washout of the first day of Test cricket at the ground, in 1884; was fortified when the Tests of 1890 and 1938 were abandoned without a ball bowled (Old Trafford is the only ground in England to hold this dubious distinction); and reached a peak in the summer of 1953, when eight whole days of cricket were washed out at the ground. The last day of the 1987 match against Pakistan, played in June, was the 27th to be completely washed out in 56 matches: Lord's, with 16 days lost in 81 matches over the same period, stands a distant second in this watery catalogue, which also accounts in large part for Old Trafford staging a higher proportion of drawn Tests than any other English ground.

Enough, though, of meteorology, for Old Trafford has a long and distinguished history as a cricketing centre and can claim seniority to every ground but the Oval in Test match terms. The present ground, some $3\frac{1}{2}$ miles from the city centre, was opened in 1857 – also the year of foundation of another great Manchester institution, the Hallé Orchestra. It was sited on eight acres of land leased from the de Trafford estates after the Manchester club's previous site nearby had been claimed for the Art Treasures Exhibition, itself used subsequently for botanical gardens, which themselves were supplanted by a somewhat different art form, the White City greyhound track.

Manchester defeated Liverpool by 31 runs in the inaugural match, and *Bell's Life* reported: 'The new ground ... consists of about eight acres of good, level, sandy land. The pavilion is erected on the north side; and while it is a great ornament to the ground, it is well adapted for the purposes for which it will be used. It consists of a centre compartment (intended for a dining hall) and two wings, a turret surmounting the centre. The dining hall is 36 feet long by 22 feet wide ... Underneath the building is an excellent wine cellar, no unimportant acquisition in a cricket pavilion. The entire front of the dining hall, which commands a view of the whole field, is composed of glass.'

The Lancashire county club was formed in 1864 and was a tenant of Manchester at Old Trafford until the two clubs amalgamated in 1880. The first inter-county match was played against Middlesex in 1865, Lancashire winning by 62 runs despite V.E. Walker, one of a famous cricketing family, taking all ten wickets in Lancashire's second innings. The event seems not to have captured the imagination of the Manchester public for the gate money amounted to only £25. The Roses matches began in 1867, when Yorkshire won all three encounters by large margins; the following year the ground had its first overseas visitors, the Australian Aboriginals. Club rules in those early days were strict and members faced a 5s (25p) fine if they smoked in the pavilion before dinner or while fielding or batting; the minutes also record a reprimand for the ground manager, Fred Reynolds, after he invited friends to a pigeon shoot over the ground. It was not the shooting which upset the committee, for this was one of the perks of his job, but the fact that the friends were not members of the club.

As Lancashire grew in strength, so their cricket grew as an attraction, and when Gloucestershire, fielding the three Graces, visited Old Trafford for the first time in 1878, the accommodation was inadequate for the crowd of over 16,000 which turned up for the final day and which frequently encroached on to the playing area. Their action culminated in a riot in which lumps of turf were hurled about before order was restored. This match – at least the cricketing part – was the inspiration for Francis Thompson's famous poem, *At Lord's*, which immortalized the county's opening batsmen of that era, 'my Hornby and my Barlow long ago'. The pugnacious Hornby, a rugby international and first-rate boxer, played a significant part in quelling the riot, as he was to do when Lord Harris was attacked by a spectator at Sydney that winter.

After these unsavoury incidents two stands were hastily erected for the visit of the Australians the next month and the 1880s saw the addition of a members' dining-room and a ladies' pavilion. Incidentally, Barlow was an avid collector of cricketana and after he retired he turned his home in Blackpool into a virtual cricket museum. One of the most striking items was a stained-glass window depicting Barlow, Hornby and the Lancashire wicket-keeper, Pilling, and it is now incorporated in the entrance hall of the executive suite at the Stretford end of Old Trafford, which stands more or less opposite the stand which bears Hornby's name.

Hornby, as captain of Lancashire, though by then past his best form, was invited to captain England in the first Test match at Old Trafford on 10–12 July 1884, when Australia played more than a single-match rubber in England for the first time. Barlow was also included, though he did not open the innings with Hornby, and two other Lancashire players, Steel and Pilling, were in the side. As already mentioned, rain prevented play on the first day and England escaped with a draw after Boyle and Spofforth had bowled them out for 95 in the first innings. Old Trafford was thus confirmed as a Test match venue and from then until 1957 (with the exception of 1907) it always had a Test during

a major tour; in summers when only three Tests were played, Old Trafford would be awarded the northern game alongside the two London grounds, Lord's and the Oval.

Old Trafford in the early days was out in the country. It had the advantage, however, from the outset of a station in Warwick Road, adjoining the ground and only a few minutes' journey from the centre of Manchester (confusingly Old Trafford station is one stop up the line). This gives it an asset unique among English Test grounds – although the Oval and Lord's have nearby underground stations – and if the setting is less rural now, the ground retains an open environment, which has happily remained despite its being situated in an area of industrial development and dense population. A feature of the ground, which has repeatedly drawn comment over the years, is the good light this affords, allowing play to proceed in conditions which cause its suspension on grounds in more built-up areas.

Led by Lancashire's outstanding all-rounder, Steel, England were victorious against Australia in 1886, with Barlow taking 7 for 44 in the second innings, and in a remarkable match in 1888 they won by an innings despite themselves scoring only 172. On a real 'sticky dog' Peel (11 for 68), Lohmann and Briggs claimed 18 wickets and the match was over before lunch. It had lasted little more than $6\frac{1}{2}$ hours, the shortest completed Test in England, and Australia's second innings of 70 occupied a mere 69 minutes, their briefest ever. The 1890 match, scheduled for late August, was totally washed away; but in 1893 the batsmen had a happier time, with William Gunn, of Nottinghamshire, scoring the first hundred in an Old Trafford Test, although England, one up going into this final match of a three-match series, ignored a target of 198 in $2\frac{1}{4}$ hours despite Australia

bowling 63 five-ball overs. W.G. Grace's skill as a doctor as opposed to cricketer has often been disparaged, but in this match he replaced Turner's dislocated finger during a match-saving innings and it was also at Old Trafford, in 1887, that Grace saved the life of his Gloucestershire colleague, Croome, after his throat was spiked by one of the boundary railings as he tried to make a catch.

As Manchester was transformed in 1894 by the opening of the Ship Canal, so the face of the Old Trafford ground changed with the demolition of the old pavilion and its replacement with a new, three-storey building. It offered spacious accommodation, including three baths for the amateurs, while the professionals, in particular, benefited, for previously they had had to change on the 'popular' side of the ground, in a cramped, ill-appointed room. The frontage of the pavilion, with its twin copper domes, dark brick and black stone, has changed little to the present day and if it seems to echo the Oval pavilion, that is not surprising, for Thomas Muirhead designed them both. It now has a fine, bow-windowed committee room, offering a panoramic view of play, plus dining room, library and a central feature on the ground floor, a Long Room, filled with cricketing mementoes, such as scorecards and pictures of famous old Lancashire

Old Trafford in the 1890s.

warriors such as MacLaren, Spooner, Makepeace and the Tyldesleys.

Unusually among Test grounds the pavilion is sited at right angles to the square, but has the compensatory advantage of facing south and thus benefiting when the Manchester sun does shine, as well as being adorned by hanging baskets of flowers. This feminine touch belies the fact that, until the rules were changed in the winter of 1989, Old Trafford barred women spectators from the pavilion – although men were allowed into the adjacent Ladies' Pavilion, albeit accompanied by a 'lady subscriber' (as they were termed before graduating to member status).

There were some hiccoughs in the pavilion's early stages, as the plans involved the demolition of the house occupied for many years by Reynolds, the ground manager, and his moving to another near the ground. He set out to obstruct the builders in any way he could, largely by delaying the removal of his possessions. However, the builders had the last laugh, when they welcomed him convivially one morning: in stripping the roof of his house they had discovered his supplies of whisky and helped themselves. The initial cost of the project was expected to be £6000, but it cost half as much again, and soon afterwards the club was involved in further large expense when it was offered the chance of buying the ground at a cost of £24,082. Although strapped for funds, it could not let the opportunity pass and issued 200 bonds of £100 each to raise the necessary cash. The debts entailed by these and the upkeep of the ground were not paid off until nearly 40 years and two public appeals later.

The 1896 Old Trafford Test was one of the most memorable at the ground. After England had followed on 181 behind Ranjitsinhji, on his debut and the first Indian to play Test cricket, scored a magnificent 154 not out, the last 113 coming on the last morning of the match; Stoddart was the only other batsmen in the innings to exceed 19. In the priceless words of one contemporary writer Ranji 'stroked and turned the crimson rambler to the confines with oriental splendour. In between he lofted the ball at catchable height to all the places where no catchers prowled'! Left to make 125 to win, Australia were made to fight all the way by Richardson, who bowled unchanged for 42.3 overs and took six wickets to add to his seven of the first innings; however, Australia got home by three wickets. The next match in 1899, the fourth of the first five-match series in England, was drawn after two staunch innings by Noble for Australia; there were large crowds, 23,226 paying for admission on the first day and 21,144 on the second, and it was estimated that 10,000 were turned away when the gates were closed on the first two days.

If the 1896 Test had been memorable the 1902 match was nothing short of sensational and produced the closest finish to any Test match in terms of runs, 3, until it was equalled at Melbourne in 1982–83. Trumper's brilliant century before lunch on the first day, making light of a damp pitch and slow outfield, gave Australia a sizable initial advantage. Jackson replied with a fine hundred for England and then Lockwood (11 for 76 in the match) took advantage of a damaged pitch to dismiss Australia for 86 and leave England 124 to win. The target might have been smaller had Fred Tate, controversially selected for his first Test in place of Hirst and usually a close-to-the-wicket fielder, not dropped Darling at deep square leg when he had scored 16; he went on to make 37 and arguments about his selection and MacLaren's field-placing were still rumbling in the cricketing press in 1987. England reached 92 for 3 but collapsed against Saunders and Trumble on a drying pitch and 8 runs were still required when the luckless Tate came in at number 11. Then the local mischief, rain, arrived and held up play for nearly three quarters of an hour. The agony of the crowd was as nothing to poor Tate's. Fate at the last seemed to smile on him as he snicked the first ball he faced from Saunders to the fine-leg boundary – 4 to win. Alas, the fourth ball came in with the left-arm Saunders's arm, kept low and shattered Tate's wicket. England had lost and Tate never played another Test, but he sought solace in the young son at home in Sussex who would one day win a Test for England; it was 22 years later that Maurice Tate restored family pride.

The 1905 match at Old Trafford saw England retain the Ashes with an innings win after Jackson, in his 'year', had repeated his feat of 1902 by scoring a hundred at the ground, his fifth in all against Australia in England (still a record), and shared a glorious partnership with a local favourite, Spooner. Another local hero, the fast bowler, Brearley, who used to leap over the pavilion railings in his eagerness to reach the middle rather than take the orthodox passage through the gate, contributed eight wickets to England's triumph. By the 1909 match Australia were already two up in the series and were thus merely intent on avoiding defeat, which they did with the help of the rain and Laver's 8 for 31, still the best figures by a visiting bowler in an English Test.

Old Trafford had two of the nine games in the 1912 Triangular Tournament: the second meeting between England and Australia, in which the old enemy allowed only five hours' play, and the opening fixture of the tournament, between Australia and South Africa, which brought a feat unique in Test cricket. Matthews, the Australian leg-spinner, achieved a hat-trick in each innings, his third victim on both occasions being the South African wicket-keeper, Ward. So unexpected and late in the day was the second feat that one correspondent merely reported: '... Matthews repeated his former feat'. No sports editor would allow him to get away with that today.

For the duration of the First World War cricketers' whites gave way to doctors' coats and nurses' aprons. The Old Trafford pavilion (and latterly the members' dining and tea rooms) was transformed into the Pavilion Hospital with 100 beds for wounded soldiers, of whom some 1800 were tended by the Red Cross. However, the playing area was kept regularly mown and rolled against the day when cricket could resume.

Test matches returned in 1921 with the visit of the Australians, who had beaten England eight times in succession. Rain, inevitably, accounted for the first day when a strong force of police ensured that there was no trouble after the crowd had waited until 5.30 for the decision to call play off; the second day produced an extraordinary incident when the Hon. Lionel Tennyson, grandson of the poet, tried to declare England's innings at ten to six so as to have half an hour's bowling at the opposition. However, he – and the England selectors and three former England captains who advised him – were unaware that, in what had now become a two-day match, he could not declare unless at least 100 minutes' playing time remained before the close. Carter, Australia's Yorkshire-born wicket-keeper, it seems was the only one who knew the laws and after a protracted debate, causing a 25-minute hold-up, the Australians returned to the field and England continued their innings. Some sections of the crowd of 25,000 booed the Australians, and when their captain, the massive Armstrong, staged a sit-down protest while the noise continued, Tennyson and one of the umpires had to go to explain the position to them. Amid the confusion, once play had resumed, Armstrong contrived to bowl two overs in succession either side of the break. Australia saved the game on the final day despite the Lancastrian Parkin's best Test return, but their run of wins was halted. A footnote on Carter: he was an undertaker who often turned up to matches in a hearse and after the Second World War was one of the earliest subscribers to Lancashire's rebuilding appeal, his £500 donation reflecting his gratitude for hospitality extended to him by the club and by Lancastrians.

With rain permitting only ten balls on the first day the 1926 match was doomed to a draw, though it added to the clamour – particularly from Australia – for four-day Tests in England and saw Hobbs taking over the England captaincy for the last two days after Carr went down with tonsillitis over the weekend. The last professional to lead England was Shrewsbury in 1886–87. It was, incidentally, that season which had seen the largest ever attendance at Old Trafford, 46,000 (38,906 paid) for the bank holiday's play in the supreme northern test of strength, the Roses match.

West Indies were new visitors to Old Trafford

Old Trafford from the air during the visit of the 1934 Australians.

in 1928 but went down by an innings, as did the 1929 South Africans; Tich Freeman, the Kent leg-spinner, took 22 wickets in these matches. In 1930, by when Tests against Australia had been extended to four days, rain removed most of the last two so the match was drawn but large crowds flocked to Old Trafford, whose facilities were complimented by an MCC committee of inspection. They reported that the ground 'was in every respect most desirable, and in fact the only ground they had visited where no improvement could be suggested'. When New Zealand made their debut in 1931 play could not begin until 3.15 on the last afternoon, the sun making such an unexpected reappearance that there were problems in locating some players, who had sought entertainment elsewhere.

West Indies were back in 1933 with a sparkling 169 from Headley and England had a taste of their own medicine when Martindale and Constantine bowled bodyline; Jardine passed his own comment on the situation by scoring his only Test hundred, never flinching and showing how it could be coun-

tered by drawing himself up to his full height and playing the ball down with a dead bat. The following year 'from first to last the sun blazed down, the heat being at times almost unbearable' (*Wisden*) and a perfect batting pitch brought a high-scoring draw, 1307 runs for the loss of only 20 wickets. O'Reilly, the great Australian leg-spinner, struck a blow for the bowlers by dismissing Walters, Wyatt and Hammond in the space of four balls on the first morning, although Allen's opening over for England contained 13 balls, including three wides and four no-balls, as he tried to avoid the deep footmarks left by O'Reilly. It was in 1934 too that the Old Trafford crowd, often noted for its partisanship, paid a moving tribute to Jack Hobbs, in his last season, singing 'Auld Lang Syne' as he returned to the pavilion after scoring a century in Duckworth's benefit match.

Draws followed in the next two years against South Africa and India, the second day of the latter match producing a still extant record of 588 runs (including a memorable 167 from Hammond) on another easy-paced pitch, but England defeated New Zealand in 1937 when Hutton scored the first of his 19 Test centuries. The Manchester weather struck again with a vengeance in 1938 to cause a total washout – not even the final elevens were announced – and in 1939 severely curtailed the match against West Indies.

Old Trafford suffered more severely than any other English Test ground during the Second World War, when it was occupied first by the Royal Engineers, then used, after Dunkirk, as a transit camp for the evacuated troops, and latterly taken over by the Ministry of Supply for stores and vehicles. A sentry stationed at the main gate was killed during the air raids of December 1940, buildings were heavily damaged – the pavilion took a pounding, the catering facilities were destroyed and all but one stand on the popular side was badly damaged – and the playing area, renowned for the velvety texture of its grass, was covered with craters, although the square was unscathed; there was a limit, however, to what could be done by way of restoration, for the heavy roller had been requisitioned to help lay out airfields in the Middle East. The club's furniture and valuable relics were at least kept safe, stored in banks or out of town in members' houses.

Cricket did at least resume in 1944 and Mancunian appetite for the game was reflected in a crowd of over 72,000 for the three days of the fourth Victory Test of 1945. The Army got the pavilion and other bomb-damaged buildings back in shape for the match and German prisoners of war were paid three farthings an hour for assisting in the work. A rebuilding appeal for £100,000 was launched at the end of the war and plans drawn up for an elaborate new pavilion and other accommodation, which would extend the capacity of the ground to 40,000. Although there was a generous response to the appeal, the development of the pavilion was restricted to repairs of the old structure. However, steady refurbishment of the stands followed, even if for several years Old Trafford had a rather makeshift appearance.

The resumption of Test cricket after the war revealed no change in the Manchester weather, rain preventing play until after lunch on the first day of the 1946 match against India, whose last pair saved the match by batting out the final 13 minutes. Compton and Edrich in their golden year of 1947 were largely instrumental in England's victory over South Africa and it was a bandaged Compton in 1948, with an heroic hundred after he had mishooked a bouncer from Lindwall on to his forehead, who gave England the better of another draw. A high-scoring draw against New Zealand in 1949 was most notable for the debut of Brian Close at 18 years 149 days, the youngest man to play for England.

Wanting to even out the balance between bat and ball, Lancashire instructed their groundsman before the 1950 season to make less use of water and the heavy roller in pitch preparation and throughout its course spin bowlers prospered. It certainly made for cricket full of incident, even if batsmen were not too enamoured of the conditions. The Test match was no exception and England gained their only victory of that summer against West Indies on a crumbling pitch, described by John Arlott as 'like an ash heap'; for once England's spinners, including Lancashire's own Berry with nine, outdid Ramadhin and Valentine.

Bedser claimed another 12 wickets when England beat South Africa in 1951 on another

lively pitch, the second day being washed away, and in 1952 England routed India by an innings and 207 runs. Trueman took 9 for 40 and Bedser 7 for 46 as India were dismissed for 58 and 82 in only $3\frac{3}{4}$ hours. Play in the 1953 match against Australia was confined to less than 14 hours and it was drawn, though the visitors crashed to 35 for 8 in their second innings. Three more were lost when Pakistan first appeared at Old Trafford the following year and were spared almost certain defeat. The unfortunate Ghazali made a pair within two hours of the third afternoon.

1955 brought England's first defeat at Old Trafford for more than half a century when South Africa, needing 145 to win in $2\frac{1}{4}$ hours, got home with nine balls to spare. The match marked the last Test appearance of Alec Bedser on one of his most successful grounds, and the next Old Trafford Test will forever be remembered for the unique, still

barely credible feats of another legendary Surrey bowler, Jim Laker, against Australia. He captured 9 for 37 (the last seven for 8 runs in 22 balls) in the first innings and 10 for 53 in the second, all the wickets taken from the Stretford end, as a bemused Australia could manage only 84 and 205 in reply to England's 459. England had won two matches in a home series against Australia for the first time

---

Above More than 133,000 attended the 1961 Test, which Australia won on the last afternoon.

Right Jim Laker leaves the field after his astonishing 19 for 90 at Old Trafford in 1956.

since 1905, the last time there had been a definite result between them at Old Trafford. No one before or since has taken 19 wickets in a first-class match or ten in a Test innings – nor perhaps ever will do. Much was written and said at the time and subsequently about the pitch, from which Laker made his off-breaks lift and turn, but as the Australian captain, Ian Johnson, said afterwards: 'When the controversy and side issues of the match are forgotten, Laker's wonderful bowling will remain.' Indeed it does. 'Do people remember it, Jim? Do they still ask you about it now and again?' Laker would be asked years afterwards. 'Only about three times a day,' he would reply with typical dry humour.

Under the rota system recently introduced Old Trafford ironically did not get a Test match in its centenary year, 1957, although MCC sent a side of near Test strength to meet Lancashire, but in the next two years England easily beat weak opponents from New Zealand and India. The latter match was distinguished by a hundred on Test debut by Baig, an Oxford freshman summoned to his country's colours, and by 131 from Pullar, who succeeded where the likes of MacLaren, Spooner, the Tyl-

desleys, Paynter and Washbrook had failed and became the first and so far only Lancashire player to score a hundred for England on his home ground.

When the opening two days of the 1960 match against South Africa were washed out, Old Trafford had then been responsible for 23 of 48 days lost on all English Test grounds; thereafter the match was destined for an inevitable draw. The following year Australia gained a measure of revenge for Laker's ravages in one of the most exciting of post-war Tests in England, attended by more than 133,000, a record for Old Trafford, with a full house of 34,000 on the fourth day. The hero of the hour was Benaud who, delivering his leg-spin round the wicket and pitching it in the rough, snaffled five wickets in 25 balls on the last afternoon and wrecked the bold efforts of England – particularly Dexter, who scored a sparkling 76 – to reach a target of 256 in 230 minutes. At one stage England were 150 for 1, but they were shot out for 201. Benaud, despite a damaged shoulder, finished with 6 for 70.

Spin continued to feature prominently in Old Trafford Tests. In 1963 the off-breaks of Gibbs brought West Indies their first Test win at the ground, but the 1964 match against Australia was notorious for the fact that only two innings plus two overs were completed in a virtually uninterrupted five days. On a too perfect pitch Australia, one up in the series and determined to make sure of retaining the Ashes, batted for over two days to score 656 for 8 – Simpson, their captain, making his first Test century and a remarkable 311 in all – and England replied to this highest Test total at Old Trafford with 611, Barrington 256, Dexter 174 and Veivers, the Australian off-spinner, bowling 95.1 overs. With an election in the offing the Leader of the Opposition, Harold Wilson, attended on the second afternoon and the Prime Minister, Sir Alec Douglas-Home, was there the following day.

It was Gibbs again in 1966 whose ten wickets brought West Indies victory by an innings and inflicted England's first three-day defeat since 1938; the weather, in early June, was hot throughout! England were beaten by Australia in 1968, well short of a target of 413, but they returned to winning ways the next year against West Indies, the first match under Illingworth's leadership. The first three days were played in superb weather and *Wisden* noted: '. . . on Saturday, when 21,000 people were present, the well-appointed Old Trafford arena presented a most pleasing sight. There is no better place for cricket when the sun shines on a goodly company, a perfect pitch and a green outfield.'

There were even more people at Old Trafford in 1970, nearly 33,000, though not for a Test match; they were there to see Lancashire win the John Player Sunday League with a victory over Yorkshire and the devoted support shown for the county in one-day matches at this time was more appropriate to the other Old Trafford, home of Manchester United, a few hundred yards up the road.

Despite the large crowds Lancashire reported a record deficit that season, mainly because of the loss of revenue from the cancellation of the South African tour, and in order to reduce its overdraft (from nearly £67,000 to less than £1700) the county sold the lease on the office blocks at the western corner of the ground. At least they retain the names of famous Lancashire cricketers – Duckworth, MacLaren, Statham and Washbrook – and the cricketing tenor of the area is emphasized by nearby street names such as Barlow Road, Hornby Road, Headingley Drive and Trent Bridge Walk.

In 1971 rain saved India from likely defeat; Lever, the Lancashire fast bowler, shone unexpectedly with the bat, an undefeated 88 preceding five wickets in India's first innings. It was that year which also saw a famous match in the Gillette Cup between Lancashire and Gloucestershire, which ended at ten to nine in near darkness and was won by Hughes taking 24 off an over from Mortimore as BBC television's main evening news bulletin was delayed to accommodate the climax of the match. Australia were defeated in the opening Test of the 1972 series in bleak conditions, although Old Trafford on this occasion perversely managed to miss heavy storms which afflicted nearby areas, and England won on their next appearance at Old Trafford in 1974 against India, a match which was the first in which the regulation allowing an extra hour's play on the first four days if more than an hour of a particular day was lost. Manchester being true to form, play continued until 7.30 on the first and third days.

In 1975 *Wisden* ran an article by Sir Neville Cardus titled 'Old Trafford Humiliated' in which he lamented that the ground was, for the first time since becoming a Test ground in 1884, not to have a match against Australia, an insult to 'have provoked A.C. MacLaren to a purpled vocal indignation'. The Test and County Cricket Board had decided that Old Trafford must take its turn alongside Trent Bridge and Edgbaston for an Australian Test because of smaller than expected Test match attendances there in recent years – Mancunians had been turning more and more towards the instant brand of one-day cricket – and also because only four Tests were to be played in 1975 because the inaugural World Cup occupied the first part of the summer. Old Trafford's next Test, in 1976, was accompanied by devastating cricket from West Indies, who won by the enormous margin of 425 runs on a cracked, often unpredictable, pitch. It was symptomatic of England's plight that the largest contributor in the match to their pitiful totals of 71 and 126 was extras (44); for the winners Greenidge scored a century in each innings, the first batsman to accomplish the feat in an Old Trafford Test. Much anger was rightly aroused on the third evening when the West Indies fast bowlers unleashed a concerted and unacceptable fusillade of bouncers at England's venerable openers, Edrich and Close, neither of whom played another Test. Holding was eventually warned, but the damage had been done and this style of attack was late to form the basis of West Indies' run of success in the ensuing years. Their captain then was Clive Lloyd, a dearly adopted son of Lancashire.

The Australians were back at Old Trafford on their next visit in 1977 and England marked the occasion with a nine-wicket victory thanks in no small part to the Kent pair, Woolmer and Underwood. Old Trafford did not have another Test until 1980, when Lloyd scored his only Test hundred at Old Trafford.

The 1981 Test against Australia was the one in that never-to-be-forgotten series in which England retained the Ashes. It produced some extraordinary feats and contrasts: Botham scored a devastating hundred off only 86 balls, including a Test record in England of six sixes, while Tavaré was making the slowest half-century ever recorded in English first-class cricket (306 minutes); Australia's first innings, lasting only 30.2 overs, was their shortest since 1902 but Border, bravely defying England in the fourth innings despite a broken finger, took 377 minutes to reach his hundred, the slowest by an Australian in Tests. The catering returns give an indication of the major operation that constitutes a modern Test match: the turnover was almost £200,000 and the operation involved 300 waitresses, 100 kitchen staff, 200 bar staff, 2500lb of meat, 5000 sandwiches and 60,000 pints of beer.

Another weather-disrupted match in 1982 against India was drawn and a total attendance of less than 22,000 on the four days on which play was possible confirmed the waning interest in Test cricket in Manchester. Old Trafford celebrated its centenary as a Test match ground in 1984 and the 52,000 who turned up over the five days saw another crushing defeat for England. Greenidge made a double-hundred for the winners, Lamb – in adversity – his third in successive matches for the losers. It was a painful return to Test cricket for the Surrey off-spinner, Pocock, after a gap of 86 matches and more literally painful for the Hampshire batsman, Terry, who had his left arm broken but returned to the wicket to bat one-handed and enable Lamb to complete his hundred. A slow pitch and interruptions brought another draw against Australia in 1985, and in 1987, as mentioned at the outset, the rain was at it again. Two years later Australia went some way towards exorcizing unhappy memories of Manchester when they won there by nine wickets to regain the Ashes for the first time in England since 1934. Maiden Test centuries by Robin Smith and Russell at least salvaged home pride.

Old Trafford is now as well appointed as any ground in the country thanks to a continuing programme of development. The Conference Centre centred around the pavilion has become a valuable local amenity, used throughout the year and bringing the club valuable revenue – as does the tented village which springs up during Tests and can play host to 3000 guests. In 1982 a ground appeal raised more than £200,000 to pay for a new complex on the east side of the pavilion and two years later this was followed by a £500,000 executive suite at the Stretford end. This has since been matched at the opposite, Warwick Road end by the Red Rose Suite, which is topped by the Neville Cardus Gallery, a commodious press box offering a splendid view of play and named after the most famous of all cricket writers, whose reports in *The Manchester Guardian* immortalized Lancastrian cricket and cricketers. It replaced the unlamented, former box which perched precariously on the roof of the Ladies' Pavilion at the other end of the ground and is now consigned to that fund of history, with which the place is suffused. How appropriate that in 1984 Old Trafford should have opened its own well-appointed museum, in which many of the great players and their deeds can be recalled.

Manchester

Ref/No	Season	V	T	Result	Ref/No	Season	V	T	Result
14/1	1884	A	1	Draw	353/31	1952	I	4	E-I&207
22/2	1886	A	1	E-4w	374/32	1953	A	3	Draw
30/3	1888	A	3	E-I&21	389/33	1954	P	3	Draw
–	1890	A	3	Abandoned	410/34	1955	SA	3	SA-3w
41/4	1893	A	3	Draw	428/35	1956	A	4	E-I&170
51/5	1896	A	2	A-3w	457/36	1958	NZ	4	E-I&13
63/6	1899	A	4	Draw	477/37	1959	I	4	E-171
73/7	1902	A	4	A-3	495/38	1960	SA	4	Draw
86/8	1905	A	4	E-I&80	510/39	1961	A	4	A-54
104/9	1909	A	4	Draw	543/40	1963	WI	1	WI-10w
	1912 Triangular Tournament				564/41	1964	A	4	Draw
121/10		AvSA	1	A-I&88	605/42	1966	WI	1	WI-I&40
126/11		EvA	2	Draw	637/43	1968	A	1	A-159
143/12	1921	A	4	Draw	653/44	1969	WI	1	E-10w
156/13	1924	SA	4	Draw	691/45	1971	I	2	Draw
166/14	1926	A	4	Draw	698/46	1972	A	1	E-89
174/15	1928	WI	2	E-I&30	739/47	1974	I	1	E-113
184/16	1929	SA	4	E-I&32	779/48	1976	WI	3	WI-425
197/17	1930	A	4	Draw	805/49	1977	A	2	E-9w
211/18	1931	NZ	3	Draw	882/50	1980	WI	3	Draw
228/19	1933	WI	2	Draw	907/51	1981	A	5	E-103
235/20	1934	A	3	Draw	929/52	1982	I	2	Draw
245/21	1935	SA	4	Draw	992/53	1984	WI	4	WI-I&64
253/22	1936	I	2	Draw	1020/54	1985	A	4	Draw
261/23	1937	NZ	2	E-130	1075/55	1987	P	1	Draw
–	1938	A	3	Abandoned	1100/56	1988	WI	3	WI-I&156
273/24	1939	WI	2	Draw	1124/57	1989	A	4	A-9w
277/25	1946	I	2	Draw					
287/26	1947	SA	3	E-7w	England: P 56, W 18, D 27, L 11				
301/27	1948	A	3	Draw					
316/28	1949	NZ	3	Draw					
323/29	1950	WI	1	E-202	1890 and 1938 Tests abandoned without a ball				
336/30	1951	SA	3	E-9w	being bowled and excluded from the records.				

Nottingham
TRENT BRIDGE

Given the example of Lord's and Fenner's, the main cricket ground in Nottingham might now be called Clarke's, after its founder, rather than Trent Bridge, after the nearby river crossing. For it was William Clarke – crack bowler, despot and shrewd businessman – who opened the ground in 1838, although his name remained markedly absent from the ground until the 150th anniversary appeal brought forth plans for a new stand in his honour. It was his marriage to Mary Chapman, landlady of the Trent Bridge Inn, behind which cricket had been played for many years which provided the impetus for the new venture. With an eye to the money which might be made from staging cricket Clarke enclosed the ground and imposed a 6d admission charge, resented by some and reducing attendances at his ground from the 20,000 who would assemble on the nearby Forest ground without having to pay.

The first match was played between the Forest Club and South of the Trent on 28 May 1838, South of the Trent winning by 45 runs. On 27–28 July 1840 Nottinghamshire entertained and lost to Sussex in the first county match there. The first major match on the ground followed in 1842 when Nottinghamshire lost to an England XI, led by the great Norfolk-born all-rounder, Fuller Pilch, and including Alfred Mynn, the leading batsman of the day.

Clarke, who initially followed his father into bricklaying, was idiosyncratic: his lunch, when playing cricket, was said to consist of a bottle of soda water and a cigar, though in the evening he ate a whole goose; he was an entrepreneur – as well as Trent Bridge he founded the All England XI of touring professionals, who, thanks to the spread of the railways, took the game all round the country from 1846; and he was autocratic – 'Excepting his own faults, Clarke knew more than any man alive about cricket,' his Nottinghamshire contemporary, George Parr, is quoted as saying, and it was disagreements between Clarke and his leading players which led to John Wisden founding the breakaway United All England XI in 1852. Those three attributes were perhaps summed up by his style of bowling, for in the later stages of his career, when round-arm was the vogue, he stuck to the old-fashioned underarm, adapted it to his needs and claimed many top-hatfulls of wickets after telling his opening partner: 'I'm going to bowl from this end; you can choose which end you like.'

Cricket at Trent Bridge was not the financial success for which Clarke had hoped and he turned his cricketing attentions to the All England XI. His stepson took over the lease to the inn and ground and it passed through several other landlords before the county cricket club, now firmly established and boasting the strongest side in the land, took out a 99-year lease in 1881; the club bought the freehold in 1919, retaining the ground but selling off the inn, though the latter remains very much part of the cricketing scene at Trent Bridge. The current building, which dates from 1885, is a popular meeting-place for cricketing folk and during big matches customers are offered refreshments and a panoramic view of the cricket from a stand on the roof.

The first pavilion, erected around 1860, stood at the rear of the Trent Bridge Inn, a modest building of brick and slate. It was superseded in 1872 by a two-storey building at the opposite end of the ground and that in turn gave way to the present pavilion in 1886. Designed by H. M. Townsend, of Peterborough, and costing £5000, it is distinguished by its balustrades and decorative iron-

The Trent Bridge pavilion in its full glory in 1930 (Australia going out to field) and in 1989.

work and by the contrast of white woodwork and red brick. Pre-1953 representations show the building in its full glory, for in that year a copper and cast-iron canopy was removed to accommodate, perched on stilts above the main forecourt, a spacious but unattractive cabin to house radio, television and scorers. The pavilion houses an excellent library and, since 1987, a small museum. In addition, a splendid range of cricketing photographs and paintings, not to mention more than 130 historic bats, is spread throughout the building,

the collection owing its origins to A.W. Shelton, a club stalwart for more than half a century and president in 1933.

The playing area, which now covers about half of the ground's current ten acres, was first tended by an official groundsman in 1855 and 1876 saw the appointment to the groundstaff of 'Fiddler' Walker, a diminutive figure distinguished by his white hair and whiskers and so nicknamed because he used to play the violin not because he doctored pitches. It was he who discovered the lasting properties of Nottinghamshire marl, which became the bane of bowlers not only at Trent Bridge but on other grounds around the country. In Walker's words his pitches would taunt bowlers thus: 'I'm better this match than ever I was. They'll never be able to wear me out; I shall be just as good on the third day as I was on the first.' This was the beginning of the traditional pitch at Trent Bridge – the one on which Arthur Shrewsbury, the best professional batsman of the late 19th century, was so sure of staying in that he would tell the pavilion attendant to bring him out a cup of tea at half past four (there was no tea interval in those days) and where it was always afternoon and 360 for 2 wickets, as Cardus wrote in the 1920s. Over 50 years after Walker retired the pitches were still too perfect and in the end the committee had the square dug up and the marl taken away. The critics of the 1980s would laugh in their boots after the controversies generated by Allsopp's 'result' pitches, tailor-made it was alleged, to suit the home county's attack. In his defence it should be said that the Test match pitches at Trent Bridge during this time have proved rather more durable.

The years prior to 1900 witnessed extensive development at the ground and this meant that the whole playing area was now surrounded with permanent seating or stands; the east side of the ground was occupied by football stands, which had been used by the cricket club's tenants, Nottingham Forest, for two seasons from 1880 and Notts County from 1883 to 1910; England played an international match there, too, in 1897, defeating Ireland 6–0. Both clubs eventually moved to their own grounds nearby and their floodlight pylons are a familiar sight to television viewers of cricket at Trent Bridge. Apart from soccer, Trent Bridge has also staged bowls, cycling, athletics, pigeon and sparrow shooting, rabbit coursing (around 1870 this attracted two or three times as many spectators as soccer!), lacrosse and, in the inter-war years, international hockey.

The spur for the end-of-century building was that Trent Bridge had been awarded its first Test match, the opening encounter of the 1899 series against Australia. Sides from overseas had appeared many times previously on the ground, starting with the Australian Aboriginals side of 1868 who gave their usual display of spear and boomerang throwing after the game against the Nottingham Commercial club, and the next Australian side of 1878 played their first game in England at Trent Bridge, routed by the famous Nottinghamshire pair of Alfred Shaw and Fred Morley and losing by an innings but proving a great attraction. Now, however, the decision to extend series against Australia from three matches to five meant that Trent Bridge received full international status: W.G. Grace, scorer of the first century in a county match at Trent Bridge in 1871, was chosen to lead England in what transpired to be his final Test. Coincidentally the match marked the first appearance of Wilfred Rhodes, who went on to become one of the greatest all-rounders and the only cricketer to have played for England at a more advanced age than Grace, who was 50 years 320 days when this match ended.

The capacity of the ground had risen to 20,000–25,000 and although the estimated attendance over the three days of the Test was 40,000, generating receipts of £1211 11s, *Wisden* commented that it 'scarcely justified the elaborate preparations that the Notts committee had made in erecting new stands'. Other special arrangements included the moving of the pitch and the incorporation of the football pitch into the playing area to create 85-yard boundaries on either side of the wicket. Special trains were run to Nottingham and the match was played throughout in excellent weather. Ranjitsinhji, 93 not out, saved England from defeat after they lost Grace, Jackson, Gunn and Fry for only 19 runs.

Trent Bridge staged its next Test in 1905, MacLaren making the first Test hundred on the ground and Bosanquet's leg-breaks and googlies capturing 8 for 107 in the second innings to bring England victory by 213 runs. Australia were back in 1912 to meet South Africa in the Triangular Tournament over the August bank holiday, but the match was ruined by rain and poorly attended. During the First World War the Trent Bridge pavilion was requisitioned and equipped with 100 beds for use as a service hospital – over 3500 wounded servicemen were treated there – but the ground continued to be used, free of charge, for charity and service matches.

Australian tours resumed in 1921 and from then until it had to make way for Edgbaston in 1961 Trent Bridge became the traditional venue for the first match of the series. In 1921 Armstrong's mighty side, having thrashed England 5–0 the previous winter, demolished them by ten wickets in under two days in the 100th encounter between the two countries; but after rain allowed only 50 minutes' play before flooding the ground in 1926 – when a Nottinghamshire man, Carr, was leading

England on his home ground for the first time – England gained their revenge in 1930 by 93 runs. As well as being the ninth successive win under Chapman's captaincy, the game featured a century by Bradman in his first Test in England and a superb catch at mid-on by a Nottinghamshire groundstaff member, Sydney Copley, fielding as substitute for the injured Larwood. It ended a partnership between McCabe and Bradman which was threatening to carry Australia to a formidable target of 429 and though Copley played only one first-class match for the county, a week later, he secured himself a place in cricket folklore.

By this time there had been considerable further development at Trent Bridge under the influence of Sir Julian Cahn, the businessman and philanthropist, who was twice the county's president and ran his own high-class XI. Sir Julien contributed generously towards an indoor nets area and new double-deck stands, and when the Australians next visited Trent Bridge, in 1934, a single-deck stand on the Fox Road side had completed the re-encirclement of the ground with seated accommodation and there was a new main entrance following the opening by Sir Stanley Jackson, in 1933, of the Dixon Gates, at the side of the pavilion and named in honour of J. A. Dixon, the county's first amateur captain (1889–99) and an England soccer international.

England were defeated by 238 runs in the 1934 Test, in which the unfortunate Australian, Chipperfield, became the first batsman to be dismissed for 99 on his Test debut and then the leg-spinners, O'Reilly and Grimmett, accounted for all but one of the English wickets, the last of which fell with only ten minutes of the match remaining. The match attracted large crowds: over 30,000 on the Saturday and around 90,000 in all, who had the sideshow attraction of a conflict between rival photographers in which obstructive balloons, hoisted by the company which had the exclusive picture rights, were cut adrift. Neither Larwood nor Voce, whose bodyline bowling had won England the Ashes the previous winter, played in the Test, but Voce was in the Nottinghamshire side which faced the Australians in August. There were rowdy scenes when, after he had taken eight wickets in the first innings bowling what *Wisden* quaintly described as 'direct attack', Voce did not appear in the second, officially on medical grounds although it was rumours that the county committee had

Trent Bridge during the 1934 Test.

removed him for diplomatic reasons which inflamed the crowd.

England played South Africa for the first time at Trent Bridge in 1935, rain saving the visitors after they had followed on, and the last Test there before the Second World War celebrated Trent Bridge's centenary year, 1938, with great batting deeds. Seven centuries were scored – Barnett, Hutton, Paynter and Compton (England's youngest Test centurion at the age of 20) in England's 658 for 8 declared; McCabe a brilliant 232 in Australia's reply of 411 and then Brown and Bradman when Australia comfortably saved the match after following on. It was McCabe's innings, made in only 235 minutes amid a collapse, which caused Bradman to issue the famous call to his team not to miss it for they would, he told them, never see the like again. Such was McCabe's dominance that his last 72 runs took only 28 minutes.

The Army requisitioned Trent Bridge during the Second World War, the pavilion being used as a sorting office for forces' mail, and the ground suffered some minor bomb damage, but Nottinghamshire managed to maintain the most regular programme of cricket during the war years among the counties. Test cricket returned in 1947 with the visit of the South Africans and Trent Bridge continued to be a haven for batsmen. In that first post-war encounter Melville became the first South African to score two centuries in the same Test and the following year Bradman made his 28th Test century and Compton his highest score, 184, against Australia in a match watched by a record 101,886 spectators. The splendidly detailed Australian-style scoreboard was erected in 1950, a memorial to a former committee member, T. Bailey Forman. Listing the full elevens of each side and detailing their scores and bowling figures, it made scorecards superfluous, but being electrically oper-

ated and requiring a sizable staff it proved expensive to run and fell victim to the builders and financial stringencies in 1972. In its first summer it recorded a crushing ten-wicket win by West Indies in the Third Test on the way to their first series win in England; it was also the first time Trent Bridge had staged anything but the opening Test of a rubber. The match epitomized the West Indies' success of that summer, as Worrell scored a monumental 261, Weekes 129, and Ramadhin and Valentine shared 12 wickets, bowling respectively 81.2 and 92 overs in England's second innings.

In 1951 Nourse scored South Africa's first double-century against England to help them to victory; in the same match Simpson became the only Nottinghamshire player to score a Test hundred on his home ground, a feat he repeated against the Test newcomers, Pakistan, in 1954, when Compton made the highest Test score at Trent Bridge, 278. It was a bowler, though, who dominated the 1953 Australian Test, Bedser's 14 for 99 setting a Trent Bridge record, but rain robbed England of victory. England's captain, the first professional since Nottinghamshire's own Shrewsbury in 1886–87, was Hutton, and the next year May began his run of 41 matches as England captain at Trent Bridge with an innings win over South Africa. That year, 1955, had seen the addition of the two-storey Parr Stand at the Bridgford Road side of the ground, whose capacity was thus increased to around 35,000, although it was rarely tested. The Parr, of course, was George, who during much of a career that stretched from 1844 to 1871 was acknowledged as the best batsman in England, 'The Lion of the North'. Captain of Nottinghamshire, of the All England XI after Clarke and of the first England touring team (to North America in 1859), Parr earned fame as a legside hitter and the elm tree which was the target of

Although blown down in 1975, George Parr's tree served as a fitting memorial to a great player.

many of his hits became known by his name. At his funeral in 1891 a branch from it was laid on his coffin alongside the wreaths and the tree stood against the boundary wall on the Bridgford Road side of the ground, another Trent Bridge landmark, until blown down by a gale in the winter of 1975.

In 1957 a high-scoring encounter with West Indies was distinguished by 258 from Graveney, Worrell's carrying his bat for 191, and the appearance of a pair of brothers for England, Peter and Dick Richardson, for the first time since the Hearnes in 1891–92. England beat India inside four days in 1959 and similarly the next year South Africa, whose first innings of 88 is the lowest in a Test match at Trent Bridge. An unfortunate incident in this match was the running out of McGlew after a collision with the bowler, Moss, and though Cowdrey, the England captain, recalled him, umpire Elliott stood by his decision. A rain-affected match against Pakistan in 1962 was notable for Parfitt's third hundred against the tourists within a week and for Mushtaq Mohammad scoring his second Test hundred – and he was not yet nineteen years old.

The Australian visit of 1964 brought the first of 108 caps for Geoffrey Boycott in another rain-spoiled match, but the next year saw another innings to rank alongside McCabe's in 1938.

Graeme Pollock, a left-hander of supreme elegance, scored 125 in less than $2\frac{1}{2}$ hours with a display of strokemaking to rival anything before or since; for good measure he scored 59 in the second innings and to complete a fraternal *tour de force* Peter Pollock claimed ten wickets, and South Africa won the match by 94 runs. England lost again at Trent Bridge the next year, by 139 runs to West Indies despite Graveney's third successive Test hundred at Trent Bridge, and in 1967 against Pakistan there were echoes of earlier encounters when a thunderstorm transformed the ground into a lake – the local fire brigade pumped off 100,000 gallons of water to make it playable again – and a groundstaff boy, Alan Bull, held a catch in the outfield. He played even fewer first-class games than Copley: none! The 1973 match produced a heroic effort by New Zealand to score an unprecedented 479 to win the match and that they lost by only 38 runs was due largely to a fifth-wicket stand between the captain, Congdon (176), and Pollard (116).

The face of the ground, meanwhile, had taken on several new aspects. In 1968 the Tavern was opened behind the pavilion for the use of the Supporters' club. Then, in difficult financial times for the county club, in 1970 the Ladies' Pavilion was converted into the Century Restaurant and though plans for a major redevelopment of the Fox Road side to include offices and flats were refused planning permission, in 1972 the present Trent Bridge House office block was put up on the north-east corner of the ground and required the demolition of the Fox Road stands, considerably reducing the ground's capacity, and, saddest of all, the scoreboard. A replacement was erected, next to which stands a betting office and, in confirmation of the friendly atmosphere of the ground, a children's playground, and though the new scoreboard is smaller and displays less information than its pre-

decessor, it remains the most detailed of any in England. In 1974 another of the old features disappeared, the tea gardens by the Dixon Gates being demolished to make way for more functional squash club and offices.

Trent Bridge did not have another Test until 1976, when England felt the might of Viv Richards for the first time, as he scored a masterly 232, and the following year the ground was graced by a visit from the Queen, in her Silver Jubilee year, on the first day of the Third Test against Australia. It was the second Royal visit to Trent Bridge: in 1928 King George V and Queen Mary attended the last afternoon of the match between Nottinghamshire and the West Indians, a rare honour for a provincial ground and for an occasion other than a Test match. On the cricket side the 1977 match was distinguished by England's first win over Australia at Tent Bridge since 1930 and a century from Boycott on his return to the Test scene; he owed it to the crowd, for he had earlier disgraced himself by running out the local hero, Randall. Boycott scored a hundred the next year, too, as England demolished New Zealand by an innings, Botham

The view from the Radcliffe Road end for visitors to Trent Bridge in the 1980s.

taking nine wickets, and in Trent Bridge's next Test, Botham's first as captain, West Indies squeezed home by two wickets in 1980. The press were able to witness this from a new box above the secretary's office in the West Wing; the old box at the Radcliffe Road end had been converted into hospitality boxes, fittingly named after famous Nottinghamshire players: Voce, Butler, Hardstaff, Keeton, Carr, Simpson, Whysall.

The 1981 Test at Trent Bridge, against Australia, made a small piece of history by being the first in England to contain Sunday play, and it was on Sunday 21 June, that Australia completed their first victory over England at Trent Bridge since 1948 on a green pitch, which was a far cry from the old featherbeds. The 1983 Test at Trent Bridge, the ground's next, was also the last in England to include Sunday play, the brief experiment gaining little popularity with the public, and brought England an easy victory over New Zealand.

Taylor and Marsh leave the field after batting throughout the first day of the Fifth Test, 1989.

cost Gatting the captaincy. What would the old landlord of the Trent Bridge Inn have made of that – or indeed of the trouncing England received from Australia the following year? Marsh (138) and Taylor (219) rewrote a clutch of records with an opening partnership of 329 and an increasingly depleted England subsided to their heaviest innings defeat by Australia in a home Test.

The 1985 Test against Australia – a high-scoring draw on a more typical Trent Bridge pitch – was the occasion for the opening of the Larwood and Voce stand replacing the old Hound Road stand and containing a new Tavern also bearing the name of the county's most famous partnership. Two of Larwood's daughters and Voce's widow were present at the official opening. Hadlee, a beloved adopted son of Nottingham, who with his South African colleague, Rice, became as popular as Larwood and Voce, was instrumental in New Zealand winning an English series for the first time in 1986; his ten wickets and 68 runs led to an eight-wicket win. For its 150th anniversary in 1988 Trent Bridge had the mighty West Indies as visitors and though England, thanks mainly to the patient batting of Gooch, temporarily halted a losing sequence, the match will in future be recalled as the one during which association with a barmaid

Nottingham				
Ref/No	*Season*	*V*	*T*	*Result*
60/1	1899	A	1	Draw
83/2	1905	A	1	E-213
	1912 Triangular Tournament			
127/3		AvSA	3	Draw
140/4	1921	A	1	A-10w
163/5	1926	A	1	Draw
194/6	1930	A	1	E-93
233/7	1934	A	1	A-238
242/8	1935	SA	1	Draw
263/9	1938	A	1	Draw
285/10	1947	SA	1	Draw
299/11	1948	A	1	A-8w
325/12	1950	WI	3	WI-10w
334/13	1951	SA	1	SA-71
372/14	1953	A	1	Draw
388/15	1954	P	2	E-I&129
408/16	1955	SA	1	E-I&5
425/17	1956	A	1	Draw
441/18	1957	WI	3	Draw
474/19	1959	I	1	E-I&59
494/20	1960	SA	3	E-8w
533/21	1962	P	4	Draw
561/22	1964	A	1	Draw
595/23	1965	SA	2	SA-94
607/24	1966	WI	3	WI-139
622/25	1967	P	2	E-10w
657/26	1969	NZ	2	Draw
700/27	1972	A	3	Draw
722/28	1973	NZ	1	E-38
777/29	1976	WI	1	Draw
806/30	1977	A	3	E-7w
829/31	1978	NZ	2	E-I&119
880/32	1980	WI	1	WI-2w
903/33	1981	A	1	A-4w
960/34	1983	NZ	4	E-165
1019/35	1985	A	3	Draw
1050/36	1986	NZ	2	NZ-8w
1098/37	1988	WI	1	Draw
1125/38	1989	A	5	A-I&180

England: P 37, W 11, D 15, L 11

Sheffield

BRAMALL LANE

Sheffield, the early centre of Yorkshire cricket until it was supplanted by Leeds, staged a single Test match, in 1902, on the now departed (at least as a cricket ground) Bramall Lane. Although many lamented the passing of a famous home of the game, notable for offering the epitome of the Yorkshire crowd in the Grinders' stand – knowledge of the game, forthright opinions, humorous observations, fearsome partisanship, and hostility towards visitors, though this can turn to warmth towards any visitor who proves himself by performance (as Bradman in particular discovered) – none could seriously claim that Bramall Lane had any great physical attractiveness. There were no trees, and surrounding factories and works made for a noisy, industrial atmosphere, typified by a brewery chimney which belched out soot and smoke – most copiously, it was said, when Lancashire or the Australians were batting.

The fact that Sheffield United FC occupied one end of the ground also meant that the spectator and playing facilities at Bramall Lane were never entirely suitable for cricket – or for football until the cricketers were banished in 1973, subsequently to find a home on the outskirts of the city at the picturesque but soulless Abbeydale Park, and the football club enclosed its ground.

As well as a Test match Bramall Lane staged the 1912 FA Cup final replay and several football internationals and other sports, including bowls and cycling, but it began life as a cricket ground in 1855 – chosen, ironically, because the area was then free of smoke!

The award of a Test match to Sheffield in 1902 caused some surprise, with critics pointing to the smoke and poor light, and *Wisden* reported rather

Bramall Lane in 1901, when it was still the headquarters of Yorkshire cricket.

enigmatically that 'the match ... naturally proved a strong attraction, but a mistake was made in fixing it for the latter part of the week [Thursday to Saturday], Monday being always the best day for public cricket in Sheffield.' Even in July the pall was present and bad light was held partly responsible for England's 143-run defeat before lunch on the final day. Hill's century and Trumper's rapid 62 in the second innings were key features for Australia, whose victory was seald by the bowling of Noble, who claimed 11 wickets in the match, and Trumble.

Sheffield's fate, too, was sealed, for it was never awarded another Test match – and in 1903 the county club transferred its headquarters to Leeds. Bramall Lane did, however, have one further small taste of international competition when, bombscarred but unbowed, it staged the second Victory Test between England and Australia in 1945, and around 50,000 spectators watched a match that was considered the finest of that joyful summer.

Sheffield				
Ref/No	Season	V	T	Result
72/1	1902	A	3	A-143

The journey home across the Calcutta maidan after a Test match.

❸

India

MIHIR BOSE

In India and Pakistan there are no Test match grounds, only Test match stadia. The distinction may seem academic. The Oxford English Dictionary defines 'ground' as 'the space on which cricket is played', while 'stadium' is 'a place for athletic exercises'. Yet in the sub-continent even this distinction is crucial. As cricket has developed their grounds, in the sense the term would be used in England, have become stadia. Once pleasant parks have been converted into concrete monstrosities which can be awe-inspiring when filled with spectators in the middle of an absorbing match, but ugly and naked at other times.

Cricket in India began in 1721 with an impromptu game by sailors in the bay of Cambay, in western India. The first proper cricket ground probably belonged to the Calcutta Cricket Club which played at the same site now familiar the world over as Eden Gardens. Like almost everything in India, cricket developed haphazardly, more often due to private initiative rather than planned endeavour. Despite its growth and evident popularity cricket in India remains an urban game and reflects the urban concerns of the sub-continent. Unlike England the game is hardly played in the Indian villages (which have their own games) and the nature of urban life dictates the shape of the cricket grounds. So in the sub-continent there is no tradition of blacksmith teaming up with baker to play a cricket match with the local village in the village square. The most distinctive feature of

Indian cricket is the 'maidan', often in the centre of towns or cities, where every day thousands can be seen playing the game.

The maidan is without doubt the most evocative place in Indian urban life. It has been called the equivalent of an English park but that is grossly misleading. An English park is an oasis of calm, a shelter from the hustle and bustle of city life. The maidan reproduces Indian urban life in all its noise, clamour, even dirt. True, like a park the maidan is an open area but that is about the only similarity. Even the grass, so green and smooth in an English park, is coarse and matted in an Indian maidan, struggling to stay alive amidst the dirt and rubble. Very often the maidan also acts as a thoroughfare for people crossing from one end of the city to another and during the rush hour it can be packed with commuters hurrying to and from work.

Most of the ground is hard, rugged, at times little more than dirt tracks but every few yards there is a pitch carefully prepared by the 'mali', as the local groundsman is called. Here you may see a batsman who looks like W.G. Grace, the pavilion will be a tree with a vendor selling cakes from a tin box, and as likely as not the cover point in one match will be fielding back to back with the square-leg in another, adjoining match.

But just as the lotus flower, the great Indian flower, springs from the dirtiest and most inhospitable of surroundings so amidst such confusion and noise Indians learn to play cricket.

Ahmedabad

GUJARAT STADIUM

Ahmedabad should have made its Test match debut in September 1969 during the three-Test mini-series with New Zealand but serious rioting, not connected with cricket, led to the match being transferred to Bombay. It was not until November 1983 that Ahmedabad received a second chance to stage a Test, the Third Test against the West Indies. As befits the capital of one of India's richest states, and the home state of Mahatma Gandhi, the ground is the most meticulously planned of all the cricket stadia of India, with a capacity of 60,000 and the facility to increase this to 80,000. The playing area is surrounded by a moat which can provide a curtain of water when play is not in progress. The pavilion and seating areas give due regard to players' comfort and spectators' safety and there are proper media facilities.

The first Test against the West Indies, played on an underprepared wicket, saw India's captain Kapil Dev inserting the opposition. The move backfired as in both innings West Indies recovered from early collapses and India were unable to cope with Marshall and Holding on a last-day wicket which had 'gone'. The Test marked a personal triumph for Gavaskar who passed Boycott's aggregate of Test runs to become the highest Test run-getter in history.

Four years later Gavaskar was to return to the ground to add to his record, reaching 10,000 runs in Test cricket (the only man to do so) with a delectable late cut in an otherwise dull draw against Pakistan. The match brought out the ugly communal violence between Hindus and Muslims that disfigures the city and during the Test the Pakistani outfielders were pelted with stones. Imran took his players off: when they returned many of them were wearing helmets.

Ahmedabad				
Ref/No	*Season*	*V*	*T*	*Result*
966/1	1983–84	WI	3	WI-138
1069/2	1986–87	P	4	Draw

Ahmedabad's Gujarat Stadium during a one-day game between India and England in December 1981.

Bangalore

KARNATAKA STATE CRICKET ASSOCIATION (CHINNASWAMY) STADIUM

Bangalore, in the southern India state of Karnataka, ranks with Kanpur as the fifth major Test centre after Bombay, Calcutta, Delhi and Madras. But that is its only similarity with its northern rival. In every other way, Bangalore's Karnataka State Stadium is vastly superior. The stadium is situated in the old cantonment area of the city. During the Raj the British built up the city as a garrison city and developed fine boulevards with the mandatory statue of Queen Victoria and elegant parks. Despite recent development, and the inevitable growth of high-rise buildings, much of this elegance remains and the stadium mirrors this.

The grass has been artificially grown and one can see the red earth underneath, but like Madras's Chidambaram Stadium – which it closely resembles – this is an excellent Test centre, soundly administered and with good facilities. The game has a loyal following there and in recent years the local team has provided a great deal of talent for the national team: Chandrasekhar, Prasanna, Viswanath, Brijesh Patel, Roger Binny. All this has

produced a knowledgeable crowd which appreciates good cricket and apart from one occasion when political disturbance in Bangalore city led to the loss of a day's play there has been hardly any trouble at the Test matches.

Although it only gained Test status in November 1974 when India played the West Indies in the first of the five-Test series, Bangalore has quickly established itself as a Test centre which players, spectators and administrators like. The arrival of Test cricket coincided with an economic boom: Bangalore is now talked of as the 'silicon valley' of India and there is excellent provision for hotels and other amenities. It is certainly fit to rank as a major Test centre but because of regional claims and counter-claims it has hosted fewer Tests than deserved since its debut in 1974.

Perhaps the Indian victory over England in February 1977 and the Pakistan victory over India more than ten years later in March 1987 are the highlights of Bangalore's Test career. Both matches

The Second Test between India and England at Bangalore, December 1981.

Scooters and motorcycles parade in segregated ranks at Bangalore's 'patrons only' cycle park.

Bombay

GYMKHANA
BRABOURNE STADIUM
WANKHEDE STADIUM

Nowhere is maidan cricket more diligently played than in Bombay, home of Indian cricket. The very first Test ever to be played in India neatly juxtaposed maidan cricket with Test cricket. This was played at Bombay Gymkhana in December 1933 when India, under C.K. Nayudu, played a strong England side led by Douglas Jardine. Bombay Gymkhana stands at one end of what used to be known as Esplanade Maidan but has been renamed Azad. On the Maidan's hard, stony ground criss-crossed with pitches and make-shift tents, ordinary Indians learn to play cricket amidst all the confusion and bustle of commercial Bombay.

Bombay Gymkhana is a world removed: a private club which seeks to recreate an English village green. A neat, colonial pavilion with a mock-Tudor facade faces a lush green, well tended by an army of malis whose job it is to produce good cricket pitches. Open on three sides and separated from the surrounding Indian chaos by nothing more than a hedge, its nearest English equivalent would be the Bank of England ground at Roehampton. With no fixed seating available for the spectators, the Test match saw vast 'shamianas' (Indian for marquees) erected to house the spectators. The Test also saw the club make another, temporary, concession. This was the height of the Raj, Bombay Gymkhana was the ultimate English club and, as with most such clubs in the sub-continent then, no Indian was allowed to become a member. The only Indians allowed in the club were servants. For the Test that rule had to be suspended so that the Indian players had access to the dressing-rooms.

Despite this, and the almost inevitable Indian

took place on turning wickets. The Indian victory came after England had won the series 3–0 but Bedi and Chandrasekhar caused such havoc that at one stage in England's second innings the scoreboard read 8 for 4. England never recovered and lost by 140 runs. The Pakistan victory was much narrower, by 16 runs in an absorbing match on an obviously underprepared wicket, with Gavaskar making a brilliant but futile 96 in his last Test.

Bangalore				
Ref/No	Season	V	T	Result
745/1	1974–75	WI	1	WI-267
791/2	1976–77	E	4	I-140
841/3	1978–79	WI	2	Draw
856/4	1979–80	A	2	Draw
861/5	1979–80	P	1	Draw
913/6	1981–82	E	2	Draw
961/7	1983–84	P	1	Draw
1070/8	1986–87	P	5	P-16
1107/9	1988–89	NZ	1	I-172

India: P 9, W 2, D 5, L 2

Townsend batting in the first Test on Indian soil at the
shamiana-lined Gymkhana in December 1933.

work on Saturday – that thousands were shut out
and they made alternative arrangements. The roof
top of Ralli Brothers provided a fine view as did
the trees surrounding the ground; some even clam-
bered on to the roof of some of the shamianas.
Those who got a seat watched, perhaps, in greater
comfort than most other Indian spectators have
done over the years. They had an individual
wooden chair resting on wooden planks underneath the canvas roof of the shamiana. There were
food stalls behind the shamiana and the harshness
of the wooden seats could be reduced by cushions.

Even today the memory of the Test brings a
warm nostalgic glow for older Indians as they recall
Lala Amarnath's Test hundred on his debut – the
first by an Indian in a Test match – and the first
Test anywhere to see Sunday play. Perhaps the
romantic glow is greater for this was the only Test
ever to be played there.

When Test cricket returned to Bombay, after the
war and after India's emergence as an independent
country, it was at the Brabourne Stadium, barely a
mile away. The colonial power had gone and the
colonial cricket ground, so reminiscent of 'home',
was replaced by modern stadia, as increasingly
became the norm in the sub-continent.

To be fair, the Brabourne Stadium had come
into existence before the war, in 1937, when it was
conceived as the sort of Lord's of Indian cricket.
For almost four decades until the mid-1970s it did
occupy this unique position. Named after Lord
Brabourne, then Governor of Bombay, the con-
ception belonged to a remarkable Goan called
Neville de Mello who saw the Cricket Club of India
which owned the stadium as the MCC of India. It is
a testimony to De Mello's skill that until Brabourne
Stadium lost its Test status in the mid-1970s this
is how most people in India and abroad saw it.

As at Lord's, the only people who could gain

defeat, vast crowds thronged this match. Also, the
spectators had perhaps the most intimate feel about
a Test match that has ever been possible. There
was neither a picket fence nor barbed wire, only a
few policemen to keep out the crowds. Until half
an hour before play began the policemen allowed
the crowd to congregate across the ground though
the actual square was roped off and guarded by a
couple of sepoys (Indian military police). They saw
the two captains toss, the wickets pitched, the
players practise and it was only 15 minutes before
11 o'clock that the police ushered the crowd away.

The first Test set another pattern that was also
to be part of Test cricket on the sub-continent:
spectators who watch the game without paying or
even entering the ground. Such was the enthusiasm
for this first Test – increased by the fact that the
first day, a Friday, was declared a holiday by the
Governor with the law courts, secretariat and other
government offices closed and restricted hours of

entrance to the pavilion of the Brabourne Stadium were members of the CCI and at its height of glory membership of CCI was about as rare as the chance of a drink in then 'dry' Bombay. There was a long queue for the membership and it cost an exorbitant sum. This reflected its status as India's premier Test match ground, one that had a wonderful array of sporting facilities. Much ahead of its time, it could be a multi-sports complex and has hosted tennis internationals and, after it lost its cricket status, football matches. But perhaps De Mello's most radical idea was that it would also be a hotel for members, guests and players. So the upper floors of the clubhouse contained luxurious rooms where visiting cricketers stayed and so convenient was this that Frank Worrell always marvelled that he could watch cricket in his dressing-gown and only shed it when required to bat. Then he would quickly don his pads, walk down the stairs and on to the ground.

The end of the day's play would also see the ground itself converted into an open-air dance-hall with a wooden floor erected on the outfield near the clubhouse complete with dance bands playing smoothing melodies. Unlike Lord's, CCI made no effort to discourage ladies in the pavilion. Indeed they quite encouraged ladies to attend Test matches, so much so that Test matches at the CCI were very much part of the Bombay social calendar when society ladies, in their glittering sarees, would like to be seen, seated in the governor's pavilion next to the clubhouse.

Brabourne Stadium had other differences with Lord's or other English grounds. Despite stands and permanent structures you can walk all the way round any English ground. Not so in the sub-continent. Different sections are sealed off with fencing and gates. You would no more think of walking all the way round a Test match ground in India than you would a football stadium in England. In that sense most Test grounds of the sub-continent bear a resemblance to the Old Trafford of footballing rather than cricketing fame.

Since the Brabourne Stadium has been a model for nearly all the sub-continent's cricket stadia it is worth describing it in some detail. The stadium itself has perhaps the greatest backdrop any cricket ground would wish for: the Arabian Sea is just over mid-on or third man depending on which end the bowling is from. But such is the enclosed nature of the stadium's construction that once inside the ground you see nothing of the sea or the beautiful Marine Drive seafront that for generations has provided Bombay with a magnificent promenade. And while the clubhouse with its clock and its ornate balconies is attractive, the stands that surround it are functional. The most famous, perhaps notorious, of stands is the East stand, the popular stand whose nearest equivalent would be the terraces of an English football ground with the same mixture of loyalty, boisterousness and clamour.

It was the East stand which developed many of the chants and cries one can hear on Indian cricket grounds. Perhaps the most famous was the rhythmic shouts of 'b-o-w-l-e-d' as one of their favourite Indian bowlers ran up to bowl. The shout would begin as the bowler began his run-up and reach a crescendo as he delivered the ball. Not all batsmen appreciated this and visiting batsmen like Keith Carmody of the Australian Services side or Bert Sutcliffe of New Zealand complained that it disturbed their concentration. Sutcliffe was so upset by it that, eventually, the Indian captain Umrigar went over to the East stand to plead with the crowd to be quiet while the bowler bowled.

At the height of Brabourne Stadium's fame as a Test centre great masses of people would be herded in like cattle. The stand was supposed to have a

The faded splendour of the Brabourne Stadium's pavilion in the 1980s.

capacity of 13,000 but at times another 10,000 more were squeezed in. They would sit on hard concrete terracing, there being no cushioned seating, sandwiched tight against each other and at times the crush would be so great that a single movement would cause whole ranks to sway. Despite this, food vendors selling Indian snacks would move up and down the stands – though with people unable to move an empty coconut or a bottle would have to do as a makeshift toilet. Just like the terraces in an English football ground, wire fences separated this section from the rest of the ground and prevented spectators rushing on to the ground, something of an Indian habit when a local batsman scores a century. In later years a section of the East stand was converted into a stand for CCI members' children, since children under a certain age were not allowed into the pavilion during a Test match. This produced a vivid contrast between the children of the privileged and the neighbouring urban masses and sometimes led to fights.

If the East stand reflected the cricketing tastes of the urban working classes, other stands in the stadium reflected the well-off middle classes. Exactly opposite the Clubhouse the North stand had proper seats, even cushions, and consisted of the more affluent members of society, while next to it was the most prestigious stand, the Gymkhana stand, reserved for the various cricket clubs and gymkhanas which were members of the Bombay Cricket Association. The members sat on comfortable wicker chairs of the type they would have in their own clubhouses and this stand reflected the cricketing elite of Bombay, as opposed to the social elite to be found in the pavilion.

Brabourne Stadium also set another, at times more dubious, precedent. This was in the sale of what were called 'season' tickets. A spectator who wanted to watch the match had to buy a book of tickets which covered all five days of the Test. Such was the demand for these tickets, particularly in the popular East stand, that it was common for people to sleep outside the booking offices the night before tickets were due to go on sale. Tickets would be sold out within a few hours. Daily tickets were virtually unobtainable and the casual spectator keen to watch a day's play stood little chance unless he was prepared to pay exorbitant black market prices. Such demand inevitably led to black-marketing and the Brabourne Stadium Tests saw the touts make a lot of money. In recent years as Test cricket has begun to wane in popularity, daily tickets are once again on sale in Bombay as an inducement to get the casual spectator to come and watch cricket.

The enthusiasm for Tests in Bombay grew through the 1950s and 1960s. The first Test to be played at the Brabourne Stadium was during the 1948–49 season when the West Indies toured India for the first time. Brabourne Stadium hosted two Tests, the second in December 1948 when India after following on saved the match comfortably. This led Sarder Patel, then a prominent Indian politician, to quip that India should play her second innings first. It was the pattern for many an Indian performance: a bad first innings followed by a good second.

In the final Test in Bombay in February 1949 India came close to winning her first-ever Test. Needing 361 to win in 395 minutes, India fell just 6 runs short with one wicket left. Their victory bid was thwarted by some desperately negative tactics by the West Indian bowlers Gomez and Prior Jones when India, at one stage 275 for 4, looked like coasting to victory.

Those inaugural Tests set the pattern for the subsequent 15 Tests that were played at the Brabourne Stadium. India very rarely lost a Test, occasionally won but more often drew. Of the 17 Tests played there, 12 were drawn and Bombay became famous for shirt-front wickets where batsmen reigned supreme. On the first morning of a Test match the hot sun drying the early morning dew occasionally produced some help for the bowlers but the only bowler to be really happy there was the Bombay-born leg-spinner Subhash Gupte who enjoyed many a magical day in a Bombay Test, regularly bamboozling visiting batsmen with his own brand of leg-spin. As he did in December 1955 when he took 5 for 45 in the New Zealand second innings, having taken 3 for 83 in the first, to help India win the match by an innings and 27 runs. Then in November 1958 he took his hundredth wicket in Tests and his 4 for 86 helped bowl out a powerful West Indian side for 227 on the first day. But faced by the pace of Hall and Gilchrist, Indian batsmen struggled and only a desperate rearguard action in the second innings saved the match.

The Bombay wicket was relaid in 1964 and this led to a dramatic change in the nature of Tests there. That same year saw the Australians visit India at the fag-end of a tour of England. In one of the most dramatic matches ever seen in Bombay, India won by two wickets with half an hour to spare. Australia were reduced to ten men at the start when O'Neill withdrew due to stomach problems. He did not bat in the match at all. Undoubtedly his presence would have made a difference for the Australian batsmen, apart from Peter Burge and Bob Cowper, never came to terms with the spin of Chandrasekhar and Nadkarni. India were left 256 to win but looked doomed at 122 for 6. Then a crucial stand between Pataudi and Manjrekar nearly took them to victory. Both fell and at 224 for 8 India again looked like going down, before Borde with some cool strokeplay saw India home.

The remarkable victory set the pattern for the remaining Tests played at the Brabourne Stadium. After that every Bombay Test provided some excitement and many of them produced definite results. Six months later, in March 1965, New Zealand shot out India for 88 but following on India recovered so strongly that in the end New Zealand on 80 for 8 were hanging on for dear life.

The following year India lost a Test for the first time at the Brabourne Stadium. This was against the West Indies led by Sobers. The batting of Conrad Hunte and Clive Lloyd and the bowling of Gibbs was too much for the Indians, despite Chandrasekhar taking 11 for 135.

India's only other Brabourne defeat was against Australia in November 1969, a Test which for the first time saw a riot in Bombay. Before this, Bombay crowds had been noisy, occasionally disruptive but always proud of their reputation as keen, knowledgeable followers of the game. Their rapport with the players was evident. During the 1959 Test against Australia, once it was certain that India could not lose, vociferous crowd demands, particularly from the East stand, 'declare, declare', led to the Indians doing just that. Favourite players like the left-handed Salim Durani would be asked to hit sixes and he would oblige. However, during the 1969 Test a combination of factors led to a riot. There was serious overcrowding and anger with the Indian performance. As the Indians slid to defeat, Venkataraghavan was given out caught in what the crowd considered were dubious circumstances. The riot, starting from the East stand, spread to all sections of the crowd including the posh CCI pavilion, but despite this play continued and India were beaten.

It was problems about the allocation of seats that eventually led to the demise of the Brabourne Stadium as a Test match venue. The official cricket body which runs the game in Bombay, the Bombay Cricket Association, resented the haughty, imperial style of the CCI. It may have seen itself as the Lord's of India but this was a status that the Bombay Cricket Association was not prepared to accept. They had to run cricket in the city and they felt that they did not get enough money from the Brabourne Stadium Test matches. Every Test saw

The Brabourne Stadium in November 1981 during the match between an England XI and the Cricket Club of India President's XI.

a battle between the CCI and the BCA about tickets. While a whole block of seats, over 17,000, was given to the BCA for distribution to its various clubs, gymkhanas and associations this was never enough.

Personality also played a part. The CCI was run by the autocratic Indian Test player Vijay Merchant, who saw CCI as his second home, while the BCA was led not by a cricketer but by a shrewd politician and the then state finance minister, S.K. Wankhede. Eventually after the last Test against England in 1973 the split could not be contained. BCA decided it must have its own stadium and in record time one was constructed half a mile away and just further along the same seafront of Marine Drive that Brabourne backed on to. The CCI remained the model, and the Wankhede Stadium looks very like the Brabourne Stadium complete with residential accommodation. The growth in five star hotels in Bombay means that few Test players stay there during Tests, but it is used by visiting players for lesser matches.

Like the original, Wankhede even has flats and houses surrounding it and during Tests people throng the roofs of such houses hoping to catch a glimpse of play. In some cases some enterprising landlords erect shamianas on roof tops and charge people to watch the game from there. But for many people in Bombay nothing can remove the glow and charm of the Brabourne Stadium and Wankhede is seen as an uglier, shabbier copy of the original. This is partly an argument between new money and old money in Bombay. Brabourne represented the old well-off classes of Bombay; Wankhede is firmly representative of those who have made their money in more recent years, with many whispers that some of them may have made it through the operation of 'number two' accounts, the one that avoids paying income tax.

Brabourne Stadium supporters have more justifiable grievance against the usurper in terms of crowd behaviour. Since the new stadium came in to being, crowd behaviour in Bombay has taken a turn for the worse with even the crowd in the pavilion behaving like the East stand crowd,

A general view of the Wankhede Stadium during the World Cup semi-final between India and England in November 1987.

pelting players and joining in any commotion going. The first Test at the stadium in January 1975 was to see this. This was the last Test against the West Indies. When the West Indies had passed through Bombay on their arrival in India the previous November, the stadium was little more than a hole in the ground. They returned in January to see a full-blown stadium, and the series marvellously poised at 2–2. Clive Lloyd's team had taken a 2–0 lead, then been pegged back by a remarkable Indian comeback.

The cricket at this inaugural Test was superb. Clive Lloyd made 242 not out, there was great bowling by Gibbs who took 7 for 98 and some stout resistance by the Indian batsmen. In contrast with the pattern established in the Brabourne Stadium India crumbled, not in the first, but in the second innings. They responded to the West Indian 604 with 406 but then collapsed in the second innings to lose by 210 runs.

But the match was marred by the second incident of crowd violence in a Bombay Test when police overreaction to a spectator who ran on to the pitch to congratulate Lloyd led to rioting and the loss of 90 minutes play. This time not only the popular stands but also those in the new Garware pavilion were involved, regular fires were lit and some twenty spectators were injured in running battles with the police.

Nothing like that has ever been repeated again but certainly the general crowd behaviour at the Wankhede Stadium has been poor, with the pavilion, far from giving the lead, often expressing its displeasure with the cricket it did not like. This has even included booing and catcalling Sunil Gavaskar, the local hero. Some of this may reflect disenchantment with Indian performance though after the inaugural Test defeat Wankhede has followed the Brabourne pattern in being a Test ground where India rarely lose. Indeed, of the 11 Tests played there until the 1987–88 season, India had won five, twice defeating England and once each New Zealand, Australia and Pakistan. There have been two other defeats, one by New Zealand in 1988, but the one following the inaugural Test against the West Indies was quite remarkable. It came in a Test held to celebrate the Golden Jubilee of the Indian Cricket Board.

This was the third Test in Bombay in four months, Australia having been beaten in November by an innings and 100 runs and Pakistan in December by 131 runs. Those results were achieved on slow turners, which has been the norm at the Wankhede. But for this sole, celebratory occasion the Indians left so much grass that Mike Brearley, the England captain, was astonished. It proved ideal for Botham who took 13 for 106. He also featured in a stand of 171 with Taylor which turned the match England's way and began in

the most controversial circumstances. Taylor was given out caught behind. He protested he had not touched the ball and the Indian captain, Viswanath, persuaded the umpire to revoke his decision. In stark contrast, Boycott when given out just ignored the umpire's decision and went on batting. But then it was a very unusual match. There was an eclipse of the sun which superstitious Indians regarded as an evil omen. The second day of the Test, a Saturday, thus became a rest day.

Bombay				
Ref/No	Season	V	T	Result
Gymkhana				
230/1	1933–34	E	1	E-9w
Brabourne Stadium				
305/2	1948–49	WI	2	Draw
308/3			5	Draw
340/4	1951–52	E	2	Draw
357/5	1952–53	P	3	I-10w
417/6	1955–56	NZ	2	I-1&27
432/7	1956–57	A	2	Draw
459/8	1958–59	WI	1	*Draw
484/9	1959–60	A	3	Draw
497/10	1960–61	P	1	Draw
513/11	1961–62	E	1	Draw
554/12	1963–64	E	2	Draw
567/13	1964–65	A	2	I-2w
581/14	1964–65	NZ	3	Draw
610/15	1966–67	WI	1	WI-6w
659/16	1969–70	NZ	1	I-60
665/17	1969–70	A	1	A-8w
707/18	1972–73	E	5	Draw
Wankhede Stadium				
749/19	1974–75	WI	5	WI-201
785/20	1976–77	NZ	1	I-162
792/21	1976–77	E	5	Draw
840/22	1978–79	WI	1	Draw
860/23	1979–80	A	6	I-1&100
863/24	1979–80	P	3	I-131
876/25	1979–80	E	–	E-10w
912/26	1981–82	E	1	I-138
967/27	1983–84	WI	4	Draw
1005/28	1984–85	E	1	I-8w
1054/29	1986–87	A	3	Draw
1081/30	1987–88	WI	2	Draw
1108/31	1988–89	NZ	2	NZ-136

India: P 31, W 9, D 16, L 6

Calcutta

EDEN GARDENS

This is now perhaps India's most famous Test ground, and rightly so. The sheer enthusiasm of the native Bengali for Test cricket when in the rest of the country the craze for one-day cricket – ever since India won the World Cup in 1983 - is predominant makes it one of the few places where crowds are guaranteed for Test matches. Even in Bombay spectators are getting choosy about watching Test cricket, but in Calcutta almost any Test is a guaranteed sell-out. Calcutta cricket officials, while acknowledging that there is a fall-off in demand for cricket, say this does not affect their position: when demand is 300 per cent of capacity, 'house full' is no problem.

Unlike Bombay, Calcutta has never been a great centre for the game. The list of great cricketers it has produced can be counted on the fingers of one hand. The only explanation for such demand is that in this city of 'hujuks' (a Bengali word meaning roughly 'intoxicated enthusiasm') watching Test cricket ranks as one of the city's great pastimes. The city is a centre for Bengalis, the first to fall to the British, the first to develop a vibrant Indian culture that fused British and Indian traditions. But during the last sixty years Calcutta has declined from being the the second city of the Empire and capital of the Raj to a poor, overpopulated, pollution-ridden place famous for Mother Theresa and communist governments. Plagued by power cuts which can last for several hours a day and a loss of economic power to other Indian communities, cricket forms a delectable release. Calcutta's 'hujuks' have included riotous welcome for such disparate characters as Kruschev and Pelé. Test cricket fits somewhere in between.

The intoxication is such that Calcutta has a unique method of selling tickets. Here you can get neither day tickets nor even the 'season', meaning five-day tickets common elsewhere in India. The only source of tickets open to the general public – those for places like the pavilion are catered for differently – is a curious lottery where some 900,000 tickets are sold out of which emerge 8500 lucky ticket holders. Otherwise it is a case of knowing somebody or belonging to the right organization which is entitled to a ticket. This odd system evolved in 1969. Then, on the morning of the fourth day's play against Australia, upwards of 25,000 queued up for 7000 daily tickets. When the counters opened at 7.00 am there were not enough police to control the crowds and several youths suffocated.

Ironically the local government had made massive police arrangements for the match as this was a time of violent political struggle in the city with the Naxalities, local Maoists, urging boycott of the Test because Doug Walters had served with the Australian army in Vietnam. But the police were meant to control the crowds during the match which would begin several hours later, and were not there when the thousands queued for tickets. All this was compounded by a common practise then of Calcutta cricket administrators to issue more tickets than there were seats – such characters then went 'underground' to escape the wrath of the public.

This wrath was seen at its worst on 1 January 1967. It was the second day's play in the Second Test against West Indies. There had been massive overselling of tickets by the authorities. The surplus spectators tried to find seats on the grass around the boundaries. This is something never allowed in India where, generally, spectators remain penned behind fences. The Calcutta police mounted a baton charge and even threw tear gas

The pavilion at Eden Gardens during Calcutta's Test debut in January 1934.

grenades into the crowd. The crowd replied with a counter charge and when the outnumbered police fled stands and furniture were burned. Stumps and bamboo canes were dug into the pitch and three buses were set on fire in the neighbourhood of the ground. By general consent it was one of the most frightening moments ever seen on a Test ground. Some West Indian fielders were so frightened that they ran off the ground into the streets of Calcutta vowing never to play there again. The Test only resumed two days later after assurances from high authority that there would be no further incident. After this the match itself was almost an irrelevance with the West Indies making the most of batting first and India, demoralized by having to face Sobers and Gibbs on a damaged pitch, collapsing ignominiously.

The 1967 riots had come after a series of earlier disturbances in Calcutta Tests. In 1964 police had to lathi-charge spectators who wanted to watch the practice of the Indian and English teams; during the Test itself spectators set fire to awnings, producing a ten-minute delay. Later that year the rain-interrupted Test against Australia saw more arson which left the ground looking like a shanty town. The Sen Commission which investigated the riot

of 1967 had no doubts that while the police over-reacted the ground authorities were responsible for selling too many tickets and providing few facilities. It recommended that the stadium should be remodelled with due regard to spectators' comfort, safety and convenience.

That Eden Gardens, of all India's Test grounds, should see such crowd trouble (more than anywhere else in the country) is all the sadder because when Test cricket first came to this ground, in January 1934, it had the look and feel of a real garden. Situated on the banks of River Hooghly, it is one of the oldest grounds in the world and was once the property of the Calcutta Cricket Club. Like the Bombay Gymkhana Test, there were improvised stands and shamianas to accommodate the crowd. The scene would be both vivid and picturesque. In the far distance one could see the river, whose proximity explained the green pitches, and the smoke from the funnels of passing ships would often aid swing bowling. On the other side, at the end of the great maidan, was the high court. The river end and high court end still constitute

Eden Gardens sometime in the 1940s, with the River Hooghly – a tributary of the Ganges – in the distance and the buildings of Governor's House on the right.

the two ends of the ground.

By the time Test cricket returned to Eden Gardens fifteen years later, on New Year's Eve 1949, the nature of the ground was changing. The lease had been transferred to the National Cricket Club and now steps were taken to convert it into a concrete bowl of a stadium. It was many years before this process was completed, and it was only in the early 1980s that Eden Gardens assumed its present imposing form: a huge bowl with seating capacity all round of just under 80,000 and a sumptuously appointed pavilion with one of the most modern press boxes in the country. During a packed Test match day – and every day is a packed Test match day in Calcutta – it has an imposing grandeur unrivalled in the cricket world, apart

from Melbourne. The improved facilities have so moderated the crowd's behaviour that trouble of the type that plagued cricket there in the 1960s has virtually disappeared. But it remains a place where good cricket is much appreciated and not merely from the Indians. This was most evident when the World Cup final played between Australia and England drew a capacity crowd, despite the fact that India had been beaten in the semi-finals.

However, it is not afraid to show its displeasure of what it considers bad cricket. This so upset Gavaskar, who was convinced the crowd did not like him, that in February 1987 he withdrew for 'personal' reasons from the Test against Pakistan.

Two traditions have been maintained. First, the Calcutta Test is always played over the New Year holiday. This colonial legacy of celebrating Christmas and the New Year in style still holds in the city and this is seen as the best time for the Test match. Second, more than any other ground in

India it helps seam bowling, particularly in the morning when the wicket has a tinge of green and late in the evening if the bowler can align himself to the prevailing smog and breeze.

Such help for seam has not decisively turned Tests and the first five were all drawn. It was not until November 1956 that Australia, led by Benaud and Johnson on a turning wicket, produced the first result – an Australian win by 94 runs. The next Test in January 1959 saw Rohan Kanhai blast 256 and India lose by an innings and 336 runs, its most humiliating margin ever. India registered its first victory at Calcutta in January 1962, beating England by 187 runs. Perhaps the most gripping Test at Eden Gardens was in January 1973 when Tony Lewis's England were beaten by 28 runs, unable to cope with the great spinning quartet of Prasanna, Bedi, Chandrasekhar and Venkat. The spinners were also responsible for bringing India back into the series against the West Indies when, in January 1975, they bowled India to an 85-run victory. The Indians were hoist by their own petard of preparing turning wickets when, in January 1977, Greig – overcoming fever – scored a hundred in 413 minutes, one of the slowest ever, to give England her first victory in Calcutta. Perhaps the most dramatic moment came on the evening of 3 January 1979 when, with their last pair at the wicket and 11 balls still to face, bad light came to the rescue of the West Indies. Since then Calcutta Tests have reverted to type, producing draws almost as a matter of routine but with no loss of enthusiasm from the crowd.

Eden Gardens filled to capacity for the World Cup final of 1987.

Calcutta				
Ref/No	Season	V	T	Result
231/1	1933–34	E	2	Draw
306/2	1948–49	WI	3	Draw
341/3	1951–52	E	3	Draw
359/4	1952–53	P	5	Draw
419/5	1955–56	NZ	4	Draw
433/6	1956–57	A	3	A-94
461/7	1958–59	WI	3	WI-I&336
486/8	1959–60	A	5	Draw
499/9	1960–61	P	3	Draw
516/10	1961–62	E	4	I-187
555/11	1963–64	E	3	Draw
568/12	1964–65	A	3	Draw
580/13	1964–65	NZ	2	Draw
611/14	1966–67	WI	2	WI-I&45
668/15	1969–70	A	4	A-10w
704/16	1972–73	E	2	I-28
747/17	1974–75	WI	3	I-85
789/18	1976–77	E	2	E-10w
842/19	1978–79	WI	3	Draw
859/20	1979–80	A	5	Draw
866/21	1979–80	P	6	Draw
915/22	1981–82	E	4	Draw
968/23	1983–84	WI	5	WI-I&46
1007/24	1984–85	E	3	Draw
1067/25	1986–87	P	2	Draw
1082/26	1987–88	WI	3	Draw

India: P 26, W 3, D 17, L 6

Cuttack

BARABATI STADIUM

Cuttack, the ancient capital of the eastern state of Orissa, hosted its first Test in January 1987. It shares one quality with Kanpur. During the Test the cricketers, the officials and the media are housed in Bubaneshwar, the new capital which has the facilities for modern travel – an airport – and also the hotels considered necessary for international cricket. So every day the players have a two-to-three hour coach ride back and forth from their hotel.

For the first Test the Barabati Stadium provided an underprepared wicket and Indians were relieved to win the toss and bat. Despite the variable bounce Vengsarkar made his highest Test score (166), an innings of high class. India made 400 and this proved too much for the Sri Lankans who lost by an innings.

Cuttack				
Ref/No	*Season*	*V*	*T*	*Result*
1065/1	1986–87	SL	3	I-I & 67

Right The lunch interval at Delhi.

Opposite page Delhi's Feroz Shah Kotla ground, makeshift in appearance when compared with the concrete stadia so common in India.

Delhi

FEROZ SHAH KOTLA

Delhi's Feroz Shah Kotla staged its first Test in November 1948 against Goddard's West Indians. The fact that it was the capital of the country and that Jawaharlal Nehru, India's first prime minister, was keen on cricket (having learned it at Harrow) had more to do with it becoming a Test centre than any native cricketing tradition.

The ground itself is well located on the borders of old Delhi – of Indian princes and Mughal Emperors – and the New Delhi that Edward Lutyens designed for the imperial Raj. But it has neither the pomp and majesty of the Mughals nor the elegance and administrative convenience of Lutyens's Delhi. Unlike other Test grounds, there is no stadium. Makeshift stands are erected on an open, flat ground and the only permanent building is a poky pavilion which barely has room for the two dressing-rooms. Everything else is in the open and while this makes a change from the enclosed

stadia common in other cities it means the facilities are poor for spectators, players and journalists. It was in the open air, makeshift press box during the English Test in December 1963 that something like an international incident took place when E.M. Wellings, then cricket correspondent of the *Evening News*, refused to vacate the seats traditionally reserved for the Maharajkumar of Vizianagram, whose generosity had done much to make Delhi a Test centre. Eventually the British High Commissioner became involved and Vizzy and his assistant, who carried a big book of Neville Cardus cuttings as an instant reference for his master, regained their natural seats.

The Delhi crowd seems to show little appreciation of the finer points of the game which is why it has never been a popular Test centre with the Indian players. All Indian Test crowds are a mix of the genuine cricket lover and the man who hopes to use the Test match to further his own interest. Delhi has rather fewer cricket lovers than other centres and many more government officials, businessmen and politicians who see the Test match as an occasion to develop their contacts.

The Indian players' unhappiness with Delhi may also be due to the fact that the local cricket association is a hot bed of intrigue and infighting which can be bewildering to the player and has done much to retard the development of Kotla as a major stadium. Nor, in recent years, has it been a happy place for Indian cricket.

The initial history of Delhi as a Test centre suggested it might be different. After following on in the First Test against the West Indies in November 1948, India saved the match and should have beaten England in November 1951. In October 1952 it did defeat Pakistan, playing its first ever Test. Indeed India did not lose a Test in Delhi for ten years until December 1959 when Richie Benaud's all-conquering Australian side won by an innings. This defeat was reversed ten years later when Lawry's team was defeated in November 1969 by seven wickets.

But since then India has not won a single Delhi

Test, with both the West Indies and England winning two of the last three they have played there. The rest have been drawn on slow wickets where batsmen have had plenty of time to run up huge scores. It was such Test in December 1981 which saw Boycott score a painstaking 105 and in the process become the world's then highest Test run-getter, going past Garry Sobers' 8032 runs. Boycott greeted the moment in typical style, bemoaning Yorkshire criticism that he was obsessed with records. As it turned out, it was the last full Test he played for England. In the next one in Calcutta he took time off in the middle of a match to play golf, returned to England and never played again for his country.

Delhi

Ref/No	Season	V	T	Result
304/1	1948–49	WI	1	Draw
339/2	1951–52	E	1	Draw
355/3	1952–53	P	1	I-I & 70
418/4	1955–56	NZ	3	Draw
463/5	1958–59	WI	5	Draw
482/6	1959–60	A	1	A-I & 127
501/7	1960–61	P	5	Draw
515/8	1961–62	E	3	Draw
556/9	1963–64	E	4	Draw
582/10	1964–65	NZ	4	I-7w
667/11	1969–70	A	3	I-7w
703/12	1972–73	E	1	E-6w
746/13	1974–75	WI	2	WI-I & 17
788/14	1976–77	E	1	E-I & 25
844/15	1978–79	WI	5	Draw
858/16	1979–80	A	4	Draw
862/17	1979–80	P	2	Draw
914/18	1981–82	E	3	Draw
965/19	1983–84	WI	2	Draw
1006/20	1984–85	E	2	E-8w
1053/21	1986–87	A	2	Draw
1080/22	1987–88	WI	1	WI-5w

India: P 22, W 3, D 13, L 6

Hyderabad
FATEH MAIDAN (LAL BAHADUR STADIUM)

Hyderabad, in southern India, made its Test debut in November 1955 when it staged the First Test against New Zealand. The newly laid turf pitch provided a stackful of runs with India making its then highest Test score of 498 and Umrigar hitting a double-hundred. But despite making New Zealand follow on, the Indians could not force a win. It was another 14 years before Hyderabad saw another Test match, in October 1969. Again the opponents were New Zealand. Much had been changed, including the name of the ground – from Fateh Maidan to Lal Bahadur Stadium after an Indian Prime Minister.

This time India were lucky to escape with a draw. The umpires forgot to have the wicket cut on the rest day and, batting on a pitch unmown for three days, India were bowled out for 89. This dramatic collapse saw a boy run on to the field to congratulate the players. But he was beaten severely and the blood on his shirt so incensed the crowd that it resulted in a riot. There was more drama on the final day when India, set 268 to win, had collapsed to 76 for 7. A heavy downpour halted play but although the sun soon came out the

Hyderabad's garrison-like stadium, c1970.

groundstaff failed to dry the ground and this prevented New Zealand from winning their first series in India.

The New Zealand connection with the ground resumed ten years later when, during the World Cup, they scraped home by 3 runs against Zimbabwe in a group match. They were less fortunate in the 1988–89 Test series against India whose comprehensive ten-wicket victory owed much to the off-spin of Arshad Ayub, playing in front of his home crowd.

Hyderabad				
Ref/No	Season	V	T	Result
416/1	1955–56	NZ	1	Draw
661/2	1969–70	NZ	3	Draw
1109/3	1988–89	NZ	3	I-10w

Jaipur

SAWAI MANSINGH STADIUM

This is India's princely city, known as the pink city and built by Man Singh, one of the great Rajput warriors. The stadium named after him became India's 16th Test ground – and the world's 61st – when it staged the Third Test against Pakistan in February 1987. The match produced a dull draw but was notable for some off-the-field controversy. The second day saw the unexpected visit of Pakistan's General Zia as part of his policy of 'cricket for peace'. Whatever effect this had on the diplomatic front, by the end of that day a storm was brewing on the cricketing front. This controversy

Jaipur's Sawai Mansingh Stadium, where a fine backdrop makes up for fairly primitive facilities.

centred on repairs to the pitch following a thunderstorm and heavy winds which swept aside the covers and soaked the ground. The Pakistanis claimed the Indians had sprinkled sawdust to dry the pitch, thus changing the nature of the pitch; the Indian officials claimed that sawdust had been blown on to the pitch from the outfield. Imran refused to bat, the umpires dragged their feet and play was abandoned for the third day.

Jaipur				
Ref/No	Season	V	T	Result
1068/1	1986–87	P	3	Draw

Jullundur
BURLTON PARK

Burlton Park staged its only Test match during the same 1983–84 series against Pakistan which provided Test outings for Nagpur and Bangalore. It made sense to have a Test there as Jullundur is in the Punjab, the land that is divided between India and Pakistan. However, given the weather, early morning mist and a very early dusk it is doubtful whether Jullundur can often provide a full day's play. In looks it is like most Indian stadia: a large expanse of playing surface surrounded by concrete stands. For the Test against Pakistan the stands had not been finished. A day was lost due to rain and this almost inevitably condemned the match to a draw.

Jullundur				
Ref/No	Season	V	T	Result
962/1	1983–84	P	2	Draw

Kanpur
GREEN PARK (MODI STADIUM)

Green Park is fairly low in the popularity stakes with cricket lovers and players. One of the problems is that while the match is played in Kanpur the players are put up in hotels in Lucknow, a two-to-three hour coach ride away. So for the players a Kanpur Test is always a strange occasion. True, this is much more of a park than other Test grounds in India, and the outfield is well watered and comparatively lush. But its clay pitches now produce some of the dullest cricket on the sub-continent.

The first three Tests all produced results. In January 1952, Hilton and Tattersall exploited a turning wicket so well that the match was over in $2\frac{1}{2}$ days with an English victory by 8 wickets. Kanpur's next Test was in December 1958 when Gupte almost did a Laker – in the West Indian first innings he took nine wickets, a tenth victim was dropped and the West Indies were bowled out for 222. India also made 222, the second first-innings tie in Test cricket, but after that lost control of the match to lose by 203 runs. Just over a year later on a newly laid pitch Jasu Patel, an off-spinner, took 14 for 124 (India's best analysis in Tests) and India beat Australia by 119 runs, their first victory over Australia.

Since that dramatic victory Kanpur has been notorious for draws with the bare, slow wickets providing plenty of scope for the accumulation of vast scores and little else. Not surprisingly, this has done little to foster the game in this part of the world and the Kanpur crowd remains the one least versed in good cricketing tradition. It has always had a big problem encouraging spectators to take to the game and it has been common to sell low-price tickets to students and mill workers, while some higher-priced seats are sold to the very rich in the pavilion. What is missing, as one Indian cricket administrator analyzed, are the middle-class supporters that other Test centres have – ones who appreciate cricket and can afford to pay reasonable prices to see it. But despite such subsidized seats, Kanpur rarely attracts good crowds. In the final Test of the 1981–82 series against England, a match they had to win if India were not to win the rubber, only one stand was full. If it had not been for the presence of 7000 policemen in a ground that can hold 30,000, there would have been the distinct impression that this was an Indian version of two old men and a dog watching cricket. Perhaps those who stayed away knew what was in store as the match ended in a tame draw.

Kanpur				
Ref/No	*Season*	*V*	*T*	*Result*
342/1	1951–52	E	4	E-8w
460/2	1958–59	WI	2	WI-203
483/3	1959–60	A	2	I-119
498/4	1960–61	P	2	Draw
514/5	1961–62	E	2	Draw
557/6	1963–64	E	5	Draw
666/7	1969–70	A	2	Draw
706/8	1972–73	E	4	Draw
786/9	1976–77	NZ	2	Draw
845/10	1978–79	WI	6	Draw
857/11	1979–80	A	3	I-153
864/12	1979–80	P	4	Draw
917/13	1981–82	E	6	Draw
964/14	1983–84	WI	1	WI-I&83
1009/15	1984–85	E	5	Draw
1063/16	1986–87	SL	1	Draw

India: P 16, W 2, D 11, L 3

Green Park, Kanpur, in February 1985 during the Fifth Test between India and England.

Lucknow

UNIVERSITY (GOMTI) GROUND

This city is now more famous for the fact that its hotels house the Test cricketers when the Test is staged at Kanpur. The Gomti Ground, also known as the University Ground, has staged only one Test. This was in October 1952 when on a jute matting wicket Fazal Mahmood, the king of mat, took 12 for 94 and bowled Pakistan to an innings victory. The other incident of note was that Nazar Mohammad, who opened the batting for Pakistan and hit 124 not out, became the first player to remain on the field throughout the entire Test match.

The ground has never had further chances for a record as Test cricket has never returned there – but then Test cricket very nearly did not come. Four years before its solitary Test Lucknow could not raise the 10,000 rupees guarantee money to stage a match between East Zone and the West Indies. For the Pakistan match the money was raised but the facilities provided did not come up to scratch. The ground did not look like a Test match venue nor were there adequate dressing-rooms. Hardly surprising that it has remained one of those one-Test wonders.

Lucknow				
Ref/No	Season	V	T	Result
356/1	1952–53	P	2	P-I & 43

Right and opposite page Madras's Chepauk ground, transformed into a major stadium but retaining its links with the past.

Madras

CHEPAUK (CHIDAMBARAM STADIUM) CORPORATION (NEHRU) STADIUM

The South, they say, is a different country and this is certainly true of its cricket. The Madras Test grounds may look like the conventional bowl stadia of Bombay and Calcutta but the cricket produced on them has been more vibrant than at any other ground. From the administrative point of view, the southern cricket grounds are far ahead of their northern and eastern rivals.

Madras has come full circle in terms of Test grounds. Chepauk staged the Third Test of the 1933–34 series, in February 1934, and hosted Tests until 1955 when, for nearly ten years, Test cricket shifted to the Corporation Stadium in the city. The

Chepauk ground had once been part of the grounds of the palace of the Nawab of Arcot and it retained some of the feel of princely splendour. The East India Company passed the ownership to the Madras Club in 1861 and the early Tests here resembled the first-ever Test at Bombay Gymkhana, a club ground also acting as Test centre. When the club's lease expired, and while the Tamil Nadu Cricket Association was renegotiating the lease, Test cricket in Madras moved from a lovely ground to a modern, custom-built stadium. Test cricket returned to Chepauk in January 1967, by which time the old gardens had gone. It too had become a modern stadium, renamed the Chidambaram Stadium, but it had better facilities and better management than other stadia in India.

Despite its modernity, Chepauk will always have a very special place in Indian cricket for it was here on 10 February 1952 that India – after 20 years and at the 25th time of asking – won her first Test match. England, led by Donald Carr in the absence

through illness of tour captain Nigel Howard, were completely bamboozled by the spin of Mankad who took 12 for 108, and there were centuries from Roy and Umrigar.

Four years later when the Corporation Stadium staged its first Test, in January 1956, there was another record. Pankaj Roy and Vinoo Mankad, opening the innings, batted throughout the first day and part of the second scoring 413 for the first wicket, the highest first-wicket partnership in the history of Test cricket. Roy just missed his double-hundred but Mankad went on to score 231. New Zealand, finding the spin of Gupte too much, lost by an innings and 109 runs.

Mankad's 231 was the highest Test score by an Indian and stood for almost thirty years when, in another Madras Test, back at Chepauk, Gavaskar broke it. Coming in to bat at 0 for 2, one of the few occasions in Test cricket when he did not open, he made 236 not out and in the process scored his 30th Test hundred, passing Sir Donald Bradman's world record number of centuries by an individual batsman. He also became the first batsman to score 13 hundreds or double-hundreds against the West Indies.

Perhaps Chepauk's proudest moment came on a hot, humid September day – 22 September 1986 - when in front of 30,000 spectators India and Australia produced only the second tie in Test history, the first also having involved Australia. India were asked to make 348 to win in a minimum of 87 overs on the final day, at 4 runs an over, and when the last over began India had one wicket left and still needed 4 to win. They got 3, then at 5.18 pm Maninder Singh pushed forward to Matthews and was given out lbw.

Not all Tests in Madras have provided such record- breaking feats but the good pitches, in recent years providing more pace and bounce than elsewhere, have always produced good cricket and some gripping moments. In a land of draws, Madras has produced more outright results than any other Test centre in the country. High drama has been interspersed with comedy and some low intrigue. Allegations of the latter were made in January 1977 when the Indian cricket captain Bishen Bedi accused John Lever of using vaseline to maintain the shine on the ball and thus produce unnatural swing. Lever vigorously denied the charge, but to this day many Indians remain convinced that he used underhand methods to gain an advantage.

The comedy had been provided some years earlier after the 1964 Test against England, when Barrington allowed Nadkarni to bowl 21 consecutive maidens, a record for six-ball overs in Test cricket, and the Test match petered out into a draw. After play had ended, some 200 fans chanting and banging cymbals escorted a flower-decked bier bearing a young boy in white in a mock cremation

service for the death of Test cricket. This was entirely in keeping with tradition as the Test is normally held while Madras is celebrating the Pongol Festival, a bit like Wakes Week in the north of England.

Madras				
Ref/No	Season	V	T	Result
Chepauk (Chidambaram) Stadium				
232/1	1933–34	E	3	E-202
307/2	1948–49	WI	4	WI-I&193
343/3	1951–52	E	5	I-I&8
358/4	1952–53	P	4	Draw
Corporation (Nehru) Stadium				
420/5	1955–56	NZ	5	I-I&109
431/6	1956–57	A	1	A-I&5
462/7	1958–59	WI	4	WI-295
485/8	1959–60	A	4	A-I&55
500/9	1960–61	P	4	Draw
517/10	1961–62	E	5	I-128
553/11	1963–64	E	1	Draw
566/12	1964–65	A	1	A-139
579/13	1964–65	NZ	1	Draw
Chepauk (Chidambaram) Stadium				
612/14	1966–67	WI	3	Draw
669/15	1969–70	A	5	A-77
705/16	1972–73	E	3	I-4w
748/17	1974–75	WI	4	I-100
787/18	1976–77	NZ	3	I-216
790/19	1976–77	E	3	E-200
843/20	1978–79	WI	4	I-3w
855/21	1979–80	A	1	Draw
865/22	1979–80	P	5	I-10w
916/23	1981–82	E	5	Draw
934/24	1982–83	SL	–	Draw
969/25	1983–84	WI	6	Draw
1008/26	1984–85	E	4	E-9w
1052/27	1986–87	A	1	Tie
1066/28	1986–87	P	1	Draw
1083/29	1987–88	WI	4	I-255

India: P 29, W 9, D 10, L 9, Tied 1

Nagpur

VIDARBHA CRICKET ASSOCIATION GROUND

Nagpur is India's equivalent of Crewe. Lying almost at the centre of India, it is a natural change station. The town is hardly noteworthy but the ground, lined by trees, has none of the concrete monstrosities to be seen at other Test centres. This makes it unexpectedly attractive. Its first Test was against New Zealand in October 1969. That year there was also an Australian visit so the Indian Board decided to allocate New Zealand, who are not a great draw in India, to some of the newer Test centres. The experiment came unstuck at Nagpur where New Zealand beat India for the first time in India by 167 runs. It was not until October 1983 that Test cricket returned to this pleasant ground with a visit from Pakistan. This time the draw more accurately reflected the nature of cricket between the two countries. But there was an unusual moment of the type more associated with club cricket. Before the start of the match, Mohinder Amarnath withdrew because of fever and Sandeep Patil, not in the squad of 14, was called up. The only problem was that he was 600 miles away and despite a flight by a specially chartered plane he arrived after the first day's play had finished. In December 1986 India recorded an innings victory over Sri Lanka in Nagpur's third Test.

Nagpur

Ref/No	Season	V	T	Result
660/1	1969–70	NZ	2	NZ-167
963/2	1983–84	P	3	Draw
1064/3	1986–87	SL	2	I-I & 106

The tree-lined Vidarbha Cricket Association ground at Nagpur.

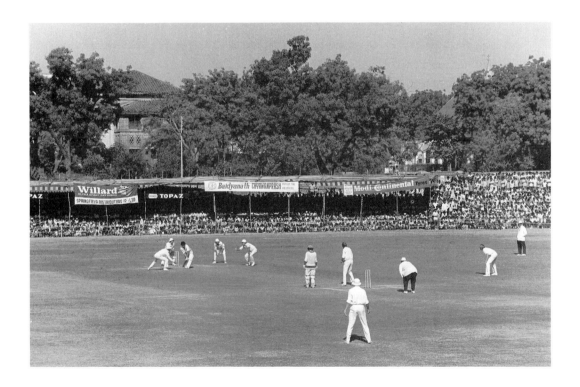

Wellington's Basin Reserve, 'the biggest traffic island in the world'.

4

New Zealand

JOHN COFFEY

New Zealand celebrates its 150th anniversary in 1990. The early British settlers took their cricket gear with them to the new colony. Within a quarter of a century, and in spite of severe communications and transport difficulties, representative fixtures were being played.

First-class rating has since been given to Otago's match with Canterbury at the South Dunedin Recreation Ground in 1863–64. George Parr's All England XI brought international cricket to Dunedin and Christchurch in the same summer. But it was to be another 66 years before New Zealand was accorded Test status when Harold Gilligan captained an England side considered to be somewhat short of full strength to an eight-wicket victory at Lancaster Park, Christchurch, on 10, 11 and 13 January 1930.

Unfortunately, the pioneers of the sport did not live to see their labours recognized. Modern officials and players could not envisage how hard their predecessors worked to develop even the basic facilities required for cricket to prosper. New Zealand's Test grounds were far from attractive in their infancies. All were low-lying and sodden. Indeed, the Basin Reserve was reduced from lake to swamp by an earthquake; part of the original Lancaster Park was known as the 'frog pond'; Carisbrook and Eden park were unkempt, marshy areas; McLean Park is reclaimed land.

By financial necessity they are multi-purpose sports arenas. The Otago Rugby Union owns Carisbrook, cricket and rugby union admin-

istrators fill the majority of the seats on the Eden Park and Lancaster Park trust boards, rugby union is also McLean Park's winter tenant, and rugby league has recently joined association football in playing feature matches at the Basin Reserve. Because of the surface damage caused by the football codes, and climatic considerations, the home international cricket programme has invariably been fitted in between January and March.

When rain ruined the third Test of the original 1929–30 series, a fourth match was added. Only the 1955–56 West Indian and 1967–68 Indian teams have also taken part in four-Test series.

For many years overseas squads arrived in New Zealand weary after long treks around the Australian continent. England, South Africa, West Indies and Sri Lanka made their first New Zealand appearances at Lancaster Park. Australia made its debut at the Basin Reserve and Carisbrook was India's first host.

Since 1972–73 New Zealand has welcomed an overseas visitor every summer, almost always for three-Test series. Over the decades most series have begun in Christchurch or Wellington and been completed in Auckland. Carisbrook joined the circuit on an irregular basis in 1954–55, and McLean Park became the 50th Test ground in 1978–79. Eden Park, Basin Reserve, Lancaster Park and Carisbrook have also dominated the allocation of international limited-overs games. Only McLean Park and Seddon Park in Hamilton have interrupted their monopoly.

Auckland

EDEN PARK

Eden Park concedes seniority in terms of age to the other regular New Zealand Test centres. But it is the country's premier sports stadium, the most thoroughly developed, and the best equipped – as would be expected of a ground situated in the biggest city.

Representative cricket had been centred on Auckland Domain in the latter part of the nineteenth century, and as late as 1899 the land upon which Eden Park now majestically sits was rough, swampy farmland, pitted with tussock and scarred by low stone walls. Some friendly games were held by the local Kingsland Cricket Club. In 1903 district inter-club competition was introduced, Kingsland disbanded, and the Eden club made a successful bid for the area, which was ploughed, levelled and sown. On the official opening day, 9 November 1903, Eden's first XI played Grafton.

The Domain and Victoria Park hosted inter-provincial games for the next decade while Eden club officials were tenaciously fighting against financial and flooding problems, a losing battle which led to the Auckland Cricket Association

assuming responsibility for Eden Park in 1911–12. After one winter of rugby league, the cricket administrators entered a lease agreement with their rugby union counterparts and development started in earnest. The $12\frac{1}{2}$ acres were valued at six thousand pounds, an amount increased when the cricketers had a pavilion (still in use 77 years later) built and the rugby union provided a grandstand to accommodate 2500 spectators.

Financial difficulties continued. An Eden Park Retention Fund was launched and money was raised from concerts, raffles and levies imposed on the club cricketers who used the six pitches on the park. Damage from the pounding of rugby boots was another perennial problem.

But Eden Park has exuded prosperity in modern times. Two huge grandstands and high terracing lifted the winter capacity to over 55,000 (subsequently reduced to 46,000 as seating replaced standing room) and it staged World Cup finals in rugby union (1987) and rugby league (1988). A national cricket attendance record of 43,000 was

---

A general view of Eden Park in the 1920s seen from what is now the No. 2 ground. The pavilion on the extreme right of picture still stands today.

created at a limited-over international with Australia on 13 February 1982. The electronic scoreboard was added soon afterwards, and plush private boxes became a feature of the South Stand in 1989.

The main oval is complemented by an adjacent No. 2 ground, a pleasant well-grassed area given first-class status in 1975–76. A combined grandstand and indoor wicket was completed in 1982.

Arthur Sims's Australian XI were distinguished visitors in Eden Park's maiden first-class season, 1913–14. They beat both Auckland and New Zealand with more than an innings in hand.

The third and intended final Test of England's original 1929–30 series at Eden Park was washed out after Ted Bowley and K. S. Duleepsinhji had scored centuries. A fourth Test was agreed upon, much to the delight of the powerful Kent captain, Geoffrey Legge, who made 196 in a drawn encounter.

Legge's record did not last for long. When Auckland next held a Test, in 1932–33, Walter Hammond discovered his batting garden of Eden, Hammond's 336 not out overtook Don Bradman's 334 at Leeds in 1930 as the highest individual score in Test cricket. Hammond needed only 47 minutes to reach his third hundred, and the entire innings took 318 minutes and included 10 sixes and 34 other boundaries.

Earlier, the match had a sensational start, Stewart Dempster was late and could not open the New Zealand innings. But he was at the crease in the second over facing a hat-trick after Bill Bowes got rid of Jack Mills and Lindsay Weir with his first two balls. Dempster, in one of his most skilful exhibitions, was unbeaten on 83 when his last partner was out at 158. Rain forced a damp draw.

It was not until 1951–52 that Test cricket was played again in Auckland. Cricketing thrill seekers might have considered the wait worthwhile as Jeff Stollmeyer (152), Frank Worrell (100), Clyde Walcott (115), Allen Rae (99) and Everton Weekes (51) flayed the New Zealand attack. Verdun Scott defied Alf Valentine, Sonny Ramadhin and the rest for 84 of New Zealand's first innings 160 before the weather again saved the situation.

Eden Park was the backdrop for New Zealand's blackest day in cricket, 28 March 1955. There was no hint of imminent disaster when New Zealand

Eden Park in 1984 before the installation of electronic scoreboard and private boxes atop the South Stand (to the left of the old pavilion).

registered 200, then held England (with Len
Hutton scoring 53 in his last Test innings) to a lead
of 46. But in just 105 minutes and 162 balls Frank
Tyson, Brian Statham, Bob Appleyard and Johnny
Wardle reduced New Zealand's second innings to
rubble – all out 26, a world record Test low.

Yet less than one year later New Zealand finally
broke through for its first Test victory. No matter
what else is achieved, 13 March 1956 will ever be
a red-letter date in New Zealand cricket history.
Denis Atkinson's West Indians were set 268 runs
to win in four hours. By tea the scoreline was an
improbable 77 for 9. Soon after the resumption
the expatriate West Indian, Sam Guillen, stumped
Valentine to complete the Kiwi coup. Harry Cave
claimed eight wickets in the match, and John R.
Reid top-scored with 84.

Little Barry Sinclair made centuries against
South Africa and England in the 1960s, hundreds
by Ken Barrington, Peter Parfitt and Barry Knight
led to an England innings victory in 1962–63,
and Bishen Bedi and Erapally Prasanna spun the
1967–68 Indians to a big win.

The 1968–69 West Indian Test contained plenty
of drama. It was Glenn Turner's debut, and his
only 'duck'. But Bruce Taylor's amazing century
in 86 minutes helped the home side to a first-
innings advantage. Given less than even time to
make 345 for victory, the visitors mostly thanked
Seymour Nurse (168) for their five-wicket success.

A draw with Pakistan in 1972–73 is remembered
for Rodney Redmond's unique achievement of
scoring a century and half-century in his only Test,
and also the world record tenth-wicket stand of
151 runs between Brian Hastings (110) and Richard
Collinge (68 not out).

Ian Redpath (159 not out) became the first player
to carry his bat through a Test innings in New
Zealand when Australia won easily in 1973–74, and

The scramble for souvenirs at Eden Park in 1956 after New
Zealand's first Test victory

Mike Denness (181) and Keith Fletcher (216) were
largely responsible for an Eden Park record Test
total of 593 for 6 and an innings winning margin
for England in 1974–75.

Prasanna (8 for 76 in the second innings) and
Bhagwat Chandrasekhar reaped 19 wickets
between them for India's successful 1975–76 side.
Australia also beat New Zealand before Geoff
Howarth delighted his fellow Auckland citizens
with a century in each innings of the 1977–78 draw
with England. Bruce Edgar's hundred and Gary
Troup's ten wickets ensured a draw and the clin-
ching of the 1979–80 series against the West Indies.
John Wright patiently gathered his maiden Test
century in the 1980–81 draw with India.

A monumental 161 by Edgar laid the foundation
for a five-wicket defeat of Greg Chappell's 1981–
82 Australians; Wright, Jeff Crowe and Ian Smith
exceeded 100 in New Zealand's biggest Eden Park
total of 496 for 9 to complete a series win over
England in 1983–84; John F. Reid's unbeaten 158
and the seam bowling of Richard Hadlee, Lance
Cairns and Ewen Chatfield put paid to Pakistan 12
months later; and John Bracewell became the first
New Zealand spinner to take ten wickets in a Test

as Australia crashed by eight wickets in 1985–86.

New Zealand's purple patch was ended by the 1986–87 West Indians, Gordon Greenidge's 213 prompting a ten-wicket decision, but Mark Greatbatch will always have affection for Eden Park as the setting for his century on debut against England in 1987–88.

The next summer New Zealand conceded more than 600 runs in a Test innings for the first time, Pakistan's 615 for 5 declared including a magnificent 271 from Javed Miandad. New Zealand followed on but comfortably avoided defeat.

Auckland				
Ref/No	*Season*	*V*	*T*	*Result*
188/1	1929–30	E	3	Draw
189/2			4	Draw
226/3	1932–33	E	2	Draw
350/4	1951–52	WI	2	Draw
371/5	1952–53	SA	2	Draw
402/6	1954–55	E	2	E-1&20
424/7	1955–56	WI	4	NZ-190
473/8	1958–59	E	2	Draw
540/9	1962–63	E	1	E-1&215
560/10	1963–64	SA	3	Draw
577/11	1964–65	P	2	Draw
604/12	1965–66	E	3	Draw
636/13	1967–68	I	4	I-272
650/14	1968–69	WI	1	WI-5w
686/15	1970–71	E	2	Draw
713/16	1972–73	P	3	Draw
738/17	1973–74	A	3	A-297
758/18	1974–75	E	1	E-1&83
770/19	1975–76	I	1	I-8w
797/20	1976–77	A	2	A-10w
819/21	1977–78	E	3	Draw
848/22	1978–79	P	3	Draw
875/23	1979–80	WI	3	Draw
902/24	1980–81	I	3	Draw
923/25	1981–82	A	2	NZ-5w
977/26	1983–84	E	3	Draw
1011/27	1984–85	P	2	NZ-1&99
1037/28	1985–86	A	3	NZ-8w
1072/29	1986–87	WI	2	WI-10w
1092/30	1987–88	E	2	Draw
1116/31	1988–89	P	3	Draw

New Zealand: P 31, W 4, D 18, L 9

Christchurch
LANCASTER PARK

Hagley Park was the first headquarters of cricket in Christchurch, and it was there that George Parr's All-England XI appeared in 1864. But Hagley was a fair haul for the prominent players who lived in Opawa, about five miles away, and A. M. Ollivier, who was skilled in rugby football as well as cricket, led a move to find playing fields closer to home.

He wanted an all-purpose ground. Though now used almost exclusively by the Canterbury cricket and rugby union bodies, Ollivier's wishes were carried out in the days when Lancaster Park hosted cycling and harness racing, Davis Cup tennis, New Zealand athletics and Australasian swimming championships, field hockey, association football, a rugby league Test, wartime baseball featuring United States servicemen, marching, even an exhibition of hurling. Big crowds have attended rugby union and cricket matches, Royal visits, a Billy Graham crusade, a Pope John Paul II blessing. But the attendance record of 62,000 was set at a Dire Straits concert.

The ground was purchased from the Lancaster Estate, owned by Benjamin Lancaster of 'Sunnyside', Bournemouth, and was opened in 1881. Alfred Shaw's England XI and XVIII of Canterbury met in the first representative cricket match.

Lancaster Park was a potato patch in the First World War before money was raised to free it of debt. Rugby union revenue has largely financed the massive grandstands on the east side, protecting the playing area from the prevailing winds. The western embankment was demolished and replaced by concrete terraces during the summer of 1988–89. Oval in shape, the park is set in an industrial area close to the centre of Christchurch.

Plaques attached to No. 1 stand pay tribute to world records set on the Lancaster Park turf – Bert Sutcliffe's best first-class score by a left-hander (385 for Otago against Canterbury in 1952–53) and Peter Snell's 800 metres and 880 yards track double in 1962. The cricketing world expected Richard Hadlee, then tied on 373 Test wickets with Ian Botham, to join them in February 1988 but Hadlee bowled without success and suffered an injury in front of his fellow Cantabrians.

New Zealand entered Test cricket on 10 January 1930 – with a thud. Morris Nichols claimed two quick wickets and the home side crashed to 21 for 7 when Maurice Allom took four wickets in five balls. England eventually won a low-scoring encounter by eight wickets.

Jim Christy and Bruce Mitchell hit centuries and featured in an opening partnership of 196 when South Africa won by an innings in 1931–32.

Christchurch Tests either side of the Second World War were dominated by the great Walter Hammond. In March 1933 New Zealand spirits were lifted when Ted Badcock dismissed Herbert Sutcliffe first ball and Denis Smith bowled Eddie

Paynter with his first ball (for his sole wicket) in Test cricket. Hammond watched that dismissal from the non-striker's end, then led an annihilation of the New Zealand bowlers. He made 227, Les Ames 103, and Freddie Brown and Bill Voce thrashed 108 runs in 45 minutes. New Zealand, following-on, were saved by the weather. It was a more corpulent but still masterly Hammond who scored 79 in his final Test innings at Lancaster Park in 1946–47. His career was ended by Bert Sutcliffe's first Test catch. On his debut Sutcliffe scored a highly promising 58, of a 133-run partnership with Walter Hadlee (116), but the final day was washed out.

Sutcliffe had his own innings of 116, and Trevor Bailey made his only Test century, in a 1950–51 draw. The wiles of the West Indian spin twins, Sonny Ramadhin and Alf Valentine, twice bamboozled New Zealand's batsmen in the 1950s. Ted Dexter posted his maiden Test hundred and Tony Lock spun an 11-wicket web in a big 1958–59 England victory. In 1962–63 Fred Trueman had a first innings analysis of 7 for 75 – still the best by a visiting bowler at the park – and John R. Reid's

Left Lancaster Park in February 1903 during the match between Lord Hawke's team and Canterbury.

Above The old pavilion, photographed during MCC's 1906–07 tour of New Zealand.

outstanding 100 of New Zealand's second innings 159 could only reduce the losing margin to seven wickets.

There were centuries from Hanif Mohammad and Bevan Congdon in separate Tests in the midsixties. But Graham Dowling, and the 1967–68 team he captained, were to surpass all previous New Zealand performances in Christchurch. Dowling's personal 239 broke Sutcliffe's national Test record, the total of 502 is still New Zealand's highest at Lancaster Park, and fiery fast bowling by Dick Motz and Gary Bartlett consigned India to a six-wicket defeat.

That was the first of five New Zealand triumphs in Christchurch. But for a time overseas players were again in centre stage, Seymour Nurse reached 258 for the 1968–69 West Indians; Derek Underwood gathered 12 inexpensive wickets and Basil D'Oliveira scored a century two seasons later.

Nothing brings out a Kiwi's competitiveness more than the challenge of toppling his 'big brother' from across the Tasman Sea. For years Australia would not rate its neighbour as a worthy opponent at cricket. The second official Test was not played until 1973–74, when a home-and-away programme was scheduled. New Zealand was robbed by rain at Sydney, well beaten in Melbourne and Adelaide, drew at Wellington, before doing the improbable by achieving a five-wicket win in Christchurch. Glenn Turner, the first New Zealander with a century in both innings of a Test, served his country magnificently.

Turner continued to display his affection for the Lancaster Park pitch, scoring 98 against England and 117 against India in the next two years. Doug Walters restored Australian pride when he made 250 in 1976–77, but all those games were drawn. In 1977–78 Ian Botham became the second England player to complement a Test century with a five-wicket haul, and New Zealand lost heavily again the next summer when Javed Miandad put together innings of 81 and 160 not out for Pakistan.

Cricket has had no uglier incident than that at Christchurch in February 1980 when the West Indian bowler, Colin Croft, deviated in his run-up to charge into an umpire, Fred Goodall. A drawn Test was also marred by a West Indian dressing-room sit-in after tea on the second day. The actual

New Zealand playing England in a one-day game in January 1984. The embankment at Lancaster Park has since been replaced by concrete terracing, but the scoreboard remains.

cricket included centuries by Geoff Howarth, Richard Hadlee, Desmond Haynes, Lawrence Rowe and Collis King, and two 90s by Gordon Greenidge.

John F. Reid accumulated his first Test century in a rain-wrecked match against India. Next season, 1981–82, Greg Chappell rattled up the last 100 of his 176 runs before lunch on the second morning; John Wright's 141 only delayed the inevitable.

Sri Lanka's inexperience showed in their innings defeat within three days in March 1983 – the first Test between the two countries – but there was no such excuse available to England 11 months later. In playing time the game lasted less than two days. Richard Hadlee's 99 bolstered New Zealand's batting. In reply to 307, England managed just 82 and 93, the first time this century they had been dismissed under three figures in both innings of a Test. Hadlee, with eight cheap wickets, Lance Cairns, Stephen Boock and Ewen Chatfield shared the spoils.

Criticism of the pitch caused Lancaster Park to be 'rested' as a Test venue in 1984–85, when Pakistan and the Canterbury provincial side indulged in a high-scoring contest. One year later Allan

Border (140 and 114 not out) and Martin Crowe (137 after a temporary retirement because of injury at 51) found it to their liking before rain prevented a positive result.

However, Hadlee ruled in his home town in March 1987. Given unstinting support by Chatfield, Hadlee humbled the mighty West Indies. All out for 100, the tourists trailed by 232. They left New Zealand 33 runs to win. Five wickets were lost in getting them.

There was no such excitement when England returned in 1987–88. Rather, Hadlee's failure to take his 374th Test wicket seemed to extract the life from a match to which Chris Broad contributed a century but which drifted into a dull draw.

Christchurch				
Ref/No	*Season*	*V*	*T*	*Result*
186/1	1929–30	E	1	E-8w
217/2	1931–32	SA	1	SA-I&12
225/3	1932–33	E	1	Draw
284/4	1946–47	E	–	Draw
332/5	1950–51	E	1	Draw
349/6	1951–52	WI	1	WI-5w
422/7	1955–56	WI	2	WI-I&64
472/8	1958–59	E	1	E-I&99
542/9	1962–63	E	3	E-7w
578/10	1964–65	P	3	Draw
602/11	1965–66	E	1	Draw
634/12	1967–68	I	2	NZ-6w
652/13	1968–69	WI	3	Draw
685/14	1970–71	E	1	E-8w
737/15	1973–74	A	2	NZ-5w
759/16	1974–75	E	2	Draw
771/17	1975–76	I	2	Draw
796/18	1976–77	A	1	Draw
818/19	1977–78	E	2	E-174
846/20	1978–79	P	1	P-128
874/21	1979–80	WI	2	Draw
901/22	1980–81	I	2	Draw
924/23	1981–82	A	3	A-8w
954/24	1982–83	SL	1	NZ-I&25
976/25	1983–84	E	2	NZ-I&132
1036/26	1985–86	A	2	Draw
1073/27	1986–87	WI	3	NZ-5w
1091/28	1987–88	E	1	Draw

New Zealand: P 28, W 5, D 13, L 10

Dunedin

CARISBROOK

The Presbyterian Church Board of Property owned what is now the southernmost Test cricket ground virtually from the founding of the Otago province until it sold out to the Otago Rugby Union in 1968. During that time it had been changed from marshland to an arena ringed on three sides by stands and on the other by a low terrace overlooked by a railway embankment which permits free viewing of activities at Carisbrook.

In 1880 the Carisbrook Cricket Club had leased the area, named, drained and fenced it, and erected a small pavilion. The prime mover in this development, Henry Rose, has a grandstand named in his honour. Rugby authorities took over the lease in 1907.

Carisbrook became a first-class venue, at least in status, when Tasmania toured in early 1884 – but not before the fire brigade pumped off hundreds of gallons of water to make the field barely playable. Exactly 100 years on more modern drainage work

required the entire oval to be stripped bare and relaid.

Only Bert Sutcliffe batted with much confidence against Frank Tyson and Brian Statham when England won Carisbrook's first Test in 1954–55. But even Otago's favourite adopted cricketing son could not prevent an innings loss to the 1955–56 West Indians.

Graham Dowling made New Zealand's highest Carisbrook Test score (143) against the 1967–68 Indian team. When Pakistan routed the home side by an innings and 166 runs five years later Mushtaq Mohammad (201) and Asif Iqbal (175) put on 350 runs for the fourth wicket. Intikhab Alam had 11 wickets, Mushtaq seven.

Two of New Zealand's most dramatic victories occurred in consecutive matches at Carisbrook. In February 1980 New Zealand needed only 104 runs to beat the West Indies. But the seventh wicket fell at 54, the eighth at 73. Lance Cairns and Gary

Carisbrook under reconstruction in November 1983.

Troup got to within 4 runs of their goal before Cairns was out. In an atmosphere of nearly unbearable tension New Zealand staggered home by one wicket courtesy of a leg bye from Stephen Boock's pads. Richard Hadlee bagged 11 wickets, Desmond Haynes (55 and 105) scored almost half of the 326 runs from West Indian bats.

Five years and one day later New Zealand held its breath again as Jeremy Coney and Ewen Chatfield shared a match-winning partnership of 58 runs to foil Pakistan's bid to square the series. The only other available batsman, Cairns, was lying on the dressing-room table, dazed after being struck on the head by Wasim Akram. Chatfield (21 not out) courageously faced most of the bowling, his support of Coney (111 not out) elevating him to the rank of sporting hero in his homeland. Akram, only 18, became the youngest man to claim ten wickets in a Test.

When Pakistan returned in 1988–89 Carisbrook's Test was abandoned after rain prevented play on the first three days. A limited-over match was substituted on the fourth day.

Dunedin

Ref/No	Season	V	T	Result
401/1	1954–55	E	1	E-8w
421/2	1955–56	WI	1	WI-I&71
559/3	1963–64	SA	2	Draw
603/4	1965–66	E	2	Draw
633/5	1967–68	I	1	I-5w
712/6	1972–73	P	2	P-I&166
873/7	1979–80	WI	1	NZ-1w
1012/8	1984–85	P	3	NZ-2w
–	1988–89	P	1	Abandoned

New Zealand: P 8, W 2, D 2, L 4

1988–89 Test abandoned without a ball being bowled and excluded from the records.

Napier

MCLEAN PARK

Bequeathed to the city of Napier by Sir Douglas McLean in memory of his father, Sir Donald McLean, in 1908 as ten acres of partly reclaimed land, Test cricket's fiftieth venue has a far from happy history.

Ruined by the disastrous 1931 Napier earthquake, damaged by army occupation in the Second World War, the park was on standby for the possible transfer of an England Test (from a suspect Lancaster Park) in January 1984 when the main Harris Stand was razed by fire. Napier was also to have hosted one of the Tests of a short England itinerary arranged and then aborted in 1988–89.

Fiji met Hawke's Bay in the first cricket match of note on this renowned rugby union ground in 1947–48. Four years later Central Districts and Otago played in the maiden first-class game.

Batsmen did best in McLean Park's rain-affected Test debut. Geoff Howarth (114) and John Wright (88) accumulated 195 runs for New Zealand's second wicket, and Asif Iqbal and Majid Khan were century-scorers for Pakistan in February 1979.

Napier

Ref/No	Season	V	T	Result
847/1	1978–79	P	2	Draw

McLean Park during a one-day game between England and New Zealand in March 1988.

Wellington
BASIN RESERVE

It can truly be said that Wellington's international playing field was given to cricket by an act of God. Not long after the first settlers arrived in 1840 plans were drawn up for the lake at the top of Kent Terrace to be utilized as a Basin, or inner port, where trading vessels could take shelter from the frequently strong winds. A stream trickling from the lake was to be widened into a canal. However, lack of finance and other priorities caused the proposal to be shelved.

If the architects of young Wellington ever intended to reintroduce the scheme they were foiled by an earthquake in 1855 which raised by six feet the whole of the Te Amo end of the town and transformed the Basin Lake into a swamp.

Two years later Wellington's cricket enthusiasts, frustrated by not having a permanent pitch, petitioned the Provincial Council to set aside the Basin as a public park. Their plea was granted and initial work was done by prison labour.

The first match was held on 11 January 1868 between Wellington Volunteers and officers and men from HMS *Falcon*. There was no fanfare – just a few words by an umpire, Bruce Wallace, to the players apologizing for the rash of thistles and stones. The Basin Reserve was the fourth New Zealand ground given first-class status, when Wellington hosted Auckland in 1873–74.

The once humble surrounds have changed dramatically, especially in recent times. An original grandstand was replaced in 1923–24 but the Basin Reserve for many years offered most spectators only ageing, splintering wooden forms to sit upon, and could be a desolate place in a cold wind.

Various proposals were put forward to renovate the Basin Reserve, until increasing costs forced

Wellington's Basin Reserve in 1875. The canal was dug by prison labour to drain the ground. The grandstand was replaced in the 1920s.

cricketers and city councillors to abandon them. But Bob Vance, a former Wellington captain who became chairman of the Wellington Cricket Association and New Zealand Cricket Council, would not take no for an answer. His dream was realized when the handsome R. A. Vance Stand was opened in November 1980. The whole complex was given a facelift, with new seating and landscaping of the concrete and grassy embankments, the installation of a semi-electronic scoreboard, erection of a picket fence, and a complete overhaul of the oval itself.

Emerging from the Hataitai road tunnel, the Basin presents a pretty picture, if hardly a somnolent one. Close to the city centre, it earned its nickname of the 'biggest traffic island in the world' because of the surrounding circular, one-way, two-lane road. Screeching fire engines set off from their nearby station, and across the street a car sales proprietor signals notable cricketing achievements with his private siren. Overlooking the scene are the Governor General's residence and Wellington College.

The old stand houses the Cricket Museum, a marvellous recent addition to the amenities, and in 1989 the main entrances were named after two of Wellington's greatest players, Stewart Dempster and John Reid. The Basin is a welcome contrast to the impersonal Eden Park and Lancaster Park stadiums.

There are few crosswinds at the modern Basin, with its north-south pitch. A Wellington legend, Ewen Chatfield, spent a sporting lifetime willingly bending into everything from a light breeze to a near-gale.

Wellington was awarded New Zealand's second Test match in 1929–30 and Frank Woolley's 7 for 76 for England in the first innings has yet to be surpassed by an overseas bowler at the Basin. But New Zealand, after their defeat at Lancaster Park, were greatly encouraged by a remarkable opening partnership between Dempster and Jack Mills. Worth 276 runs, their stand is the second most prolific in New Zealand's Test history. After being struck on the head in Stan Nichols's first over, Dempster scored 136 (and an unbeaten 80 in the second innings), while Mills, on his debut, made 117. New Zealand, 440, led by 120 in an inevitable draw.

Innings of 100 and 73 by 19-year-old Giff Vivian could not prevent an eight-wicket loss to the 1931–32 South Africans. Much, much worse was in store for the next New Zealand team to assemble in Wellington. In a lopsided encounter given official Test recognition two years later, New Zealand batsmanship bowed to the Australians Ray Lindwall, Ernie Toshack, Bill O'Reilly and Keith Miller in late March 1946. New Zealand were humbled for 42 (having been 37 for 2) and 54. Six wickets did at least earn Jack Cowie credit.

Trevor Bailey, Doug Wright and Roy Tattersall undermined the New Zealand batting when England won by nine wickets in 1950–51, Jackie McGlew's ground Test record of 255 not out set up South Africa for an innings win in 1952–53, and Everton Weekes registered his third century in as many Test innings when the 1955–56 West Indians won by nine wickets.

The courage of Colin Cowdrey, who scored an unbeaten 128 after batting with a damaged hand at number eight, highlighted England's innings win in 1962–63. But the decade closed triumphantly for New Zealand against the West Indies when Brian Hastings guided his side through to its 163-run target with the loss of five wickets – the first New Zealand victory at the Basin, the fifth anywhere.

The Chappell brothers, Ian and Greg, established all sorts of family and other records in the high-scoring draw of March 1974. Ian made 145 and 121, only to be upstaged by his sibling's 247 not out and 133. Bevan Congdon and Hastings had three-figure replies in New Zealand's only innings.

It was not long before the Basin was looked upon as a 'result' ground. Between 1975–76 and 1982–83 New Zealand won four Tests; the only other, against Australia, was washed out.

A youthful Richard Hadlee – most people's pick for twelfth man before the match – spearheaded New Zealand's first innings win in mid-February 1976. Hadlee captured 4 for 36, then (as India collapsed for 81) 7 for 23, the best Test figures by a New Zealand bowler.

Two years later Hadlee had another ten wickets, and a most effective new-ball partner in Richard Collinge, a big left-armer, when New Zealand embellished its burgeoning reputation by beating England for the first time. Geoffrey Boycott's team needed only 137 runs but lost by 72.

The Basin went into Test recess until 1980–81

while it was redeveloped. But the sequence of New Zealand successes continued when India returned. Geoff Howarth contributed a handsome unbeaten 137, Lance Cairns chimed in with five wickets, and a poor New Zealand second innings was only a temporary setback before Hadlee and his fellow seamers finished off the tourists.

Sri Lanka came and were conquered in March 1983. Not without a struggle though, for they led by 39 runs. Hadlee, Martin Snedden and Ewen Chatfield demolished the Sri Lankan second innings and New Zealand had six wickets to spare.

Heavy scoring and draws characterized Tests at the Basin over the next few summers. Martin Crowe compiled centuries against England in 1983–84 (his first), West Indies in 1986–87, England in 1987–88 and Pakistan in 1988–89.

During the 1983–84 England Test Jeremy Coney reached his maiden Test century and created a new ground record for a New Zealander of 174 not out, a mark equalled by Crowe against Pakistan. John Wright defied the West Indians for 582 minutes, then the longest Test innings in his homeland, only to have that marathon surpassed by Shoaib Mohammad who batted exactly 12 hours for his 163 runs in 1988–89.

A fine view of Basin Reserve on the occasion of MCC's match against Wellington in March 1933.

Wellington

Ref/No	Season	V	T	Result
187/1	1929–30	E	2	Draw
218/2	1931–32	SA	2	SA-8w
275/3	1945–46	A	–	A-I&103
333/4	1950–51	E	2	E-6w
370/5	1952–53	SA	1	SA-I&180
423/6	1955–56	WI	3	WI-9w
541/7	1962–63	E	2	E-I&47
558/8	1963–64	SA	1	Draw
576/9	1964–65	P	1	Draw
635/10	1967–68	I	3	I-8w
651/11	1968–69	WI	2	NZ-6w
711/12	1972–73	P	1	Draw
736/13	1973–74	A	1	Draw
772/14	1975–76	I	3	NZ-I&33
817/15	1977–78	E	1	NZ-72
900/16	1980–81	I	1	NZ-62
922/17	1981–82	A	1	Draw
955/18	1982–83	SL	2	NZ-6w
975/19	1983–84	E	1	Draw
1010/20	1984–85	P	1	Draw
1035/21	1985–86	A	1	Draw
1071/22	1986–87	WI	1	Draw
1093/23	1987–88	E	3	Draw
1115/24	1988–89	P	2	Draw

New Zealand: P 24, W 5, D 12, L 7

The Lahore crowd anticipating victory over India in October 1978.

Pakistan

MIHIR BOSE

Pakistan, formed in 1947 by partitioning the old Raj India, first played Test cricket in October 1952 in Delhi. By the time Pakistan played its first Test at home it had already played two series abroad, losing 1–2 in India and, unexpectedly, squaring the 1954 series in England, albeit with some help from the weather.

The first home Test was played in Dacca in January 1955 and remains a curious moment: Dacca is now the capital of another country and Pakistan's captain had first played Test cricket for yet another country. Dacca was to witness six further Tests over the next 15 years before it became the capital of Bangladesh, born through the war in 1971 which split the eastern wing of the country from the western one. In that first home Test, as in all Pakistan's early Tests, the captain was Abdul Hafeez Kardar who had played for India when the sub-continent was one country.

Before partition, cricket in the area that is now Pakistan was concentrated mostly in Karachi in the Sind desert and in Punjab, particularly Lahore. Pakistan's early years as a newly independent country did not immediately expand the cricketing arena, nor was there a dramatic increase in first-class matches. The Quaid-e-Azam Trophy, the Pakistani equivalent of the county championship, was not established until 1953–54 and in the preceding five seasons first-class matches nearly always involved a touring side.

The pattern of international tours gave those early days of Pakistani cricket a rather unusual feel for visiting teams treated the sub-continent as if it had never been divided. Thus a tour would begin in northern India, then go over the border to Pakistan, then return to India to play the remaining Tests there and finally round off the tour in Pakistan. This was the pattern followed on the MCC tour of 1951–52 when, after playing the First Test in Delhi, the MCC team played a series of matches in Pakistan including two against the full Pakistan side which were treated by the Pakistanis as little short of full scale Test matches. When the MCC next visited the sub-continent in 1961–62, they began the tour in Pakistan, playing the First Test in Lahore, moved to India to play five Tests and a number of other first-class matches there, and then returned to Pakistan for the remaining two Tests. Other visitors like the West Indies followed a similar touring pattern.

Such a pattern of touring probably suited the Pakistanis for one of the factors which hindered the development of the game in those early years was the paucity of grounds suitable for first-class cricket. In 1948 there were only four associations, with no tradition of the game in the eastern wing and the North West Frontier Province an unlikely growth area for cricket with its many mountains and sparse population. But the bias towards matches against touring teams did mean that cricket in Pakistan quickly acquired glamour. It also meant that an inaugural first-class match on a ground was often a Test match or a match against a touring team and the local administrators were proud to display their grounds and amenities to the visitors

The first Test series in 1954–55 with bitter rivals India took Test cricket far and wide, from the dusty plains of the Punjab to a ground not very far away from the Khyber Pass. The subsequent years have seen the number of Test centres expand: by the end of the 1988–89 season Pakistan had played on 11 grounds at 10 centres, as against India's 16 grounds at 13 centres. Given the relative size of the two countries, this shows the depth of Pakistan cricket, even if it is still concentrated in the two regions of Punjab and Sind. In the 1986–87 season a record 126 first-class matches were played but international cricket continues to dominate the Pakistani cricket calendar. In the 1987–88 season the staging of the World Cup in the sub-continent, followed by an English tour, reduced this number dramatically to 54. As ever, international cricket pushed the domestic season into the background.

While the Indian expansion has come in recent years, particularly after the World Cup victory in 1983 when the decline in Test cricket made the authorities realize the need to take Test cricket away from the traditional centres, Pakistan has added only slowly to the five centres used in 1954–55. The World Cup allowed many grounds that had staged a solitary Test once again to stage international cricket, albeit of the one-day variety, and most of them were renovated and improved. Such changes confirmed the established sub-continental pattern of converting once open grounds into covered, multi-purpose stadia where cricket is one of many games played.

Bahawalpur
DRING (BAHAWAL) STADIUM

Bahawalpur was the venue for the Second Test against India in January 1955. It was only a little more than a year before, in November 1953, that the ground had hosted its first first-class match since the creation of Pakistan when Bahawalpur played Sind in the inaugural Quaid-e-Azam Trophy. Bahawalpur, a princely state, owed the development of the game to the Amir of Bahawalpur and for the national championship he had organized a strong side including Hanif Mohammad. Hanif scored 147 not out in this match and played an important part in helping Bahawalpur become the first winners of the trophy.

In the Test against India Hanif scored another century, the first of his 12 in Tests, but with less than 2 runs scored per over throughout the match the game turned into one of the dullest draws of all time. This is the only Test that has been played on the ground and as the princely influence declined so did the importance of Bahawalpur in domestic cricket. They won the Trophy again in 1957–58 but since then teams like Pakistan International Airlines, Habib Bank, National Bank and United Bank – reflecting the clout of the new commercial princes – have taken over.

The ground itself has remained more or less as it was developed by the Amir: pretty to the eye, lined with trees and temporary stands constructed to accommodate spectators, some of whom are women in purdah watching intently through the slits in their costumes.

Bahawalpur				
Ref/No	Season	V	T	Result
397/1	1954–55	I	2	Draw

Dacca

DACCA STADIUM

Dacca, now the capital of Bangladesh, which is not a full member of the ICC, is no longer a Test centre. Its brief reign lasted from January 1955 to November 1969. Wickets at Dacca alternated between matting and turf laid on a surface composed of rolled mud, which meant it was always difficult to get a result.

Of the seven Tests played there, only two produced results and both of those came in the same year. In March 1959 Fazal Mahmood (12 for 100) proved the matchwinner in a low-scoring game against the West Indies. But in November 1959, when the conditions should have suited him, Fazal was outwitted by Benaud and Mackay. Heavy rain made it impossible to use the new grass pitch, matting was laid and despite Fazal's 5 for 71 the Australians led by 25 runs after the first innings. Then Benaud (4 for 42) and Mackay (6 for 42) bowled Pakistan out for 134 – their lowest total against Australia in a home series – to pave the way for Australia's first win in Pakistan.

Of the three draws which followed, perhaps the most notable was that with England in 1968–69. With East Pakistan, as it then was, in turmoil and agitating to break free from the Punjabi control of West Pakistan this was, ironically, the only Test in the series free from riots. There was neither army nor police presence, authority being provided by the East Pakistani student leadership who were shortly to play such a heroic role in freeing their country. On the field of play, the pitch of hardened mud broke up during England's first innings and they collapsed to 130 for 7, but D'Oliveira (114 not out) and the tail resisted stolidly, overhauled Pakistan's 246 and saw England to safety.

Even without the extraordinary political events that marked Dacca's last Test it was always an unusual ground. It was an all-purpose ground that was used not only for sports other than cricket but also for all sorts of 'tamashas' – a rich sub-continental word that covers anything from a film stars' gala night through a night of singing and dancing to political meetings. In 1971 the stadium was to see some amazing rallies in favour of an independent Bangladesh, some horrific killings by the Pakistani army seeking to thwart it and a massive rally to celebrate the birth of the new state.

Dacca				
Ref/No	*Season*	*V*	*T*	*Result*
396/1	1954–55	I	1	Draw
415/2	1955–56	NZ	3	Draw
470/3	1958–59	WI	2	P-41
479/4	1959–60	A	1	A-8w
518/5	1961–62	E	2	Draw
648/6	1968–69	E	2	Draw
664/7	1969–70	NZ	3	Draw

Pakistan: P 7, W 1, D 5, L 1

Faisalabad
IQBAL STADIUM

This is a city named after a king with a cricket stadium named after a poet. Faisalabad is named after King Faisal – it used to be known as Lyallpur – and is the classic third world city: the textile capital of Pakistan, it attracts villagers in droves from the surrounding countryside looking for work in the dark, satanic, dirty mills. The city has been cleaned up in recent years but it is still a city of dirt and grime and smog. The stadium is named after the poet Iqbal who coined the concept of Pakistan, land of pure, though there is nothing to suggest that he took any interest in cricket. As befits the only Test ground named after a poet, it is quite pretty with one side open and the concrete terracing covering the other side not quite as obtrusive as elsewhere in the sub-continent. The wicket is slow and the first Test there against India in October 1978 resulted in a draw.

Since then there have been some impressive victories by Pakistan, but this ground will always be associated with one of the most acrimonious incidents in Test history. This occurred at the end of the second day's play on 8 December 1987 as England looked like getting on top in the match. Already unhappy with the umpiring from the previous Lahore Test and also during this match, the flashpoint came three deliveries from the end of the day's play when Gatting became embroiled with umpire Shakoor Rana. Gatting moved Capel's fielding position, the umpire claimed he was moving the fielder behind the batsman's back and stopped play to inform the batsman.

This resulted in a furious exchange between Gatting and Shakoor Rana, with choice four-letter words flowing, and this was all picked up by microphones close to the wicket and broadcast round the

Faisalabad's Iqbal Stadium and the view beyond during the Second Test between Pakistan and West Indies in December 1980.

world. The next day Shakoor Rana refused to carry on until Gatting apologized; Gatting would only do so if the umpire reciprocated. A whole day's play was lost and it seemed the tour would be cancelled. Eventually, after two days' negotiations, Gatting apologized, play resumed and England carried on with the tour. Raman Subba Row and

Alan Smith, the TCCB chairman and chief executive, flew out to Pakistan and after intensive talks got Rana to express regrets – and promised the England players £1000 per head 'hardship bonus'. But English doubts that they had walked into a well laid out Pakistani plot persisted. Faisalabad had become much more than a place for slow, spinning wickets and smog-filled days. It was the place where cherished myths about cricket died: an umpire and a captain had abused each other like fisherwomen in the middle of a Test match with the world listening.

Faisalabad				
Ref/No	*Season*	*V*	*T*	*Result*
831/1	1978–79	I	1	Draw
878/2	1979–80	A	2	Draw
887/3	1980–81	WI	2	WI-156
926/4	1981–82	SL	2	Draw
936/5	1982–83	A	2	P-1&3
945/6	1982–83	I	3	P-10w
979/7	1983–84	E	2	Draw
996/8	1984–85	I	2	Draw
1026/9	1985–86	SL	1	Draw
1055/10	1986–87	WI	1	P-186
1085/11	1987–88	E	2	Draw
1105/12	1988–89	A	2	Draw
1128/13	1989–90	I	2	Draw

Pakistan: P 13, W 3, D 9, L 1

Hyderabad
NIAZ STADIUM

The ground lies in the heart of the Sind desert, 120 miles north of Karachi, and the First Test against England in March 1973 seemed a mirage. Or at least that is how it appeared to Tony Lewis, the England captain who would later call it the longest day's cricket he had ever experienced. The series was already unusual in that the Pakistan captain was Lewis's Glamorgan colleague Majid Khan and there was much joking that both of them had received instructions from Wilfred Wooller, the great Glamorgan supremo. But in this inaugural Hyderabad Test Lewis was quickly educated in the problems of preparing Test grounds in the middle of the desert.

By what seemed a magical process, the authorities had produced a lush green outfield. When the first four by a Pakistani batsman led to a pitch invasion, Lewis noticed that the grass on the route trodden by the spectators disappeared. 'The crowds', recalls Lewis, 'persisted in running on to celebrate boundaries and by lunchtime we were fielding in soft sand.' The pitch itself, made of rolled mud, had been heavily watered and rolled and was white, shiny and cracked. By midday English fielders were complaining that the glare from the pitch, reflecting the sun, made fielding impossible.

Despite the conditions, this first Test produced a bucketful of runs. Pakistan made 569 for 9 declared in response to England's 487, their highest home total against England, with Intikhab Alam making his only Test century. The second Test at Hyderabad, in October 1976, saw Pakistan scoring 473 for 8 declared in their ten-wicket victory over New Zealand. The summit of Pakistan's achievements at Hyderabad was reached in January 1983 against India when they made 581 for 3 declared. Mudassar (231) and Javed Miandad (280 not out) shared a third-wicket partnership of 451 runs in 533 minutes, a world Test record. The stand also equalled the Test record for any wicket set by Bradman and Ponsford against England in 1934. For the first time two Pakistani batsmen scored double centuries in an innings. After that India meekly surrendered to Imran's pace and movement which included a spell of 5 for 8 in 23 balls during the first innings.

Such famous victories have whetted the appetite of local crowds and when Pakistan are winning they turn up in large numbers. The stadium itself is quite pretty and surrounded by ornamental buildings and gardens.

Hyderabad				
Ref/No	*Season*	*V*	*T*	*Result*
720/1	1972–73	E	2	Draw
783/2	1976–77	NZ	2	P-10w
815/3	1977–78	E	2	Draw
946/4	1982–83	I	4	P-I&119
1003/5	1984–85	NZ	2	P-7w

Pakistan: P 5, W 3, D 2, L 0

Karachi
NATIONAL STADIUM

Pakistan cricket is dominated by the rivalry between Karachi and Lahore, which has something of the intensity of the Roses battle – if anything, the rivalry is more bitter and Machiavellian. But both cities share one thing in common: a number of first-class grounds, some of which have seen some historic matches. Thus it was at the Karachi Parsi Institute ground – no longer used for first-class cricket – that in January 1959 Hanif Mohammad set the world record for the highest score in first-class cricket, 499. He was run out going for a second run after batting for over two days. That innings was played on a coir matting wicket – in those days all the Karachi wickets were matting wickets.

The most famous mat in Karachi was of course at the Karachi Gymkhana Ground which was the premier first-class ground in the city before partition and for sometime afterwards. As was to be expected from a city on the edge of the desert, the outfield was of reddish sand and the sand-textured pitch was in the middle of a 30-yard square of grass. The pitch was covered by a coconut-fibre mat 60 feet long and the story goes that Mahomed Nissar, India's great bowler, used to be on the mat within the first few strides of his long run-up.

The first first-class match on this ground was played during the MCC tour of 1926–27 when Arthur Gilligan's side played a combined team of Parsis & Muslims. The first post-independence first-class match was between Sind and the touring West Indians on 19–21 November 1948. The first-ever domestic first-class match did not take place until March 1953 when a Pakistan XI met the Rest. The ground never saw Test cricket but in 1977–78 a one-day match between a Sind XI and England

Close of play on the last day of Karachi's inaugural Test, 1 March 1955.

was played to provide a gentle work-out before the Third Test. In the fifth over, the only ball to misbehave during the day reared off a length and struck Brearley on the arm and broke it. As a result of this Boycott became captain of England and led the team in the Third Test at Karachi. That Test, like all Karachi Tests, was played at the National Stadium which had long since superseded Karachi Gymkhana as the centre for national and international cricket.

The stadium, ten miles from the city centre, is huge though the uncovered terraces that ring it are made to look pretty by the 'shamianas' which divide them. Being on the edge of the Sind desert, watering the wicket is always a problem and the initial Tests were played on matting. The first Test at the stadium, against India in 1955, produced a dull draw, but after that Fazal Mahmood estab-

lished himself as the king of mat and could be virtually unplayable on that surface. The Australians discovered this in October 1957 when they came to play their first-ever Test against Pakistan. Fazal Mahmood took 13 for 114, including three wickets in four balls, and his analysis remains the best for this ground. The Test also went into the record books for the slowest day's play in Test history – just 95 runs in $5\frac{1}{2}$ hours of play, Australia bowled out for 80 and Pakistan 15 for 2.

Three years later, in December 1959, the first visit of a US President to a Test match – Dwight D. Eisenhower on a political visit dropped in on the cricket – perked up the run rate. A whole day's play produced 104 for 5 wickets, that being Pakistan's score at the end of the first day. It remains the second slowest day in Test history. Since then Karachi has produced almost as many draws as Pakistan victories. Indeed, the record of this Test centre is unique: 28 played, 12 wins for Pakistan, 16 draws – and no defeats.

In 1976–77 Pakistan and New Zealand had such a high-scoring draw that they made 1585 runs between them, the highest aggregate for any Test in the sub-continent. One of the most notable of the 11 wins was against the old enemy, India, in December 1982. The square had recently been relaid and Imran proved irresistible. He took 8 for 60 in the second innings, giving him 11 for 79 in the match, and his match-winning second-innings bowling included a spell of 5 for 3 in 25 balls. India at one stage were looking relatively secure at 102 for 1, then collapsed to 197 all out to lose by an innings and 86 runs. A month later when the Indians returned for the final Test, the series having been lost 0–3, they achieved an honourable draw, restricting Imran to just five wickets. But politically motivated rioting which included an attempt to damage the pitch forced the fourth day's play to be abandoned and focussed renewed attention on the riotous nature of the Karachi crowds.

This had manifested itself in a most serious way in March 1969 just before lunch on the third day of the Third Test against England. England were 502 for 7, Colin Milburn and Tom Graveney had each scored hundreds, and Alan Knott was on 96 when a crowd several hundred strong bearing numerous banners broke down the gates, stormed across the outfield and caused the match to be abandoned.

The next serious instance took place in March 1975 when, following a century by Wasim Raja, spectators rushed on to the field and there was

rioting for $2\frac{1}{2}$ hours. It could be argued that the rioting prevented a West Indian victory for in the end they had only 25 minutes to score 170 and sensibly did not attempt it.

For much of General Zia's military rule Karachi, as the capital of Sind, the home province of the Bhutto family, was the hot bed of opposition to Zia and in recent years there has been a good deal of sectarian strife amongst different Muslim sects. In such circumstances a crowd gathering in a cricket ground can be fairly volatile and Karachi has had its fair share of law and order problems.

Karachi

Ref/No	Season	V	T	Result
400/1	1954–55	I	5	Draw
413/2	1955–56	NZ	1	P-I & 1
430/3	1956–57	A	–	P-9w
469/4	1958–59	WI	1	P-10w
481/5	1959–60	A	3	Draw
519/6	1961–62	E	3	Draw
569/7	1964–65	A	–	Draw
590/8	1964–65	NZ	3	P-8w
649/9	1968–69	E	3	Draw
662/10	1969–70	NZ	1	Draw
721/11	1972–73	E	3	Draw
757/12	1974–75	WI	2	Draw
784/13	1976–77	NZ	3	Draw
816/14	1977–78	E	3	Draw
833/15	1978–79	I	3	P-8w
877/16	1979–80	A	1	P-7w
888/17	1980–81	WI	3	Draw
925/18	1981–82	SL	1	P-204
935/19	1982–83	A	1	P-9w
944/20	1982–83	I	2	P-I & 86
948/21			6	Draw
978/22	1983–84	E	1	P-3w
–	1984–85	I	3	Cancelled
1004/23	1984–85	NZ	3	Draw
1028/24	1985–86	SL	3	P-10w
1057/25	1986–87	WI	3	Draw
1086/26	1987–88	E	3	Draw
1104/27	1988–89	A	1	P-I & 188
1127/28	1989–90	I	1	Draw

Pakistan: P 28, W 12, D 16, L 0

1984–85 Test against India cancelled and excluded from records.

Lahore

LAWRENCE GARDENS (BAGH-I-JINNAH) LAHORE (GADDAFI) STADIUM

The city that Ranjit Singh made the capital of his great Sikh kingdom is the greatest city of Punjab. It was the capital of undivided Punjab, the city immortalized by Kipling's writings and widely believed to have the best Mall in the sub-continent. It is next to this Mall that the picturesque Lawrence Gardens are located. For many it resembled the Parks at Oxford; and Younis Ahmed, the Pakistani cricketer, has no doubts that it remains the most beautiful ground in the sub-continent. Originally named after John Lawrence, the legendary Raj ruler of Punjab, the very first first-class match played there was between the Muslims and Sikhs on 27–28 February and 1 March 1923 with the Muslims winning by an innings and 74 runs. The match was part of the Lahore tournament which also involved matches with Hindus and Europeans.

Soon after the creation of Pakistan the ground acquired its new name honouring the founder of Pakistan – Bagh-i-Jinnah means Jinnah's Gardens. It was under this new name that it hosted the first first-class match played in Pakistan. This took place on 6–8 February 1948 between the Punjab Governor's XI and Punjab University; in March 1949 the two teams met again. By then Bagh-i-Jinnah had seen what for Pakistanis marked the start of international cricket in the new country. This was the match against the West Indies on 26–29 November 1948. The visitors had just played a Test in Delhi where they had forced India to follow on and fight hard for a draw. But Pakistan, in a creditable draw, restricted virtually the same side to a small first-innings lead and then in the second innings two of their batsmen, Imtiaz Ahmed and Mohammad Saeed, scored hundreds, putting on 205 for the second wicket.

The game between Lord Tennyson's XI and All-India in progress at Lawrence Gardens in November 1937.

The Gardens hosted an unofficial Test against Nigel Howard's MCC team in November 1951 and the first of its official Tests began on 29 January 1955, against India. But after three Tests – a draw against India, a win against New Zealand in October 1955 and a defeat at the hands of the West Indies in March 1959, the first defeat in a home Test – cricket moved to the stadium. The Gardens could not prevent the attack of the developers who saw Test cricket in the sub-continent only in terms of massive stadia. Just as newly emergent countries believe that every independent country must have a national airline, so cricket administrators in the sub-continent can only think in terms of concrete stadia. Lawrence Gardens, for all its charm, could never be that. The days of tree-lined grounds, peace and quiet which had led to the growth of cricket in the sub-continent were coming to an end.

The Lahore Stadium (after Colonel Gaddafi of Libya bankrolled Pakistan it became known as the Gaddafi Stadium) is one of the world's largest playing areas, capable of holding 50,000 people. As such concrete structures go it is well appointed and well looked after, providing scope for sports other than cricket. In the summer (the off-season for

An aerial photo of the Lahore Stadium taken just before its inaugural Test in November 1959.

cricket in Pakistan) hockey is played there. Wickets are generally slow but they can aid the seam bowlers and are suitably adjusted to cope with the nature of the opposition Pakistan is facing. In 1976 Bert Flack, then head groundsman of Edgbaston, was flown out to advise on producing good, fast wickets – with no immediate result. Indeed, over half of the 23 Tests played there have been draws.

For a time Pakistan found it quite difficult to win at Lahore and initially it was a place that visiting sides relished. Australia won the first Test played there (when it was known as Lahore Stadium) in November 1959 when the left-arm spin of Kline proved too much for the home side. In October 1961 the spin of Barber and Allen proved just as difficult and they helped win England's first official Test in Pakistan. While this victory earned Dexter's side the rubber in the three-Test series, it remains the only Test won by England in Pakistan. In October 1969 New Zealand won by five wickets and Pakistan had to wait until October 1976 before winning a Test in Lahore – against New Zealand by six wickets.

By this time Lahore had acquired another, more dubious reputation – as a Test centre often disrupted by crowd trouble. In February 1968 the Test against England saw serious and frequent crowd disturbances, with the crowd often invading the field, leading to riots and skirmishes. Almost ten years later in December 1977, while the cricket world was reeling from Packer, another England Test produced yet more serious crowd trouble though such was the tedium of the match – the scoring rate was 31 runs per hour – that it may have enlivened the match. Both riots were more the product of the general political instability of the country than any cricket factors. In 1968 the country was entering the period of turmoil that was to end with the Bangladesh war and two of England's three Tests were badly affected by student demonstrations. The Second Test in Dacca was only riot-free because the students controlled it. The riots of 1977 reflected the political turmoil following the ousting of Bhutto by General Zia and the return of military rule.

In November 1978 Pakistan did gain a victory in Lahore when it beat India for the first time since 1952. It was the first result after 13 successive draws between the two countries but in 1982–83 the Gaddafi Stadium reverted to type and both Tests against India were drawn. This was particularly significant for this series saw some devastating bowling by Imran who took 40 wickets and so completely demoralized the Indians that they lost three Tests comprehensively. However, the first of the two Tests at Lahore in this series, in December 1982, did set a trend for tall scores by Pakistan batsmen which continued throughout the series, establishing new world records. In the first Lahore Test Zaheer Abbas made 231 and that marked his 100th first-class hundred.

In more recent years the spin of Abdul Qadir

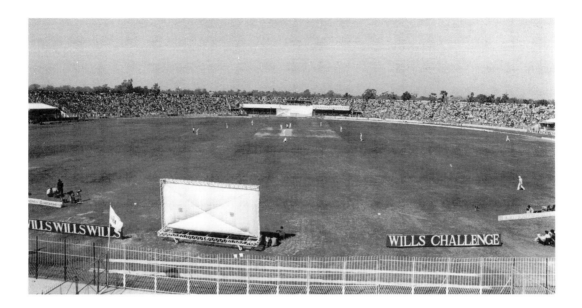

The Lahore Stadium taken during a one-day international between Pakistan and England in March 1974.

has brought Pakistan some famous, some might say infamous, victories. The most significant of these came in November 1987 when Qadir's 9 for 56 in the first innings and 13 for 101 in the match sent England crashing to defeat by an innings and 87 runs. England were upset by several decisions and in the second innings Broad, given out caught at the wicket, refused to go, stood his ground for almost a minute and had to be persuaded to leave by his partner Gooch. It was English feelings about the umpiring in this First Test that lit the fuse for the explosion that eventually came in Faisalabad ten days later. The Test, coming just after the Reliance World Cup, also provided evidence of the waning of Test cricket. Very few people watched the match, with barely 200 people at the start. Perhaps as administrators looked at the absence of crowds they might have felt a pang for Lawrence Gardens. At least there such small crowds would not have looked out of place.

Lahore				
Ref/No	*Season*	*V*	*T*	*Result*
Lawrence Gardens (Bagh-i-Jinnah)				
398/1	1954–55	I	3	Draw
414/2	1955–56	NZ	2	P-4w
471/3	1958–59	WI	3	WI-I & 156
Lahore (Gaddafi) Stadium				
480/4	1959–60	A	2	A-7w
512/5	1961–62	E	1	E-5w
589/6	1964–65	NZ	2	Draw
647/7	1968–69	E	1	Draw
663/8	1969–70	NZ	2	NZ-5w
719/9	1972–73	E	1	Draw
756/10	1974–75	WI	1	Draw
782/11	1976–77	NZ	1	P-6w
814/12	1977–78	E	1	Draw
832/13	1978–79	I	2	P-8w
879/14	1979–80	A	3	Draw
886/15	1980–81	WI	1	Draw
927/16	1981–82	SL	3	P-I & 102
937/17	1982–83	A	3	P-9w
943/18	1982–83	I	1	Draw
947/19			5	Draw
980/20	1983–84	E	3	Draw
995/21	1984–85	I	1	Draw
1002/22	1984–85	NZ	1	P-6w
1056/23	1986–87	WI	2	WI-I & 10
1084/24	1987–88	E	1	P-I & 87
1106/25	1988–89	A	3	Draw
1129/26	1989–90	I	3	Draw

Pakistan: P 26, W 7, D 14, L 5

Multan

IBN-E-QASIM BAGH STADIUM

This is the one Pakistan ground which is similar to an English county ground. When the first international match was played here, an unofficial four-day Test between a BCCP XI and a Commonwealth XI in March 1968, the dressing-room for the visitors was a 'shamiana', the sub-continental version of a marquee. Things have changed since then but it still retains some of the wonder of a cricket ground in a wild west town delighted and surprised that the brightest and the best of the cricket world should come knocking at the door. The first first-class match was played in December 1958 when one of the many reorganizations of the Quaid-e-Azam Trophy resulted in the competition being run on a zonal basis with 12 teams taking part. In this first match Multan had an easy victory over Quetta.

The only Test played in Multan was in December-January 1981 against West Indies. It started late because the umpire did not arrive, it finished early because of rain, and in between it produced a most unpleasant incident. The second afternoon saw a riot when Sylvester Clarke, the West Indian fast bowler, subjected to prolonged orange-pelting, removed a brick boundary marker and scored a direct hit on the head of the local students' union leader. There was a mini riot, though not as bad as the ones in Lahore and Karachi. Despite all this, the West Indies earned a draw to give them their first and only rubber in Pakistan.

Peshawar

PESHAWAR CLUB GROUND

The square-shaped Peshawar Club ground is not far from the famous Khyber Pass. First-class cricket arrived there in November 1949 when the North-West Frontier Province Governor's XI met the touring Commonwealth team. Pope took 5 for 46 in a low-scoring draw but generally the wickets at Peshawar have favoured the spinners. This was certainly true during the only Test played there, in February 1955, when Mankad and Gupte took 12 of the 20 Pakistani wickets to fall. But in keeping with the series, India declined to try to score 126 runs in the final hour of the Test.

Perhaps the most remarkable match the ground has ever seen was during the MCC Under-25 tour of 1966–67 when Mike Brearley scored 312 not out, the highest first-class score by an Englishman in the sub-continent. Brearley was dropped several times after reaching his double-century and there appears to have been some suggestion that at some stage the scorers may have got him and his partner Alan Ormrod mixed up. *Wisden* lamented the lack of 'competent scorers' on the tour and there is a charming story told about how the official scorer went for tea, entrusted the scoring to someone else, and never returned. It was between tea and the close that Brearley and Ormrod put on 234 with Brearley's third hundred taking only 50 minutes and MCC scoring 514 in a day.

Multan				
Ref/No	*Season*	*V*	*T*	*Result*
889/1	1980–81	WI	4	Draw

Peshawar				
Ref/No	*Season*	*V*	*T*	*Result*
399/1	1954–55	I	4	Draw

Rawalpindi
PINDI CLUB GROUND

The Pindi Club ground in the former capital Rawalpindi is in some ways Pakistan's most historic ground. It is part of the Rawalpindi Club, a complex which now has an 18-hole golf course, a swimming pool, squash courts, tennis courts, an auditorium and two main halls to cater for 600 people. The club was started in 1885, the year Lord Dufferin, then Viceroy of India, held a conference at Rawalpindi with the Amir of Kabul. Initially the cricket played there was an all-British affair with matches like Plains *v* Hills, Pindi *v* Murree, Pindi *v* Peshawar and Pindi *v* Lahore. In one match, Prince Christian Victor, Queen Victoria's grandson, scored the first double-century to be recorded in what was to become Pakistan.

After the creation of Pakistan the first first-class match to be played on this ground took place in November 1949 between a Commonwealth XI and the Commander-in-Chief's XI. The Commonwealth team were bowled out for 81 in their first innings with Miran Bux taking 5 for 19; in January 1955 he made his Test debut for Pakistan against India at the age of 47 years and 284 days, the second-oldest player on debut.

Rawalpindi hosted its only Test in March 1965, Pakistan beating New Zealand by an innings and 64 runs, its first home victory for six years. Although the ground remained a favourite of the military (Rawalpindi is the home of the extremely powerful Pakistani military side), it is not really big enough for modern Test matches. During the 1987 World Cup England met Pakistan there. Initially Donald Carr had reported that the outfield was too rough for the match, but the army reseeded parts of the ground. A crowd of 20,000 people saw a narrow Pakistan victory.

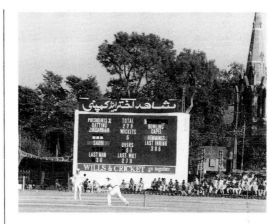

The Pindi Club ground during England's 1987–88 tour.

Rawalpindi

Ref/No	Season	V	T	Result
588/1	1964–65	NZ	1	P-I&64

Sialkot
JINNAH PARK

Pakistan reached a cricket eleven number of Test grounds in October 1985 when a Test was played in Jinnah Park, Sialkot, in the Punjab. Contrary to normal practise, the wicket helped seam. Imran found it extremely useful, taking 9 for 95, and Pakistan won with eight wickets and more than a day to spare. Four years later, India fought well to salvage a draw in the final Test of an all-drawn series.

Sialkot

Ref/No	Season	V	T	Result
1027/1	1985–86	SL	2	P-8w
1130/2	1989–90	1	4	Draw

The view from under the Oaks at Newlands, one of the world's most picturesque cricket grounds, during MCC's 1956–57 tour of South Africa.

South Africa

MICHAEL OWEN-SMITH

It must surely be one of the great ironies of South Africa's isolation from Test match cricket that by far the greatest developments of the Republic's major grounds has taken place since the last official Test in 1970. Up to that stage South Africa had four official Test venues in St George's Park (Port Elizabeth), Newlands (Cape Town), the Wanderers Stadium (Johannesburg) – and its predecessors Ellis Park and Old Wanderers – and Kingsmead (Durban) – and its predecessor Lord's.

But, if a full Test series was to be played in South Africa today, the Wanderers would almost certainly have to cede one of its normal two Tests to Centurion Park outside Pretoria and Bloemfontein's recently completed Springbok Park would qualify for a limited-overs international at least.

St George's Park claims seniority over Newlands as South Africa's oldest Test ground by a matter of 12 days. But it is highly appropriate as St George's Park is the home of the country's oldest cricket club – Port Elizabeth Cricket Club, which came into being in the early 1840s some 50 years before the first Test.

Western Province Cricket Club, the owners of Newlands, was only formed in 1864 and the ground itself only witnessed its first game of cricket in 1888.

The Wanderers club was born in the same year, 1888, and Test cricket was first played at the old Wanderers' ground, on a property that is now occupied by the Johannesburg railway station, in March 1896. The Wanderers club was originally granted a 99-year lease by the government of the day, but, in spite of this, the ground was expropriated immediately after the Second World War and rugby headquarters Ellis Park became a temporary home for Test cricket until the new Wanderers Stadium was built.

Durban came on the Test match scene at the comparatively late stage of 1910 and only four matches were played at the Lord's ground before Kingsmead became the permanent headquarters in 1922–23.

The main Test grounds have undergone surprisingly little change over the years. Newlands, of course, has been and always will be dominated by Table Mountain but the only changes at any of the grounds have been the concessions to modern commercial demands. All the grounds now have towering floodlight pylons to cater for the financially extremely remunerative night cricket and sponsors' hospitality suites are the norm rather than the exception.

The only real change in terms of public accommodation has occurred at Kingsmead where the players' box and dressing-rooms have now been incorporated in a splendid new stand, strategically placed behind the bowler's arm at the Umgeni end.

The Wanderers thus remains the only ground that can cater for a really big crowd – probably in the region of 30,000 – and any expansion in this regard will depend on the return of international cricket rather than the uncertainty of irregular unofficial tours.

Cape Town
NEWLANDS

If cricket is a visual art, then surely there is no other ground in the world that has such a perfect setting for that art to be pursued. Wherever one sits at Newlands, one can hardly be unaware of the two dominant features of this ground: the oak trees that line the one side of the ground and the mountain that dominates the other.

Alan Ross wrote in *Cape Summer* (1957): 'Newlands is so certainly, in popular imagination, the most beautiful ground in the world, that one half hopes to disagree. But in honesty one cannot. Separated from the sea and the city by Table Mountain, it lies deep under the rocks of Devil's Peak. If you sit among the plane trees with your back to Table Mountain and the railway, you look across at a thick line of oaks, the people under them stippled with light as in a painting by Pissaro or Seurat. From every other position Table Mountain flowing into its foothills dominates the eye.' And certainly these two dominant features of Newlands are the two that will have to survive the inevitable pressure on every Test ground from the commercial and public interests.

Although the Western Province Cricket Club, the owners of Newlands, came into being in 1864, Newlands itself only dates back to 1887 and the first match was played there in January 1888. Since then, Newlands has undergone remarkably little change. The pond behind what is now the War Memorial scoreboard has disappeared to make way for the B field and the practice nets, and, in turn, various new structures have been erected: the grandstand in 1956, its subsequent development into the WPCU's Protea Suite headquarters and the adjoining media facilities in the 1970s; in the 1980s, the erection of sponsors' chalets on the mountain

Newlands on 2 December 1905 during MCC's first tour of South Africa.

side of the field that have blended remarkably well into the general background; and finally, of course, the giant floodlighting pylons that have become a major feature of all of South Africa's modern Test match grounds.

There were considerable reservations expressed when the decision was taken to play the highly popular night cricket at Newlands – for financial reasons it had become absolutely essential if the Western Province Cricket Club was to survive – but nobody need have worried. The environment of Newlands is such that the floodlights have almost disappeared into the background and one is seldom aware of them.

The one major change to the environment of Newlands occurred at the turn of the century. Large pine trees extended from the B field along the Camp Ground Road boundary, around the pavilion to the railway boundary. Those bordering the present tea-room cramped spectators and obstructed their view, while the others affected the light and threw shadows over the playing area in the afternoons. It was decided to replace these pines

with oak trees and, in the 1890s, a start was made on the Camp Ground side. It was a step that has never been regretted as the Oaks have become world famous. In the late 1940s an English cricketer and his wife, having been hit on the head by acorns while having tea, took one home with them and it was planted in the assistant secretary's small garden at Lord's.

There is one other change at Newlands that is worth recording although it only lasted for a couple of days. That was the occasion of the match between the MCC and Western Province at the start of the 1927–28 tour. The two ends of the prepared pitch were far too wet for play to be possible following continuous rain, so the pitch was swung around at right angles to the mountain. Play was then possible although conditions were by no means perfect judging by the totals: MCC were bowled out for 138 and Western Province reached 67 for 6 in reply.

As befits the only ground in South Africa to have been a Test venue on every single tour – there was only one Test on the second England tour under W.W. Read in 1891 and it was played at Newlands – this ground has witnessed many moments of historic interest.

Bobby Abel of Surrey and England made the first-ever Test century in South Africa in 1889 in a match in which Johnny Briggs took 15 wickets for 28 runs, only one of which was not bowled. Jimmy Sinclair made the first Test century for South Africa at Newlands in 1899 – 106 out of only 177 – and followed this in 1902 with one of the fastest Test centuries of all time. Even by comparison with the modern standard of calculating centuries by balls bowled rather than time occupied at the crease, Sinclair's statistics that day against the Australians were remarkable. His 104 came in 83 minutes with the last 64 runs being scored in just 33 minutes. Contemporary reports indicate that 'much time was lost in recovering the ball' as a six in those days meant a hit right out of the ground.

An important event in the evolution of cricket in South Africa was the fact that Newlands was the venue for the first Test match played on a turf pitch. That was on New Year's Day 1931 against the MCC. The turf pitches at Newlands had also been used previously for the trials to select the 1929 Springbok team to England. On the subject of New Year's Day, it is also worth recording that since 1923 the Newlands Test was always played over the first few days of the New Year.

If Newlands has had many happy moments, it has been a decidedly unhappy ground for the Springboks. Apart from the two victories against MCC sides in 1906 and 1910, the Springboks were unable to secure a single victory at Newlands until 1970 when the final series of the pre-isolation era was played against Bill Lawry's Australians. Sixty years is a long time in any language for a country to go without a Test match win at a particular venue and that period included an historic first-ever win abroad for New Zealand when John Reid's Kiwi side of 1961–62 managed to share the series 2–2. The Newlands Test of that series included one of the most remarkable debuts in Springbok colours. Syd Burke returned innings figures of 6 for 128 and 5 for 68. In all he bowled more than 80 overs of fast-medium and was required to carry the Springbok pace attack after his partner, Goofy Lawrence, broke down with hamstring trouble and the up-and-coming Peter Pollock was relegated to the role of twelfth man.

There have been a number of remarkable finishes to Test matches at Newlands, two of which deserve special mention. The 1923 match against the MCC produced the closest finish with the visitors getting

home by one wicket. When the last man came in, England required 5 runs to win and one of the last two batsmen hit the ball high towards the railway stand. This one shot produced three possibilities: a catch to give the Springboks victory, a six to give England victory or a four to tie the scores. The latter course is what happened as Catterall, running round from the scoreboard position, was unable to make the ground in time. The match was subsequently won with a sharp single to gully that produced the possibility of a run out.

The other finish at Newlands is worth recalling for a totally different reason. This occurred against Ian Craig's Australians of 1957–58. The visitors batted first and made 449 to which the Springboks replied with 209. Nobody could possibly have envisaged what would happen in the follow-on when the home side were put out for a meagre 99 of which Trevor Goddard carried his bat for 56! Left-arm googly bowler Lindsay Kline, who was later to become an Australian batting hero against the West Indies in a famous drawn Test, earned his niche in history by finishing the match with a hat-trick and those three wickets were the only ones he took in the second innings.

Opposite page The tea interval at Newlands during the Second Test against England, 1 January 1939.

Above Newlands in 1983, overlooked by Table Mountain and relatively unchanged over the years.

Cape Town

Ref/No	Season	V	T	Result
32/1	1888–89	E	2	E-I&202
38/2	1891–92	E	–	E-I&189
49/3	1895–96	E	3	E-I&33
59/4	1898–99	E	2	E-210
77/5	1902–03	A	3	A-10w
91/6	1905–06	E	4	E-4w
92/7			5	SA-I&16
109/8	1909–10	E	4	SA-4w
110/9			5	E-9w
147/10	1921–22	A	3	A-10w
149/11	1922–23	E	2	E-1w
169/12	1927–28	E	2	E-87
205/13	1930–31	E	2	Draw
249/14	1935–36	A	3	A-I&78
268/15	1938–39	E	2	Draw
311/16	1948–49	E	3	Draw
319/17	1949–50	A	2	A-8w
379/18	1953–54	NZ	3	Draw
435/19	1956–57	E	2	E-312
445/20	1957–58	A	2	A-I&141
522/21	1961–62	NZ	3	NZ-72
573/22	1964–65	E	3	Draw
614/23	1966–67	A	2	A-6w
670/24	1969–70	A	1	SA-170

South Africa: P 24, W 3, D 5, L 16

Durban

LORD'S
KINGSMEAD

For a ground that has only hosted 19 official Test matches, Kingsmead – or old Kingsmead as it is known in Durban to differentiate from the local soccer ground, which is called new Kingsmead – has a remarkable history of witnessing so many of the most memorable moments of Springbok cricket. One Test match alone, the so-called Timeless Test between South Africa and England in March 1939 – has assured Kingsmead a permanent place in the history of the game. That match lasted for ten playing days, one of which was washed out, and the contest still ended in a draw!

Kingsmead came into being after the First World War, largely as the result of funds donated by the Durban Municipality and the Durban Turf Club and was completed in time for Frank Mann's MCC touring side in 1922–23. Slightly surprisingly, in view of the dominant part that Natal has played in South African cricket, particularly in the contribution of players of the highest quality to the Springbok side, Test cricket only came to Natal in 1910 with four matches being played at the Lord's ground in Durban before Kingsmead took over.

Very little seems to be known about the Lord's ground. It is presumably named after its illustrious namesake in London and appears to have been situated fairly close to Kingsmead on a sight that is now a mass of railway tracks leading to the new Durban station. If that is indeed the case, then one has the remarkable coincidence of two of South Africa's original Test grounds – the old Wanderers is the other one – suffering exactly the same fate.

The first Test played at Lord's brought the Springboks a handsome victory over England thanks to fine individual contributions from Gordon White, who made a second-innings

South Africa batting at Lord's, Durban, on the first day of the First Test against England in December 1913.

century, and Aubrey Faulkner, who took six wickets in England's second innings. The two teams had, incidentally, been tied on 199 runs each in the first innings. The Englishmen gained their revenge three years later in spite of a Herby Taylor century and the two remaining Tests at this venue were drawn against England in 1914 and against the Australians in 1921.

The decision to move to Kingsmead, which was clearly a superior ground according to contemporary reports, paid immediate dividends in that Natal was to join the Transvaal in providing two Test matches for each tour for the entire period between the world wars. The first two England tours to visit Kingsmead in 1923 and 1928 were still played on matting pitches with the first series being notable for the performance of visiting batsmen, 'Jack' Russell becoming the first player to score a century in both innings of a Test match in South Africa.

This achievement brought into being the Kings-

mead tradition of players planting trees at the ground to mark notable performances. Ever since then, other players have followed suit including Jack Fingleton, Wally Hammond, Dudley Nourse, Bill Voce and Hedley Verity, to name a few.

In 1928 Kingsmead was the venue for the final Test when the Springboks came from behind to square the series at 2–2 with a remarkable victory, England were routed for 118 in their second innings with George Bisset exploiting a strong following wind to take 7 for 29.

Nevertheless, it was the aforementioned Timeless Test that was undoubtedly the match that put Kingsmead on the cricketing map. This was the fifth contest of the series and, with England leading 1–0, it was decided to play the match to a finish. The crucial factor was the rain that fell on two days. This, coupled with the use of the heavy roller, had the effect of remaking the pitch on both occasions. Thus the match was played to all intents and purposes on three new pitches and this explained why such large totals were possible in the second half of the game.

The Springboks must, indeed, have thought they held a winning hand when they made 530, after

Kingsmead, Durban, 14 March 1928: the scoreboard recording the longest first-class match ever played.

winning the toss, and eventually led by 214 on the first innings. They then made a further 481 in their second innings to set England an improbable target of 696. Nevertheless England would surely have won had they not eventually had to catch the boat back home – the last tour match against Western Province had long since been abandoned – when they reached 654 for 5.

The match attracted tremendous public interest but it was generally agreed that a timeless test was not in the best interests of cricket and the experiment of playing a series to the finish has not been repeated.

After the Second World War, Kingsmead was restricted to a single Test in each series as Port Elizabeth rejoined the international itinerary. But the Natal ground continued to host matches of more than ordinary interest.

The finish to the 1948 match against England rivalled the excitement of the Wanderers clash in 1906. England, eight wickets down, needed 8 runs off the last over bowled by Lindsay Tuckitt with the batsmen being Alec Bedser, who had been at the crease for 15 minutes without getting off the mark, and Cliff Gladwin, who instantly became

famous with his 'Coometh the hour, coometh the man'.

The ball was wet and the Springbok attack tired and somehow the two batsmen managed to scrape together 7 runs off the first five balls. The two batsmen decided to run regardless off the last ball and this they did, scampering a leg bye.

The following year the Australians came to Kingsmead and pulled off one of the greatest escape acts of all time. Not only did they escape but they won by five wickets, thanks to an innings of unbelievable brilliance by a young 21-year-old batsman by the name of Neil Harvey.

Springbok captain Dudley Nourse came in for a lot of criticism for not enforcing the follow-on when Australia were dismissed for 75 in their first innings. The Australians had been caught on a turning pitch following rain. Apparently the Kingsmead surface that year had a greater percentage of clay than was normally the case. There were calls for the experienced Test off-spinner,

The view through the firs at Kingsmead during the drawn Test between South Africa and England in January 1957.

Atholl Rowan, when it became clear what the pitch was doing but those people need not have worried as his young understudy, Hugh Tayfield, took 7 for 23 in a superb effort.

Both Harvey and Tayfield were to become dominant figures on the cricket stage in the next decade.

Australian captain Lindsay Hassett said after the game that he would have done the same as Nourse in not enforcing the follow-on. Be that as it may, the Springboks were routed for 99 in their second innings and Harvey's 151 not out constituted nearly half of the Australian second innings winning total of 336 for 5 on a pitch that was still by no means easy.

From a purely partisan point of view, the last two Test matches to be played at Kingsmead – against the Australians in 1966 and 1970 – must surely rank among the best. The former was not so important in the sense that the Springboks came back from 100 for 6 to win easily on the back of yet another brilliant batting performance by Denis Lindsay. It was rather the debut of one of Natal's favourite sons, Mike Procter. He was to take more

than 40 wickets in seven Tests against Australia over the two tours - and, but for political interference, he would surely have matched the feats of the other great all-rounders of the 1970s and 1980s such as Ian Botham, Kapil Dev and Richard Hadlee.

But 5 February 1970 surely ranks as the greatest day in the history of Kingsmead and probably in the history of South African cricket as well. In 60 breathtaking minutes immediately after lunch on the first day, two of the world's all-time greats, Barry Richards and Graeme Pollock, came together in a partnership of just over 100.

In modern cricket such a tempo is almost unheard of. This followed a pre-lunch session when Richards, but for some delaying tactics by Australian captain Bill Lawry, would almost certainly have matched the feat of Don Bradman, Victor Trumper and Charles Macartney of scoring a century on the first morning of a Test match.

Sadly it was not to be, but Richards and Pollock more than made up for it after lunch. Their partnership almost became tip-and-run as both were determined to keep the strike. Richards's first false shot was his last one when he was bowled for 140, having played as technically perfect an innings as is possible by the purest of standards.

Springbok record after another. He finished on 274 having eclipsed Dudley Nourse's 231 best against Australia and Jackie McGlew's 255 best against any international side. The final total of 622 for 9 declared was also a South African record.

The Australians, thoroughly demoralized by this batting onslaught, were beaten by an innings in four days, which was something no Springbok side had ever come close to achieving.

Pollock and Richards, like Procter, were poised to dominate world cricket when the axe of isolation fell but at least Kingsmead – all three were born in Natal – had seen three of its most distinguished sons at their best. It was something that was to be denied to the rest of the cricketing world.

Durban				
Ref/No	Season	V	T	Result
Lord's				
107/1	1909–10	E	2	SA-95
130/2	1913–14	E	1	E-I&157
133/3			4	Draw
145/4	1921–22	A	1	Draw
Kingsmead				
150/5	1922–23	E	3	Draw
152/6			5	E-109
170/7	1927–28	E	3	Draw
172/8			5	SA-8w
206/9	1930–31	E	3	Draw
208/10			5	Draw
247/11	1935–36	A	1	A-9w
251/12			5	A-I&6
269/13	1938–39	E	3	E-I&13
271/14			5	Draw
309/15	1948–49	E	1	E-2w
320/16	1949–50	A	3	A-5w
377/17	1953–54	NZ	1	SA-I&58
436/18	1956–57	E	3	Draw
446/19	1957–58	A	3	Draw
520/20	1961–62	NZ	1	SA-30
571/21	1964–65	E	1	E-I&104
615/22	1966–67	A	3	SA-8w
671/23	1969–70	A	2	SA-I&129

South Africa: P 23, W 6, D 9, L 8

Johannesburg
OLD WANDERERS
ELLIS PARK
WANDERERS STADIUM

The world-famous Wanderers club of Johannesburg can surely be regarded as the pioneering club of sport in South Africa. Cricket is rightly the sport for which the Wanderers club has the greatest renown although its rugby, athletics and other sections have all contributed to Springbok glory. But cricket at the Wanderers was a real pioneering sport.

Unlike Port Elizabeth and Cape Town – where the first international matches were played and where both venues had the advantage of well established clubs to get the game off the ground – the Wanderers was born at virtually the same time as the first overseas tour to South Africa. Indeed it was the first tour in 1888–89 by C. Aubrey Smith's team that had a lot to do with the Wanderers club being established and having its first headquarters on a site that is now occupied by the Johannesburg railway station. In contrast the Port Elizabeth Cricket Club had come in to being in the early 1840s and the Western Province Cricket Club in 1864.

The birth of the Wanderers club in 1888 was very nearly stillborn according to the club's official history: 'Propelled by initial enthusiasm, the young men drafted rules . . . they proposed proceeding with the collection of money to prepare the playing fields, build stands, plant trees and fence the whole area. Nothing happened and, failing a responsible body to implement its undertakings, the Government made no move to confirm the lease . . . Predictably Johannesburg slid into a suffocating slump and when not playing football, the young men toiled to keep body and soul together. All through the winter of 1888, The Wanderers

Club . . . failed to exist even in name.'

One of the turning points was the news that Billy Simkins and W.H. Milton in Cape Town were negotiating with Major Warton to bring the first team of English cricketers to South Africa for the 1888–89 season. Transvaal enthusiasts obviously did not want to miss out on the tour and negotiations were revived with the government to obtain the lease to the ground. The government were not willing to do so, in view of the previous fiasco, unless it was properly established as a sporting club and a considerable sum of money was spent on it within five years. Fortunately one Jacob Swart undertook the obligations and the ground became the property of the Wanderers club and a Test venue for South African cricket from the turn of the century until the Second World War.

The original ground granted to the Wanderers was somewhat larger than that which they finally received but the leased ground basically occupied the current site of the Johannesburg railway station, bordered by Wolmarans Street on the north side and North Street on the south. The area was known as Krugers Park.

Such was the enthusiasm that the young men of Johannesburg had for the English tour that a pavilion with a limited amount of seating was built by the time the tourists arrived. The Wanderers' history records the event:

'They came at the end of January 1889. The front part of the Pavilion with bench seats on either side and a hall or dining room below ground level, was ready to receive them, the ground was in perfect condition (with very few bumpers), there were no stands, but men sat happily on the banks and scores paid three guineas each to attend the whole week of matches.

'The excitement almost paralysed the town. Twenty-two Johannesburg took on the English

J. T. Tyldesley departs, leaving 'Plum' Warner to score 132 not out during England's second innings of the First Test at Old Wanderers, February 1899.

eleven and, in one innings, the English players, totally inexperienced in such barbarous playing conditions, registered the tour's lowest score – 22 all out! – but immediately recovered.'

Clearly there were more bumpers than the historian suggests!

Such were the beginnings of the Old Wanderers. Most of its early history was to be a tale of turmoil and tragedy as much as anything. The first Test to be played there in 1896 coincided with the Jameson Raid plus a railway disaster. 'The whole of the Wanderers Hall which was our pavilion, stank of iodoform and was full of wounded,' Lord Hawke remembered. Not surprisingly, the South Africans lost by an innings. George Lohmann, who was later to die at a young age in South Africa and is buried in the Cape Karoo, returned the remarkable figures of 8 wickets for 7 runs.

Circumstances were rather better when Lord Hawke returned to Johannesburg in 1899 on his second tour. The South Africans put up a rather better show and in fact only went down by 33 runs.

A few comments on the Wanderers ground at that time seem appropriate. Plum Warner, a young man on that tour, recollects: 'The Wanderers ground is the fastest run-getting ground I know. There is not a blade of grass anywhere, the colour of the soil being a reddish-brown. The wicket is exceptionally fast and the ball simply "fizzes" to the boundary when hit. The fielding ground is as level as a billiards table and although the ball comes very fast, it always comes true.'

In addition to the strange outfield, the touring sides, of course, also had to cope with South African matting pitches. It was also the era that saw the introduction of the famous quartet of googly bowlers – Faulkner, Vogler, Schwarz and White – who provided the country's first golden era.

Warner brought the first MCC team to South Africa in 1905 and Transvaal achieved the distinction on 26–28 December of that year of becoming the first local side to win against touring opposition. The margin was a convincing 60 runs with Schwarz having a match return of 9 for 114 and Faulkner 6 for 108. Not surprisingly, the South African team for the First Test at the Wanderers was a virtual Transvaal line-up with eight members from the Wanderers and two from Pirates.

This match, played on 2–4 January 1906, must surely be the most memorable encounter at the Old Wanderers. The Springboks won by one wicket thanks to an heroic last-wicket stand of 45 between the giant Dave Nourse (he could apparently hold a soccer ball in one hand) and his captain, Percy Sherwell.

The winning hit came from a full toss bowled to Sherwell by Bert Relf. 'As soon as I saw the full toss bowled and that our skipper had hit it,' remembered Nourse, 'I started to run but never saw the ball after it left the bat. It seemed lost in an immense crowd that swept over the ground. I

The lunch interval at Old Wanderers during the Third Test against England, 1905–06. South Africa went on to record their third win of the series.

don't think the ball ever reached the boundary . . . I had made a rush in the opposite direction towards the tennis courts but was barricaded in by the crowd and shouldered into the pavilion. They took off my pads and gloves, took my bat and everything and I cannot say how pleased I was when they at last let me down on firm earth again.'

So it is not only modern crowds who behave in this fashion.

The other great match at the Old Wanderers must surely have been the first Test match played there on a turf pitch. It was the only Test of that 1935–36 tour that the mighty Australians under Vic Richardson – Don Bradman never toured South Africa – failed to win, and it took the intervention of the weather to stop them.

The Springboks looked as though they had earned the safety of a draw when Dudley Nourse made a then record score of 231 in the South African second innings to set the Australians a victory target of 399. But the South Africans had not allowed for the brilliance of Stan McCabe, who was unbeaten on 189 when the match was washed out at 274 for 2 with the Australians having both wickets and time in hand.

The Old Wanderers was to be included in only one more Test series – that in 1938–39 made famous by Durban's Timeless Test. After the Second World War the goverment expropriated the ground for the building of a new railway station, in spite of the fact that the original lease in 1888 had been for 99 years. The club took the matter to court twice to no avail – they lost the appeal on a 3–2 vote – and it was with a heavy heart that Johannesburg had to find fresh cricket head-quarters. The Wanderers, being in the centre of Johannesburg, was very much the centre of the whole community and it was seriously said that the controversy cost the United Party the 1948 election.

Fortunately the club had decided previously – in 1936 – that Wanderers was outgrowing its facilities and property was purchased in the northern suburbs to allow for the club to have town and country sections. This new ground, to become known as Kent Park, was to become the venue for the new Wanderers and South Africa's last cricket stadium was built here in time for the MCC tour of 1956–57. Meantime, Test cricket had to be played elsewhere and the rugby headquarters of Ellis Park came to the rescue – a gesture that was to be reciprocated in 1980 when Ellis Park was being rebuilt and Test match rugby was played at the Wanderers Stadium.

New Wanderers has been the setting for some magnificent sporting moments. In its first inter-national season it witnessed an inspired spell of bowling by off-spinner Hugh Tayfield, who took nine wickets in an innings and took the catch for the tenth wicket, thus having a hand in every dismissal in the innings.

Aerial views of (top) Old Wanderers, shortly before it was demolished to make way for Johannesburg's main railway station; and (bottom) the newly built Wanderers Stadium at the time of its first Test in 1956–57. The segregated stands are clearly visible.

But perhaps pride of place must go not to a Test match but to a match involving Transvaal. That was the 1966 fixture against Bobby Simpson's touring Australians. It was a match that made a young Transvaal captain by the name of Ali Bacher famous. He scored a double-century, took an unbelievable catch at short cover to dismiss the hard-hitting Bob Cowper and, above all, was responsible for the first defeat of any Australian side on South African soil.

The first Test match of that series that followed was equally memorable. The Springboks made a dreadful mess of their first innings after winning the toss and were bowled out for 199. The Australians led by 126 but the South Africans then made one of the most remarkable fightbacks in the game's history, scoring a record 620 in their second innings and going on to win by 233 runs. Denis Lindsay, who was to become the scourge of the Australians with three centuries in that series, made 182, Graeme Pollock made 90 – described as the finest non-century ever by a South African batsman – and veteran Trevor Goddard finished things off with six wickets in Australia's second innings.

Sadly, the Wanderers are faced with yet another crisis. The ground has simply become too expensive for the club to maintain on its own and the Johannesburg City Council has been tardy indeed in supplying any financial assistance. The Transvaal Cricket Council, anxious to preserve its headquarters, put in a bid to buy the Wanderers Stadium, an offer which has been matched by the city council. At the time of writing, it is likely that this latter offer will be favourably received by the club.

The cost of having to build a new Wanderers Stadium would be staggering and a great deal of money has already gone into upgrading the current facilities and building lucrative sponsors' bays. What is now needed is a fresh injection of cash to upgrade the facilities for the general public. Most of the seating is exposed to the unforgiving South African sun and has never been replaced or repaired in the ground's 30-year history. In an era when followers of the game are accustomed to watching cricket on television from the comfort of their armchairs, the Transvaal Cricket Council have a task on their hands to provide a modern, upgraded Wanderers.

Johannesburg				
Ref/No	Season	V	T	Result
Old Wanderers				
48/1	1895–96	E	2	E-I&197
58/2	1898–99	E	1	E-32
75/3	1902–03	A	1	Draw
76/4			2	A-159
88/5	1905–06	E	1	SA-1w
89/6			2	SA-9w
90/7			3	SA-243
106/8	1909–10	E	1	SA-19
108/9			3	E-3w
131/10	1913–14	E	2	E-I&12
132/11			3	E-91
146/12	1921–22	A	2	Draw
148/13	1922–23	E	1	SA-168
151/14			4	Draw
168/15	1927–28	E	1	E-10w
171/16			4	SA-4w
204/17	1930–31	E	1	SA-28
207/18			4	Draw
248/19	1935–36	A	2	Draw
250/20			4	A-I&184
267/21	1938–39	E	1	Draw
270/22			4	Draw
Ellis Park				
310/23	1948–49	E	2	Draw
312/24			4	Draw
318/25	1949–50	A	1	A-I&85
321/26			4	Draw
378/27	1953–54	NZ	2	SA-132
380/28			4	SA-9w
Wanderers Stadium				
434/29	1956–57	E	1	E-131
437/30			4	SA-17
444/31	1957–58	A	1	Draw
447/32			4	A-10w
521/33	1961–62	NZ	2	Draw
523/34			4	SA-I&51
572/35	1964–65	E	2	Draw
574/36			4	Draw
613/37	1966–67	A	1	SA-233
616/38			4	Draw
672/39	1969–70	A	3	SA-307

South Africa: P 39, W 13, D 15, L 11

Port Elizabeth

ST GEORGE'S PARK

St George's Park, home of the Port Elizabeth Cricket Club and the Crusaders Football Club, is unique in South African sports history for it was here that both the first cricket Test and the first rugby international in South Africa were held, cricket in 1889 preceding rugby by two years.

The first Test is a slight misnomer in that the match lasted less than two days, England winning comfortably by eight wickets midway through the last session of the day. The England team was also of no more than county strength. Nevertheless a start had to be made somewhere and a significant feature of the tour was that the two Test matches were the only two games in which the home side was restricted to 11 players. In other tour matches anything up to 22 players were put in the field by the provinces with no side being smaller than 15.

After such a significant contribution to the early history of South African cricket, it is surprising that St George's Park has only seen a total of 12 Test matches. After 1889, Port Elizabeth featured on Lord Hawke's first tour in 1896 and on the last tour before the First World War.

It was not until George Mann brought his England side to South Africa in 1948–49 that St George's Park again saw 'active service', but thereafter it was happily restored to the international circuit, taking over one of the two matches that had previously been granted to Kingsmead for five-match series. The Springboks had to wait almost another ten years for the visit of Peter May's England team in 1956–57 before a Test match was finally won at St George's Park. And it was a fairly narrowly run thing with the Springboks winning by 58 runs to square the series following another epic bowling performance by Hugh Tayfield who finished the second innings with figures of 6 for 78.

However, the arrival of Graeme Pollock on the Port Elizabeth scene undoubtedly helped to make St George's Park a far happier hunting ground. Pollock scored centuries in two of the three Tests he played on his home ground and, in the last two against some fairly weary Australians, the Springboks scored two big victories.

Although it fell into the realm of unofficial Test cricket, it is important to record that Pollock's last innings for the Springboks was also against an Australian side on his home ground and he duly rounded off a brilliant career with a century at the age of 42 against bowlers of Test standard almost half his age.

St George's Park has never had the beauty, charm or grace that one comes across at the great

Above St George's Park from the air in 1964.

Opposite page Cheering crowds invade the pitch at St George's Park to celebrate South Africa's win over Australia in the final Test of 1966–67.

cricket grounds. And this can largely be put down to the fact that it has, for a long time, had to double up as an international cricket and rugby ground. International rugby only moved from St George's Park in 1955 and the main concrete stand there, built after the First World War, belongs to a rugby rather than a cricket atmosphere.

In spite of the fact that Port Elizabeth has suffered severe economic hardships in the isolation period, the Eastern Province Cricket Union has done a remarkable job in modernizing and upgrading the ground. The electronic scoreboard is as efficient as anything in the country and a new three-storey block of sponsors' hospitality suites, including proper accommodation for the players, was built to mark the centenary of Test match cricket. St George's Park is also the proud possessor of the only indoor cricket facility at any of

the Test match venues.

Further redevelopment of the public seating is planned but that, to a large extent, will depend on the return of Test cricket to provide the necessary funds.

Port Elizabeth

Ref/No	Season	V	T	Result
31/1	1888–89	E	1	E-8w
47/2	1895–96	E	1	E-288
134/3	1913–14	E	5	E-10w
313/4	1948–49	E	5	E-3w
322/5	1949–50	A	5	A-1&259
381/6	1953–54	NZ	5	SA-5w
438/7	1956–57	E	5	SA-58
448/8	1957–58	A	5	A-8w
524/9	1961–62	NZ	5	NZ-40
575/10	1964–65	E	5	Draw
617/11	1966–67	A	5	SA-7w
673/12	1969–70	A	4	SA-323

South Africa: P 12, W 4, D 1, L 7

Sri Lanka's first-ever Test in progress at Colombo's P. Saravanamuttu Stadium in
February 1982, with England in the field.

Opposite Colombo's famous scoreboard recording the final
day's play of Sri Lanka's inaugural Test. Don Bradman,
writing about a match he played there in 1948, considered
that in some respects the scoreboard gave 'more
information than any board in the world – a tribute to local
enthusiasm'.

Sri Lanka

MAHINDA WIJESINGHE

Colombo is the only city in the world with three Test grounds in regular use: the P. Saravanamuttu Stadium (formerly the Colombo Oval), the Sinhalese Sports Club grounds and the Colombo Cricket Club grounds, the last two named lying adjacent to each other at Maitland Place. Another ground – the Khettarama Stadium – is waiting in the wings, with probably the best facilities. The fourth Test ground in Sri Lanka is some 70 miles from Colombo in the former hill-capital of the country, Kandy. It is the most picturesque of the lot, overlooking a majestic range of mountains.

Of the 29 Tests played by Sri Lanka since being awarded full membership of the ICC in 1981, 12 have been staged at home. Sri Lanka played her first Test, against England, in February 1982 at the P. Saravanamuttu Stadium and registered the first of her two Test victories, at the same ground, $3\frac{1}{2}$ years and 13 Tests later. This win, against India, also sealed a series win. Overall, 16 losses in 29 Tests is a gory track record, particularly as the West Indies are yet to be played.

Colombo

P. SARAVANAMUTTU STADIUM (COLOMBO OVAL)
SINHALESE SPORTS CLUB GROUND
COLOMBO CRICKET CLUB GROUND

The P. Saravanamuttu Stadium, home ground of the Tamil Union club, is located in a marshy area of Colombo known as Wanathamulla and can hold some 18,000 spectators. Ceremonially opened in January 1940, the Colombo Oval – as it was first known – dwarfed all other grounds in size and facilities. Its lush and level outfield, true and fast square, comfortable accommodation for players and spectators and massive ivy-covered scoreboard made it the pride of Ceylon. In 1976 the ground was renamed in honour of the man behind this great enterprise, Paramjoti Saravanamuttu (1892–1950), president of the Ceylon Cricket Association (1937–49) and first president of its successor, the Board of Control for Cricket in Sri Lanka. In 1982, in time for Sri Lanka's first Test, the covered stands occupying the western half of the ground were augmented by a two-tiered structure to accommodate the media and 3000 spectators.

Until recently, the renowned square – a fast bowler's dream – was maintained by a woman, first by Mariamma and then by her kinswoman Innasiamma. It was a great tribute to their expertise that bowlers of the calibre of Keith Miller and Frank Tyson extolled the virtues of the pitch. Steeped in tradition, the ground has been hallowed by the likes of Don Bradman Len Hutton, the three Ws (Frank Worrell made an unforgettable 285 runs, his highest overseas score, for a Commonwealth XI in 1951), Garfield Sobers, Sunil Gavaskar and Sri Lanka's own maestro, Mahadeva Sathasivam.

The second Test venue in Colombo – the grounds of the Sinhalese Sports Club – could rightly be termed the Lord's of Sri Lanka, for on this spacious ground is located the Board of Control headquarters. The ground has hosted two Tests, in the first of which Sri Lanka drew with New Zealand after the latter had scored only 117 runs on the final day. The match included a dazzling century by Roy Dias.

The ground is built on an old aerodrome. The club moved there from nearby Victoria Park and in their first match there on 19 October 1952 they played their rivals 'across the fence', the Non-descripts – who in turn are separated by the width of Maitland Place from the grounds of the Colombo Cricket Club, Colombo's third Test venue.

The pavilion of the SSC has been extended and improved upon to meet Test requirements, the outfield is well maintained, and the square is worthy of the claim that this is indeed the centre of Sri Lankan cricket. Other facilities are adequate but for the big occasion most of the capacity 20,000 spectators are accommodated in temporary sheds. Given the approach to the ground, its parking facilities and size and location, it has the edge over Colombo's other Test venues and with the backing of its membership – the majority of whom come from the more affluent sectors of Sri Lankan society – further development of the site could raise the capacity to about 40,000, half of them under covered stands.

The Colombo Cricket Club, the oldest cricket club in Sri Lanka, was formed by 'the merchant sportsmen of Colombo' in July 1863. It has occupied the same grounds since its origins, and until a few decades ago membership was restricted to foreign nationals.

It was on this ground in March 1986 that Sri Lanka beat Pakistan by 8 wickets in a controversy-riddled Test – and series. A year later Sri Lanka drew the First Test against New Zealand, after which the latter's tour was aborted due to the unsettled conditions in the country. In this last home Test, Brendon Kuruppu – on his Test debut – became the first Sri Lankan to score a double century when he crawled to an unbeaten 201 in 776 minutes, the third-longest innings in Test cricket.

Despite a well-manicured outfield and excellent pitches, the pavilion is small and the ground capacity could never exceed 10,000. With the Khettarama Stadium waiting in the wings, this historic ground's days as a Test venue are surely numbered.

Colombo				
Ref/No	*Season*	*V*	*T*	*Result*
P. Saravanamuttu Stadium (Colombo Oval)				
921/1	1981–82	E	–	E-7w
1024/5	1985–86	I	2	SL-149
1045/7	1985–86	P	3	Draw
–	1986–87	NZ	3	Cancelled
Sinhalese Sports Club Ground				
987/2	1983–84	NZ	2	Draw
1023/4	1985–86	I	1	Draw
Colombo Cricket Club Ground				
988/3	1983–84	NZ	3	NZ-I&61
1044/6	1985–86	P	2	SL-8w
1074/8	1986–87	NZ	1	Draw

Sri Lanka: P 8, W 2, D 4, L 2

1986–87 Third Test against New Zealand cancelled and excluded from records.

Kandy
ASGIRIYA STADIUM

The redeveloped and relandscaped playing fields of Trinity College, Kandy, became the 54th Test ground in April 1983 when it hosted the inaugural Test between Australia and Sri Lanka. The original playing fields were the inspiration of the principal of the school, Reverend A.G. Fraser, and were created by practically 'disembowelling' a hill. The first match took place on 15 January 1915, and over the years the ground and modest pavilion were to be graced by such legendary figures as Jack Hobbs, Learie Constantine, Vijay Merchant and Lindsay Hassett.

That this compact, historic school ground should be turned into a Test venue is in no small part due to Hon. Gamini Dissanayake, president during much of the 1980s of the Board of Control and, importantly, an old boy of Trinity College. Over the years a dream began to materialize and neither men, money nor materials were spared in the hectic effort to transform the ground. Heavy machinery and experts toiled for some 30 days bringing down the level of the ground by 10 feet to accommodate $7\frac{1}{2}$ acres of playing field; the square was relaid with loving care; and the massive cantilevered pavilion, new scoreboard and sightscreens were constructed in only a few months.

The ground, though relandscaped and redesigned, does not have comfortable spectator facilities for more than 10,000. But this compact, historic school playground now converted to a Test arena has had its moments. In the second of its four Tests, the First against New Zealand in 1983–84, Arjuna Ranatunga scored 51 out of 97, the lowest completed innings total in a Test where an individual fifty was registered. In the first innings, not only did Sri Lanka register their record last-wicket

Kandy's picturesque Asgiriya Stadium, redeveloped to accommodate Test cricket but retaining the old pavilion on the right of the picture.

partnership (60), but Jayantha Amerasinghe, batting at number 11 on his Test debut, top-scored in the innings.

These may be small mercies. But the proud Kandyan always has the Asgiriya grounds next to his heart and it is a tribute to the tradition-bound Trinitian that the original pavilion built in 1915, with the first donation by English army captain Ashley Arbuthnot, of £100, and named in his honour, was not demolished during the modernization programme. Sad to think that Arbuthnot died of wounds received in France on 15 May 1915 – exactly four months after the ground was ceremonially opened.

Kandy				
Ref/No	*Season*	*V*	*T*	*Result*
956/1	1982–83	A	–	A-I & 38
986/2	1983–84	NZ	1	NZ-165
1025/3	1985–86	I	3	Draw
1043/4	1985–86	P	1	P-I & 20
–	1986–87	NZ	2	Cancelled

Sri Lanka: P 4, W 0, D 1, L 3

1986–87 Test cancelled and excluded from records.

Trinidad's Queen's Park Oval, by universal consensus one of cricket's most beautiful settings.

West Indies

TONY COZIER

Although the West Indies were not granted official Test status until 1928 and the first official Test series in the Caribbean was not until 1930, West Indies cricket was established as early as 1865 when the first inter-territorial match, between Barbados and Demerara, was staged at the Garrison Savannah in Barbados. Combined West Indies teams made overseas tours from as early as 1886, when George Wyatt, of the Georgetown Cricket Club, raised a team to tour North America, while the first West Indies team to tour England in 1900 established a pattern that has been unbroken and became stronger through the years. But, more than anything else, the frequent visits to the region of English teams of increasing strengths established West Indies cricket and ensured that it reached the requisite standard to compete internationally.

While the first official Test was not until 1930, West Indians looked on earlier visits, and certainly that of the MCC in 1926, as tantamount to Test status. So, by the time the first MCC team officially representative of England arrived in 1930, the infrastructure was well in place for the staging of a Test series. The main territories and the main grounds had long since been determined – Kensington Oval in Barbados, Bourda Oval in Guyana, Sabina Park in Jamaica and Queen's Park Oval in Trinidad. All were developed and were under the control, either leased or fully owned, of private clubs. It is a system which, with a few small, but significant, alterations remains the same.

These were grounds used, under an arrangement with the recently established West Indies Cricket Board of Control (WICBC), for the inaugural series of four Tests in 1930. Kensington Oval was the venue for the first official Test on West Indian soil, mainly because of its geographical location since Barbados, as the easternmost island, was the first landfall after a sea voyage of nine or ten days out of England. The island had been the first port of call of all early English teams and has remained that way since, even with the advent of air travel. The Kensington Test started the first three series in the Caribbean, all against England, in 1930, 1935 and 1948 but, while it has hosted the opener more than any other venue, the sequence now depends on more than simply first landfall. Queen's Park, Sabina and Bourda have all been first Test venues and no set sequence has evolved.

Although the early English teams did tour extensively, including most of the Windward and Leeward Islands on their schedules, the practice was stopped by the time Arthur Somerset brought the first MCC team in 1911 and the smaller islands were kept out of the mainstream of West Indies cricket until the introduction of a regular, annual domestic tournament for the Shell Shield in 1966. So immediate was the impact of their players that their demand to be included on the rota of Test grounds could not be denied and, on 27 March 1981, the Antigua Recreation Ground, in the heart of the Antiguan capital, St John's, became the West Indies' fifth and newest Test ground with England as the touring team.

The number of Tests, and their length, has varied over the years. The first three series, all involving England, contained four Tests. When a fifth Test was added for later series, and became the norm, Queen's Park or Sabina was given the additional match prior to the introduction of Antigua. India played only four Tests on their tours of 1976 and 1989 as did New Zealand in 1985 while the briefest series has been Pakistan's in 1988, of only three. In 1981, England had their schedule truncated when the second of their scheduled five Tests was cancelled because of Guyana's decision to debar Robin Jackman from entry because of his contacts with South Africa.

Nor has the duration of matches been constant. While those in the inaugural 1930 series were of five days each – and the last actually continued for nine in an inconclusive attempt at a finish – those of 1935 were reduced to four, 1948 increased to five again and between 1953 and 1965 to six, each of five and a half hours each. Since 1968, they have been standardized at five of six hours each although there has been the occasional arrangement by which the final Test is increased by an extra day if the series has not yet been decided.

In organizing Test tours, the WICBC is beset with problems peculiar to the vast region it oversees, from Guyana on the South American mainland, $6\frac{1}{2}$ degrees north of the equator, to Kingston, 18 degrees north. Weather patterns vary greatly between the two and Bourda has been hard hit by its equatorial climate over the years. Its driest months are October and November but that is when it is usually pouring elsewhere in the West Indies.

There are also unique problems of communication, of finance – and of politics. Georgetown is 1400 miles to the south east of Kingston, as the crow flies, and, on England's 1935 tour, when travel was done by ship, the Third Test ended at Bourda on 18 February and England did not get to Kingston for their next match against the island team until 5 March, two weeks later! Even now, with jet travel, contact between the islands can be unreliable and the only daily flight from Port-of-Spain to Kingston takes five hours, minimum.

With separate governments in control of each of its member territories, and each with its own customs regulations and currencies of different values, the WICBC finds itself entwined in bureaucratic red tape organizing its matches, whether at domestic or international level. When the Guyana government decided, unexpectedly, to debar Jackman in 1981, it required a meeting of the foreign ministers of five relevant governments to determine that England's tour would continue.

With small populations, depressed economies and the fact that the cricket season coincides with the high-priced tourist season, home Test series, almost invariably, incur financial losses. In spite of generous sponsorship from the Benson & Hedges company and, since 1988, Cable & Wireless plc, the last home series to return a reasonable profit was that against India in 1971. The WICBC estimated losses of approximately £120,000 on England's 1989 tour.

As elsewhere, attendances for Tests at all venues have diminished in favour of one-day internationals. But interest remains high and crowds, at every venue, knowledgeable and volatile.

Bridgetown, Barbados

KENSINGTON OVAL

Among West Indian cricket grounds, Kensington Oval boasts three everlasting records. It was the first to host an English touring team, under R. Slade Lucas in 1895, the first venue of a match between a combined West Indies team and an official MCC side in the West Indies, under A. F. Somerset in 1911, and the scene of the first Test in the West Indies, against England, in 1930.

The explanation for such a sequence goes no deeper than the fact that Barbados is the easternmost West Indian island and was, therefore, the first landfall for ships out of England in those days. So Barbados, and Kensington, formed the first impression those pioneers had of the Caribbean and they usually encountered strong competition and ideal conditions.

The ground has been the home of the Pickwick Cricket Club since its formation in 1882 although it has never owned it. It first rented as its ground a pasture on Kensington Plantation, a mile north of Bridgetown, within quarter-mile of the coastline, from its owner, Foster Alleyne, at the nominal fee of a penny a year, soon converting it into the finest cricket ground in the island. Previously, inter-island matches had been played at the Garrison Savannah and at the Wanderers Club ground, to the south of Bridgetown, but it was at Kensington that Barbados met Lucas's team and at Kensington that all inter-territorial and international matches have since been played.

Cricket had long since become firmly established as the national game by the time Lucas's men arrived and, according to the report of the opening day of the first match in the *Agricultural Reporter*: 'The stands which were erected on the northern, western and southern sides of the ground were crowded at an early hour while the trees in the

---

Kensington Oval during one of the two matches played by Barbados against R. S. Lucas's team during their 1894–95 tour of the West Indies.

immediate vicinity were taken advantage of by a large number of the great unwashed.' As the ground, and the island, developed over the years, the trees (and the great unwashed) have largely disappeared and surrounding Fontabelle has been transformed from residential suburb to business district.

Ownership of the ground changed hands in 1914 when its four acres, three roods and ten perches was bought at public auction for £250 by a group on behalf of the Barbados Cricket Committee, an amalgamation of cricket clubs which then administered the game in the island until it was superceded in 1933 by the Barbados Cricket Association. The trustees have leased, and re-leased, the ground to Pickwick under certain agreements ever since, the present lease expiring in 2004. More and more land has been purchased for expansion so that the area now covers approximately seven acres, the playing area itself large enough to accommodate boundaries of at least 70 yards all round.

The Association has responsibility for the upkeep and development of the stands and first call on the use of ground for inter-territorial and international matches so that Pickwick's use of its facilities has been more and more limited and the club is unlikely to seek renewal of the lease when it expires.

The early wooden stands remained intact, with few occasional additions and alterations, until all were destroyed by two fires of suspicious origins in 1944. In the 45 years since, Kensington has been transfigured by the construction of several new stands and the expansion of others.

Following the 1944 fire, a new Pickwick Club pavilion, that also accommodated players' dressing-rooms, was constructed on the previous site at the northern end, a stone, rather than wooden, building. Another new stand, the Kensington Stand, spanning the western boundary and with an official capacity of 1200 but, more often than not, packed with double that number, was built at the same time as was a wall sightscreen at the southern end. Soon afterwards, public subscription raised the money to construct the George Challenor Stand following the death, in 1947, of the first great Barbadian batsman. It was opened just in time for the first Test after the war, against England, early in 1948. Located next to the Pickwick pavilion, and confined to BCA members, it incorporates a large, wall sightscreen and more recent additions include a third storey accommodating radio and television facilities and an airy President's Lounge.

New stands were added with time, some to be pulled down and themselves replaced. The Pickwick Club pavilion, the Challenor and the Kensington Stands remain intact, the Kensington extended the full length of the western boundary with the addition named after a long-serving BCA president, Eric Inniss, who died in 1973. But they no longer dominate the ground as imposing, modern stands have gone up at the northern end since the 1970s, all named in honour of the island's greatest players.

The first was the Worrell, Weekes and Walcott Stand, or simply the Three Ws Stand, a double-storied steel and concrete structure that also houses offices for the Barbados Cricket Association and the West Indies Cricket Board of Control. Financed mainly by the sale of seats, guaranteed for 25 years, at BD$400 each, it was opened in time for the 1981 Test against England and has since been supplemented by a small annexe to the east.

Profits from a highly successful lottery run by the BCA funded both the Sir Garfield Sobers Pavilion (honouring the left-handed Barbadian, generally regarded as the finest all-round cricketer of all time, who opened it himself) and the Hall and Griffith

The First Test between the West Indies and England at Kensington Oval, January 1948. On the right of the photograph at the northern end is the George Challenor Stand, doubling as sightscreen, with the smaller Pickwick Club pavilion to its left.

Stand, named after the feared fast bowling pair, who were also there for the opening.

The Sobers Pavilion offers spacious, well-appointed dressing-room and dining facilities to the players with seating for members on its top deck; the Hall and Griffith includes a dozen plush executive boxes on the middle of its three levels.

The Barbados Cricket Association, giving full vent to the policy of paying tangible tribute to the heroes who contributed to the legend that Kensington has become, installed elaborate new gates to the public car park in the 1980s, naming one the Herman C. Griffith Gate for an imposing individual whose fast bowling and personality made him a legend in his time, and the other the John D. Goddard Gate after the captain who led the West Indies on their first successful Test series in England in 1950, who was also a long-serving Barbados and Pickwick captain.

The wooden stands that these have replaced have been moved on to open areas at the southern end so that Kensington can now accommodate, in relative comfort, 15,000 spectators, although it has occasionally crammed in more. A large percentage of these in recent times have been visitors, attracted by Barbados's reputation as a vacation resort and a cricket centre. Over 5000 tourists from Britain alone came on package tours for England's 1986 Kensington Test. Their red faces were caused as much by the sun as their team's performance.

For most of its life, Kensington has been renowned for the quality of its pitches, except for those occasions, prior to mandatory covering, when they were affected by rain and became wickedly unplayable. At their best, they are even in bounce and pace, generally favouring batsmen but never completely discouraging bowlers of either pace or spin. There may have been times when the balance has been too one-sided, one way or the other, but the proof of the pudding is in the eating and the multitude of great players the island has produced, almost exclusively batsmen and fast bowlers, have been nurtured in Kensington's encouraging environment.

The effect of wet (left) and dry (right) wickets at
Kensington Oval in January 1926 when the MCC tourists
first lost heavily to Barbados then scored handsomely in
the drawn match against a West Indies XI.

There have been Test batting records in abun-
dance. Even before the initial Test of 1930, batsmen
had flourished there. The Barbados opener, Tim
Tarilton, recorded the first triple-century in the
West Indies against Trinidad in 1920 and Barbados
passed 700 twice in successive matches, against
British Guiana and Trinidad, in the 1927 inter-
colonial tournament. On the MCC's 1926 tour,
Wally Hammond followed his 281 not out against
Barbados with an unbeaten 238 against a West
Indies XI and, four years later, Patsy Hendren
emulated the feat with two unbeaten doubles
against Barbados in the match preceding the Test.

Kensington ran true to form for that historic
debut Test, a tame and high-scoring draw in which
opener Clifford Roach became the first West Indies
century-maker in Test cricket with a belligerent
122 and the great George Headley launched his
fabulous career with a second innings 176 in his

debut match, aged 20 years 230 days – still the
youngest West Indian to reach the mark.

When England returned five years later,
however, the story was far different, rain creating
a muddy monster of the previously placid surface
that led to one of the most bizarre Test matches
ever played. The West Indies' 102 was the highest
total and, after two gambling declarations, England
reached the 73 they were set to win for the loss of
six wickets. It is the one and only defeat ever
suffered by the West Indies at Kensington in its 25
Tests. Between 1978 and 1989, when the character
of the pitch was changed with more grass left in
preparation, the West Indies, with their traditional
strengths of fast bowling and attacking batting,
have won eight out of eight, a record unmatched
by any other team on any other ground.

Up until that time, there were several monumental batting feats which, for sheer endurance
and concentration, are unmatched in the history of
the game.

In 1955, after Australia had reached Kensington's highest Test total of 668 with centuries
from Keith Miller and Ray Lindwall, West Indies
captain Denis Atkinson and wicket-keeper Claire-

monte Depeiza, two Barbadians, came together on the third afternoon at 147 for 6 and were not separated until the fifth morning, having added 347 for the seventh wicket, still an overall record for all matches. Atkinson's 219 was his only Test century, Depeiza's 122, his one and only first-class century.

In the next Test at Kensington, in 1958, the first against Pakistan, the little Pakistani opener, Hanif Mohammad, started his team's second innings with a deficit of 573 and remained defiantly for 16 hours 10 minutes in scoring 337, the longest innings ever played at any level and the first of two Test triple-centuries on the ground. The first four Pakistani partnerships in a total of 657 for 8 declared were all over 100, a record as well. Two years later, when Kensington hosted its next Test, bowlers were again reduced to frustrated trundlers by a docile pitch. Sobers, with 226, and Worrell, with an unbeaten 197, batted through two days in a fourth-wicket partnership of 399 in nine hours 39 minutes, the longest on record.

And so it continued. Australia started the Barbados Test of 1965, the fourth, already 2–0 down in the series but, as they did ten years earlier, they passed 600 (650 for 6 declared) as Bill Lawry and captain Bobby Simpson became the only openers in history to score double-centuries in the same Test innings. But Seymour Nurse, before his home crowd, made his maiden Test century a double as well and, for the second successive drawn Australian Test, batsmen scored more than 1600 runs.

No batsman among the many greats who have piled up 54 centuries at Kensington has created the public stir that the stylish Jamaican, Lawrence Rowe, did against England in 1974. The sheer magnetism of his strokeplay in reaching 48 on the second afternoon swelled the crowd so that every inch of the ground was filled, the stands bursting at the seams, informed estimates of the crowd varying

between 18,000 and 20,000. He moved from century, to century, to century, until he finally skied a catch to the deep after batting $10\frac{1}{2}$ hours for 302. Yet the result was another draw, the tenth in 14 Tests at Kensington.

Apart from the freak match of 1935, the only results at Kensington until then had been achieved principally by the West Indies' spinners. Sonny Ramadhin and Alf Valentine shared 13 wickets in a victory by 142 runs over India in 1953, the only decision of the series, and were again dominant with seven first-innings wickets when England managed 128 runs off 114 overs on the Saturday of the 1954 Test and went on to lose by 181 runs.

No bowling in Kensington's history has been as devastating as that which brought India to their knees in 1962. Lance Gibbs's astonishing off-spin spell after lunch on the final day was 15.3 overs, 14 maidens, 8 wickets for 6 runs, his overall 8 for 38 the best by any bowler on the ground. They were nearly matched ten years on by the big New Zealand seam bowler, Bruce Taylor, whose 7 for 74 took advantage of an unusually grassy Kensington pitch to rout the West Indies for 133. By the time they batted a second time, 289 in arrears, the pitch had reverted to type and Sobers and Charlie Davis added 254 for the sixth wicket.

An earlier seven-wicket return had been by an off-spinner destined to become one of the finest of all time, the Englishman, Jim Laker. He was in his debut Test in 1948 and had the scarcely flattering figures of 1 for 78 at the end of the first day when overnight rain softened the uncovered pitch enough for his spin to bite next morning, transforming his figures into 7 for 103.

Spin has not featured much in contests of late. The high-scoring draws of the 1960s and 1970s influenced the ground authorities into a change in pitch preparation, leaving a layer of grass where the previous policy had been to cut it low and roll it, lengthways and crossways, so that it was as hard and bare as concrete. The effect of the new method was to supply more movement for the faster bowlers and the consequence was that the West Indies, but Barbados in particular, produced fast bowlers in even more numbers than in the past. At last, outright results were achieved, eight in succession in West Indies' favour, not simply because they were better equipped with bowlers to utilize the conditions but because they also possessed batsmen who expressed themselves on pitches that were fast and still true.

Australia were beaten in 1978, when they did not have their players contracted to Kerry Packer's World Series Cricket and the West Indies did, and again in 1984; England lost in 1981 and 1986; India in 1983 and 1989; New Zealand in 1985; Pakistan in 1988, if barely. The massive totals of the 1950s and 1960s disappeared so that the West Indies' 509 against Australia in 1984 was the only total in excess of 500 in those eight Tests. Opponents fell for less than 200 six times, Australia for 97 in 1984, New Zealand for 94 the following year in Kensington's lowest Test total when Malcolm Marshall had the only match haul of 11 wickets in a Test on the ground.

Two spells by great fast bowlers in those years have become part of cricketing folklore. In 1978, Australia's Jeff Thomson, without the support of his famous accomplice, Dennis Lillee, and others contracted to Packer, worked himself up to breathtaking speed and hostility in the final hour and a quarter of the second afternoon during which he despatched Gordon Greenidge, Alvin Kallicharran and Vivian Richards and should have had many more. In the 1981 Test, Michael Holding electrified a large crowd with an opening over to Geoffrey Boycott that ended with his off-stump cartwheeling

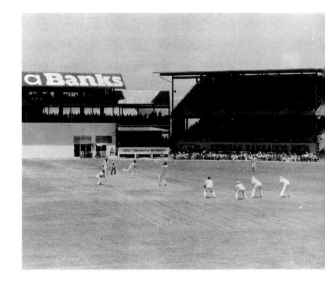

Kensington Oval during the Third Test between the West Indies and England, March 1981, the new Three Ws Stand dominating the scene. The press box is sandwiched between it and the George Challenor Stand.

out of the ground and will be talked of by all those who saw it for as long as they are *compos mentis*.

These have been among the countless moments for the Barbadian crowds to savour. Nowhere is cricket more avidly followed or discussed, nowhere does it command such a revered place in society. Barbadians are proud of their many great players, two of whom, Sir Frank Worrell and Sir Garry Sobers, have been knighted, just as they are proud of the fact that Barbados has won more West Indian championships than all the other territories put together and that it has given the West Indies more Test players than any of its neighbours.

Because they are an altogether more conservative, less cosmopolitan people than the rest of the Caribbean and treat their national sport so seriously, Barbadian crowds tend to lack the wit and spontaneity of those at other Test grounds. But there is none fairer nor more knowledgeable.

As elsewhere in the West Indies, they have disrupted the cricket with riotous bottle-throwing but, significantly, only once and never in 'official' cricket. The only time a match was halted by a Kensington riot it was part of the Packer World Series Cricket tour of the West Indies which, although widely supported in its concept, was still regarded with some scepticism.

And Kensington does have character – as well as its 'character', Redvers Dundonald Dyal, known universally (for he has travelled to England, and throughout the Caribbean for Test cricket) as 'King Dyal'. The King, surely now into his mid-70s, has never been known to miss a major day's cricket at Kensington, regaling the occasion with a variety of brightly coloured suits which he leaves the ground to change at every interval, returning to his acknowledged seat in the front of the Kensington Stand in a different ensemble to animated applause, or abuse – since he invariably supports the opposing team.

Over the years, he has gained minimal satisfaction in that regard although he does claim to have been there as a boy when the West Indies were beaten at Kensington, for the one and only time, by England. But that was a long, long time ago.

Only twice since have they come close to losing again, each time against Pakistan and each time they just managed to wriggle out of defeat. In 1977, their last two wickets held on for an hour and 35 minutes to clinch a draw; in 1988, the ninth-wicket pair, Jeffrey Dujon and Winston Benjamin, added 61 unbroken to secure victory by two wickets amidst such tension that the Pakistani leg-spinner, Abdul Qadir, stepped across the boundary to accost a spectator who was heckling him after two confident appeals had been turned down.

Kensington, as with the other Test venues of the West Indies, was the centre for all sport, and much cultural activity as well, for most of its life until the National Stadium was opened in 1971. Its hallowed turf has hosted international soccer, track and field, cycling and, even, a Davis Cup tennis tie between the USA and the West Indies in 1962. Louis Armstrong and Ella Fitzgerald performed there, calypso singers and local beauties competed for national titles, church and youth rallies were, and still are, conducted there. But it was for cricket that the Pickwick Club cleared Mr Alleyne's overgrown pasture at Kensington Plantation more than a century ago and it is cricket that has remained its main and celebrated purpose ever since.

Bridgetown, Barbados				
Ref/No	Season	V	T	Result
190/1	1929–30	E	1	Draw
238/2	1934–35	E	1	E-4w
295/3	1947–48	E	1	Draw
366/4	1952–53	I	2	WI-142
383/5	1953–54	E	2	WI-181
406/6	1954–55	A	4	Draw
449/7	1957–58	P	1	Draw
487/8	1959–60	E	1	Draw
527/9	1961–62	I	3	WI-I & 30
586/10	1964–65	A	4	Draw
630/11	1967–68	E	3	Draw
683/12	1970–71	I	4	Draw
695/13	1971–72	NZ	3	Draw
715/14	1972–73	A	2	Draw
733/15	1973–74	E	3	Draw
773/16	1975–76	I	1	WI-I & 97
798/17	1976–77	P	1	Draw
821/18	1977–78	A	2	WI-9w
897/19	1980–81	E	3	WI-298
952/20	1982–83	I	4	WI-10w
983/21	1983–84	A	3	WI-10w
1015/22	1984–85	NZ	3	WI-10w
1040/23	1985–86	E	3	WI-I & 30
1097/24	1987–88	P	3	WI-2w
1118/25	1988–89	I	2	WI-8w

West Indies: P 25, W 12, D 12, L 1

Georgetown, Guyana

BOURDA

No cricket club in the West Indies is older than the Georgetown Cricket Club (GCC) and none had as pronounced an influence in the formative years of West Indies cricket. Based on minutes of a meeting of the club in 1883, it appears certain the GCC was founded in 1858 from which time, until the formation of the Guyana Cricket Board of Control in 1943, it was responsible for the administration of the game in what was Britain's only colony in South America.

The club arranged the first inter-territorial match in the West Indies, financing and sending a Demerara team to Barbados in 1865, and organized the first West Indies team, led by its own captain, Guy Wyatt, to Canada and the USA in 1886. The next year, it hosted a USA team on a Caribbean tour.

Its home, since 1884, has been Bourda, a rectangular ground located in a southern suburb of the capital, Georgetown. Dominated by an impressive two-storied pavilion, square of the pitch on the western side, it is encircled by wooden stands and hemmed in by the wide canals that form a vital drainage system for a city that is below sea level and needs the protection of a coastal wall from the tidal fluctuations of the Atlantic Ocean. Bourda has been the venue for all 21 Tests staged in Guyana since the first, against England in February 1930, brought the West Indies their initial, historic victory.

Not always located at Bourda, the GCC originally shared the Parade Grounds at Cummingsburg and Eve Leary, elsewhere in the city, with the troops and militia stationed in the colony during the Napoleonic wars and 'with other citizens desirous of playing cricket'. It was on the Parade Grounds that the GCC hosted return

The entrance to the Georgetown Cricket Club at Bourda, below sea level and protected by canals.

matches between Demerara and Barbados in 1865 and the first triangular tournament, also involving Trinidad, in 1876. But the arrangement was unsatisfactory and, by 1884, the club was recording that several matches had to be cancelled because of the 'bad state into which the Parade Ground has lately fallen, owing to the absolute powerlessness of the club to prevent the public from playing even on that small portion of the ground which was formerly considered as entirely set apart for its members and for the keeping of which in proper order it spent nearly two hundred dollars a year.'

When a motion was put before the Town Council to withdraw the GCC's cricketing privileges at the Parade Ground, members decided the club needed a ground of its own. The lease on Bourda was obtained from the colonial government in 1884 and members raised $5000, a sizeable sum in those days, for the erection of a wooden pavilion and to enclose and put the ground in order. The club has continued its lease from government ever since.

Bourda hosted its first match in December 1885 and the ground soon became the envy of the rest of the Caribbean for its flat, immaculately maintained condition and its perfect batting pitch, easy paced and low but predictable bounce, complemented by a fast outfield.

Within a few years, Bourda had become the centre for all major sport in Georgetown. Intercolonial and international cricket have been the major attractions, of course, but, in its time, it has hosted international tennis, track and field, cycling, soccer, rugby, hockey and even quoits and croquet.

With such activity, stands have been progressively added to complement the main members' pavilion which, in keeping with architectural design in Georgetown, a former Dutch possession,

was constructed of wood and raised on stilts as protection against flooding. 'Two large and substantial stands' used for the fireworks exhibition for Queen Victoria's jubilee and the matches against Barbados and the USA team in 1877 were bought by the club, the first to be set aside for the public, and more and more have been opened over the years, the west side now dominated by two expansive double deckers. One bears the name of the sponsors, Shell; the others have been dedicated to outstanding Guyana Test players, Clive Lloyd, Rohan Kanhai and Lance Gibbs, and, in one case, a player and administrator, Kenny Wishart, to whom Bourda was a second home during his time as GCC and Guyana batsman and GCC secretary, later to become secretary of the Guyana and West Indies Cricket Boards.

Groundstaff at Bourda spreading moist palm leaves on the pitch to avoid scorching before MCC's match against a West Indies XI in February 1926.

In 1912, women 'subscribers' – a subtle, if deliberate, distinction from members – were admitted to the club, leading to the construction of a large Ladies' Stand in the south-western corner of the ground, next to the main Pavilion, which has changed little over the years and in which is to be seen during a Test a virtual fashion parade.

Apart from everything else, Bourda, at a latitude of $6\frac{1}{2}$ degrees north, is closer to the equator than any other Test match ground in the world and its weather patterns differ from those of its associates in the Caribbean Sea with which Guyana forms West Indies cricket. Yet it must share the same first-class and Test season from early January through early May, and the West Indies Board schedules its matches there with fingers crossed.

When Guyana hosted the annual inter-colonial cup between 1891 and 1937, it did so in September and October, its driest time. Not surprisingly, more playing days have been lost at Bourda than at any other venue. The 1976 Test against India was switched to Port-of-Spain when the ground was under water for a week, only two days in the India Test of 1989 were played before another deluge set in and caused abandonment. Several other Tests have had time cut while political considerations have caused the loss of three others.

The 1962 Indian team bypassed Guyana because of politically motivated violence between the two major races, those of African descent and those of East Indian, and the England teams of 1981 and 1986 did not play a Test at Bourda because the Guyana Government refused entry to members of the England team with previous South African connections. And Tests have been disrupted for more basic reasons.

When local wicket-keeper Cliff McWatt was run out in the 1954 Test against England, some sections of the crowd reacted by hurling bottles and objects on to the field, halting play for nearly half an hour. It was the first, but certainly not the last, time a West Indies Test was disrupted by irate spectators. Bourda experienced similar, if minor, trouble when local heroes Clive Lloyd was run out against New Zealand in 1972 and Alvin Kallicharran was given out lbw against Pakistan in 1977. These were minor skirmishes compared to the fearful riot that erupted when Kerry Packer's World Series Cricket visited the ground for its so-called Supertest in 1979 and the players incensed a packed crowd by their reluctance to risk fielding on a sodden outfield. The mob pushed down fences, destroyed seats, swarmed the outfield and invaded the pavilion, stealing and destroying cups and trophies and causing over £50,000 damage.

The sparks for such flare-ups were wide and varied – the heat, the packed conditions, the effect of strong Guyana rum, the position of the match and the feeling that a wrong had been done. Betting can also be a powerful catalyst for the volatility. It is perhaps more intense and widespread – and certainly as wide-ranging – at Bourda than anywhere else in the West Indies. It is pertinent that the 1954 mayhem followed the dismissal of McWatt with his partnership with J. K. Holt Jnr worth 99!

The GCC has always been fortunate in the quality and commitment of its groundstaff and its senior groundsman. None served longer, was as dedicated or as famous as Badge Menzies, a short meticulous man of East Indian ancestry whose boast was that not one blade of rogue grass could be found on his beloved Bourda during his time from the mid-1930s to the late 1960s. He was also an umpire at club level and, in one infamous case, drafted in to stand in the 1954 Bourda Test with England when the petulant England captain, Len Hutton, refused to accept the qualified umpires submitted. So Badge supervised ground prepa-

The bottles fly as parts of the crowd react to the run-out of Cliff McWatt in the 1954 Test against England.

ration then donned his white coat to supervise play, fatefully giving the McWatt run-out verdict that sparked the bottle party.

Eleven years later, Bourda was witness to another strange umpiring story for the Test with Australia. When the local umpires' association boycotted the match because only one of its members was chosen, Gerry Gomez, the former West Indies Test all-rounder who was there in his capacity as chairman of the selection panel, was hastily pressed into service as the only one on the spot with the requisite qualifications, even though he had never officiated in a first-class match. Nor did he afterwards even though, unlike Menzies, he was involved in no controversial decisions.

While it is generally accepted that Bourda is a batsman's ground, no clear pattern has emerged in its 21 Tests. It has not been a productive ground for the West Indies whose record is four wins against five defeats with the other 12 drawn and they have not won there since 1965. There have been dull, high-scoring draws yet batsmen have struggled too. Of the 40 Test centuries it has witnessed, only two have been doubles and they have completely contrasted in character.

Clifford Roach's 209 in the West Indies' initial Test victory over England in 1930 was a sparkling exhibition that included three sixes and 23 fours, 122 in 98 minutes after tea on the opening day. Forty-two years later, the New Zealand opener Glenn Turner surpassed that record with 259 that occupied $11\frac{3}{4}$ hours, sharing a partnership of 387 for the first wicket with Terry Jarvis (182) that remains the highest for New Zealand for any wicket in Tests – as does the total of 543 for 3 declared remain the highest in Tests at Bourda.

No one has scored more centuries on the ground than Garry Sobers's five. His two in successive innings against Pakistan were made in a match that yielded 1453 runs and victory for the West Indies who reached a winning target of 317 for the loss of only two wickets. Twenty-seven years earlier, the equally phenomenal George Headley marked his first Bourda Test with a similar feat, 114 in the first innings, 112 in the second against England, a major contribution to the West Indian triumph.

There was no more popular century than Kallicharran's unbeaten 101 against New Zealand in 1972 since it was his Test debut for the little Guyanese from Berbice.

Only two other native Guyanese have managed centuries in Bourda Tests – and they were some time in coming. Rohan Kanhai's 150 against England in 1968, in which he shared a fourth-wicket stand of 250 with Sobers, was 11 years into his Test career. Clive Lloyd's punishing 178 in a losing cause against Australia in 1973 was seven years after his entry into the West Indies team.

The Jamaican opening batsman, Basil Williams, whose attacking style earned him the popular nickname, 'Shotgun', followed Kallicharran's example with a century on debut at Bourda. Yet he would not have played at all but for a dispute with the West Indies Board that led to a pull-out of players contracted to Packer's World Series Cricket on the eve of the match. That match brought Australia's third victory in five Tests at Bourda, their 362 for 7 the third-highest winning Test total.

Only one touring batsman scored two centuries in Bourda Tests, India's Sunil Gavaskar, eulogized in calypso for his West Indian exploits as 'The Real Master', who had scores of 116 and 64 not out in 1971 and 147 not out in 1983, his only three innings.

Only three bowlers, none West Indian, have collected ten or more wickets in a Test in Georgetown, Pakistan's champion all-rounder Imran Khan's 7 for 80 and 4 for 41 supplementing Javed Miandad's 114 to earn his team a comfortable victory in 1988. Neil Hawke's 10 for 115 on one of Bourda's most difficult pitches was in a losing cause for Australia in 1965 when Lance Gibbs, the long-fingered Guyanese off-spinner, scythed through the Australian second innings with 6 for 29 from 22.2 overs to earn a crushing victory. Ten years earlier, another off-spinner, Ian Johnson, had created a collapse in reverse, cleverly exploiting the strong east-west breeze that cools Georgetown on its finest days. His 7 for 44 is still the most emphatic individual bowling performance on the ground.

It was appropriate that while two of the most illustrious of early West Indian players, Roach and Headley, should have set up the first Test victory, at Bourda, with their centuries, another, the dynamic Learie Constantine, should have finished it off with his fast bowling that earned him 4 for 35 in the first innings and 5 for 87 in the second as the West Indies won just in time.

Unquestionably Bourda's most remarkable all-round Test performance came from the game's most remarkable individual. Pilloried by a critical public for a daring declaration that allowed England to win the Fourth Test at Port-of-Spain, in 1968 Sobers came to Georgetown intent on personally rectifying matters in the final and deciding Test. He scored 152 and 95 not out and, bowling a total of 68 overs in all his styles, he collected three wickets in each innings. Gibbs took 6 for 60 from 40 overs on the desperate last day but England held on to draw with the last man, Jeff Jones, somehow blocking the last six balls from Gibbs amidst unbearable tension.

In common with every West Indian, the Guyanese is fanatical about his cricket, interest heightened with visits from India and Pakistani teams for whom there is still a great deal of ethnic support among the large East Indian segment of a population of 750,000 who have given West Indies and Guyana cricket so many of its outstanding players (Kanhai, Kallicharran, Joe Solomon and Faoud Bacchus most prominent among them). Even though expansion of stands has lifted the capacity of Bourda to just over 20,000, from around 10,000 in the 1930s, pressure for space is still great, particularly now for one-day internationals. Because of the size of the country, 83,000 square miles, fans travel great distances to get to Bourda, often queueing from as early as 4 a.m. to gain admission to big matches.

For the more intrepid youngsters, entry has never been a problem. The many trees that surround the corrugated-iron fences provide ideal vantage although brittle branches often snap under the strain and deposit engrossed fans into the murky canals below.

The rich, alluvial soil lends itself to the preparation of perfect pitches and practice nets are prepared and located on the outfield for international teams. Concerned about inadequate drainage that caused so many abandoned days, the entire

Part of the Bourda ground at the time of the cancelled Test of 1981.

outfield was raised six inches in 1987 with tons and tons of soil brought in from the south-east of the country.

Unfortunately, the process coincided with a rare drought and the ground was a cracked, grassless expanse, hard as concrete, for the Pakistan Test of 1988. But the pitch was in its usual order and, by the time the 1989 season came around, grass had sprouted and the outfield began to look its original pristine condition.

It is its pitch and its outfield that has given Bourda its distinctive reputation – and its knowledgeable and involved crowds.

Sir Patrick Rennison, Governor of British Guiana at the time, wrote of Bourda in 1958: 'When I am in retirement ... I know that among my clearest and most pleasant memories will be the hours I have spent in the GCC pavilion watching inter-colonial and Test cricket ... You can feel the ripple of excitement round the crowded stands when a century is coming up and the release of emotion as the century hit is happily applauded.' It is an excitement that has always rung true.

Georgetown, Guyana

Ref/No	Season	V	T	Result
192/1	1929–30	E	3	WI-289
240/2	1934–35	E	3	Draw
297/3	1947–48	E	3	WI-7w
368/4	1952–53	I	4	Draw
384/5	1953–54	E	3	E-9w
405/6	1954–55	A	3	A-8w
452/7	1957–58	P	4	WI-8w
490/8	1959–60	E	4	Draw
585/9	1964–65	A	3	WI-212
632/10	1967–68	E	5	Draw
682/11	1970–71	I	3	Draw
696/12	1971–72	NZ	4	Draw
717/13	1972–73	A	4	A-10w
734/14	1973–74	E	4	Draw
800/15	1976–77	P	3	Draw
822/16	1977–78	A	3	A-3w
–	1980–81	E	2	Cancelled
951/17	1982–83	I	3	Draw
981/18	1983–84	A	1	Draw
1014/19	1984–85	NZ	2	Draw
1095/20	1987–88	P	1	P-9w
1117/21	1988–89	I	1	Draw

West Indies: P 21, W 4, D 12, L 5

1980–81 Test cancelled and excluded from the records.

Kingston, Jamaica

SABINA PARK

Founded in 1863, the Kingston Cricket Club remains the oldest surviving cricket club in the West Indies. But it was not until 1880 that it managed to find a permanent home that was soon to become also the home of international cricket on the island – Sabina Park. Rented from a Mrs Blakely at an annual charge of £27, it was, in the words of the Kingston captain of the time, Frank Lynch, 'a derelict sort of penn'. Another contemporary member, Sir Thomas Roxburgh, described its condition in some detail.

'The field had lignum vitae trees scattered about it and the club had to set to work to cut down the trees and then cut out the roots.' Once the ground was put in some sort of playing order, one tree was left standing under which, according to Sir Thomas, was placed a 'small table ... a bottle of good "Old Jamaica" [rum] and a jug of ice water'

to refresh members after practice. The club's first match at Sabina Park was played on 16 August 1880 against the Army and Navy, the ground, according to the *Gleaner* newspaper, having been 'levelled, drained and turfed according to the most approved methods'.

At the time, a pond extended along the eastern side, limiting the outfield to a size where a boundary counted for three, not four. Soon, however, the pond was filled in and a small pavilion erected by the time Sabina Park hosted the first of its many visiting teams, the Gentlemen of America at the end of an extensive West Indies tour, in January 1888. A second, larger pavilion was opened by the Acting Governor in 1894, in time for the visit the following year of the first English team to the West

---

The northern end at Sabina Park in February 1986 with spectators sheltering under their umbrellas from the sun and the Blue Mountains rising impressively in the distance.

Indies under R. Slade Lucas of Middlesex when All Jamaica beat the visitors by eight wickets, an historic event.

The pavilion, situated square to the pitch on the western side, withstood several hurricanes that swept through Jamaica and also Kingston's great earthquake of 1907. Its size trebled in 1931 after the West Indies had gained Test status and Sabina Park was hosting increasingly more touring cricket, and soccer, teams, mainly from England.

That pavilion withstood the hurricanes of 1903 and 1916 which destroyed the adjacent main Grandstand, a wooden structure, that was rebuilt each time. Other temporary stands were erected for major matches and, in 1946, in preparation for the first MCC visit after the war in 1948, stands were built in the northwest and southwest corners of the ground.

The 1951 hurricane, however, took devastating toll of Jamaica – and of Sabina Park. The pavilion finally succumbed to the fury of the winds as did all the other stands. While the Club itself raised a mortgage to add to its insurance claim to rebuild a new, larger pavilion, with seating accommodation on the roof of the two-storied structure, the government provided a loan for stands to be rebuilt in time for India's first tour of the West Indies in 1953.

Even then, Sabina Park remained cramped and uncomfortable with a capacity of no more than 10,000. With a distance of only 127 yards end to end, its straight boundaries, north-south, were the shortest of any Test ground and fast bowlers with lengthy approaches were within touching distance of the press box that adjoined the southern sightscreen as they reached their mark. It gave the ground the appearance and the atmosphere of a bull-ring, encircled after the reconstruction by a three-deck concrete stand at the northern end and

steeply banked open stands in the south-eastern corner. Pylons for floodlights, erected in 1955 by the government specially for events commemorating Jamaica's 300th anniversary, held the overflow of spectators from the open eastern section, clinging uncomfortably to their precarious perches.

It was this congestion that was undoubtedly a major contributory factor to the two major riots that erupted during Tests in 1968 and 1978. Coincidentally both were sparked by catches by the wicket-keeper with the West Indies faltering, the first against England under Colin Cowdrey, the latter against Australia under Bobby Simpson. On each occasion, the riot squad used teargas, in 1968 an easterly wind blowing it back into the pavilion. Play was abandoned for the day in each case and, while the hour and a quarter lost was made up on an unscheduled sixth day in 1968, attempts to do the same in 1978 were thwarted by umpire Ralph Gosein who ruled there was no such provision in the playing conditions.

Sabina's expansion was stymied by a lack of space. It was located on $5\frac{1}{2}$ acres, owned by the club itself, hemmed in by private residences to the north and south. After protracted negotiations with the owners, the Jamaica Cricket Association finally managed to acquire the properties in the late 1970s and set about raising money to expand and completely redesign Sabina Park. In spite of the international oil crisis, and resulting economic downturn, that severely affected plans, all the stands adjoining the newly acquired land were demolished. Construction of a spacious, modern stand stretching the length of the southern end of the ground, with the impressive Blue Mountains before it in the distance, with comfortable seating for 6500 and 40 private boxes on two floors, was completed in 1982. It incorporated players' dres-

The enormous George Headley Stand which has enclosed Sabina Park's southern end since 1982.

sing-rooms and offices for the Jamaica Cricket Association, previously housed in the Club pavilion. A modern media centre, a three-storey structure incorporating a large sightscreen, was erected at the northern end. But the original cost jumped from J$0.75 million to $7 million and plans for more stands had to be shelved. It has completely transformed Sabina, now even more unrecognizable as 'the derelict sort of penn' that Frank Lynch described when he first saw it.

The new stand was, fittingly, almost inevitably, named the George Headley Stand in honour of Jamaica's greatest player who graced Sabina Park with some of its most memorable Test performances.

Headley was a batsman supreme and Sabina, with rare exceptions, has been a ground for batting. At its finest, its clay-like soil was prepared and

rolled until it was concrete-hard and its surface glistened like a mirror from which the players' whites clearly reflected. It was then considered the fastest, yet truest, of pitches. It lost those properties when relaid, with disastrous consequences, in 1968 and following more recent instances when its soil has been turned over. Its pace has diminished and its most striking feature recently, in every sense, has been its unpredictable bounce. Even at that, no West Indies venue has produced such a register of high-scoring.

Test cricket's first triple-century was recorded in Sabina's inaugural Test in 1930, 325 by Andy Sandham in an England total of 849 that was then the highest on record and has been since surpassed only by England's 903 for 7 declared against Australia at the Oval in 1938. Twenty-eight years later, Garry Sobers, whose phenomenal Test career began at Sabina, aged 17, in 1954, made his triple-century for the West Indies against Pakistan the highest of all, 365 not out in a total of 790 for 3 declared that rates the third highest in all Tests. That status had been Australia's for three years with their 758 for 8 declared on the same pluperfect pitch when five batsmen collected centuries, a statistic unique in Test cricket, to be answered by Clyde Walcott's century in each innings for the West Indies. India's first appearance at Sabina brought a century from each of the Ws in the same innings for the first time – 237 by Frank Worrell, 118 by Walcott and 109 by Everton Weekes.

There have been 57 three-figure innings in Sabina's 27 Tests, only four of which have gone without an individual century. Sandham and Sobers passed their 300s, seven others 200. Lawrence Rowe, an adored son of the soil, made his double, 214, on debut against New Zealand in 1972 and followed it with an even, unbeaten 100 in the second innings, a combination achieved by no one else in his first Test. In that same match, New Zealand opener Glenn Turner created another batting record for Sabina, his unbeaten 223 the highest of any batsman carrying his bat through a Test innings.

Of the 27 matches, the West Indies have won 14 and drawn 10, their only three defeats sustained in successive Tests, the last of the 1954 series against England and both the next year against Australia.

Sabina has witnessed several astonishing matches, none more so than its first, that of Sandham's triple. It was scheduled to be played to a finish, since the series was level at one match each. So England, in spite of a first innings lead of 563, batted a second time and left the West Indies a target of 836 to win and their bowlers with an eternity to complete the job. They never did. Headley kept them in the field longer than they bargained for with his 223, Karl Nunes, the West Indies and also Kingston Club captain, made 92 and, at the end of the ninth day, the West Indies were holding firm at 408 for 5. It then rained

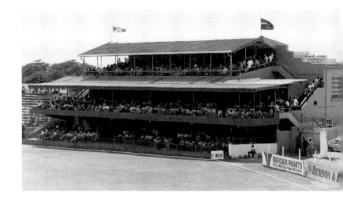

The airy, three-tiered Kingston Club pavilion on Sabina Park's western boundary.

steadily for two days and, with their county season starting in less than a fortnight, the Englishmen caught the next ship home.

When they returned for the next Test series in 1935, Headley treated his home fans to another double, an unbeaten 270, and England crumbled to an innings defeat against the kind of West Indies four-pronged pace attack (Manny Martindale, Learie Constantine, Leslie Hylton and Dicky Fuller) that was to become standard selection practice nearly half a century later. England's captain Bob Wyatt had his jaw broken by a bouncer from Martindale, the first, but not the last, injury inflicted by fast bowlers on Sabina's pacy pitch over the years.

Sobers was another batsman with a particular affinity for Sabina which saw five of his 26 Test centuries. The most extraordinary was in the extraordinary, riot-interrupted match of 1968. Dug up and relaid only months before, the pitch soon became jigsawed with a mosaic of gaping cracks off which the ball did strange things. England had first, and best, use of it, scoring 376, but the West Indies could not survive beyond 143 in reply,

Sobers bowled first ball by a shooter by John Snow, and were made to follow on. When the bottle-throwing disturbance erupted on the fall of the fifth wicket, the West Indies were still 29 in arrears and defeat appeared certain. But Sobers was still in and, when play resumed the following day, he fashioned an incredible innings of 113 not out. Then, 158 ahead, he cheekily declared and very nearly snatched a stunning victory in the hour and a quarter tacked on as the unscheduled sixth day at England's insistence to compensate for the time lost to the riot. At the end, England were 68 for 8!

Eight years later, India found a similarly devilish pitch, and perhaps more devilish bowling, too much to bear and batted five injured men short in their second innings which was recorded as 97 all out, Sabina's lowest Test total. The Indian captain, Bishen Bedi, said it was 'like war', condemning West Indian tactics as Michael Holding, in his first home Test, and his fast bowling accomplices made the ball leap alarmingly from a ridge at the northern end. Gundappa Viswanath had a finger fractured, Anshuman Gaekwad and Brijesh Patel were hit in the face in the days before helmets.

When the Indians returned in 1983, there was an altogether less controversial contest – and one of the most stirring finishes of any Test in the West Indies. With the fourth day lost to rain, a draw appeared certain when India were 164 ahead with four wickets standing at the final tea interval. Then Andy Roberts took three wickets in his first over on resumption and 4 for 1 in 20 balls and the West Indies achieved a victory target of 172 in 26 overs with four balls remaining, inspired by Vivian Richards's 61 off 35 balls.

Yet Jamaicans had to wait 13 years, and eight Tests, to see Richards, the most commanding batsman of his time, score his first century at

Sabina, 110 against India in 1989, the controversial completion of which, to a disputed catch by the wicket-keeper, stirred the crowd into a brief bottle-throwing demonstration.

The season before there had been much local resentment when Sabina, for the first time, was omitted from the Test rota during Pakistan's series of three matches. Jamaicans responded by filling the ground to capacity for the Indian Test of 1989 – and the century by Richards was a rich reward for their interest.

For all its batting records, Sabina's pitch has also promoted a string of memorable fast bowling feats. Trevor Bailey's 7 for 34 destroyed the West Indies' first innings in 1954 and set up England's victory that levelled the series 2–2 and Snow's 7 for 49 made telling use of the peculiarities of 1968. But, for sheer pace, there has been nothing to match the West Indian giants, ancient and modern, from Martindale, Constantine and Hylton of the 1930s to the more recent, more numerous crop.

None was more successful at Sabina than Wes Hall whose five Tests on the ground between 1960 and 1968 brought him 35 wickets at 15.25 each. No bowler has struck more fire from a pitch than Hall did in the 1960 Test against England when he returned his best figures of 7 for 69 and when Colin Cowdrey played two of the most courageous innings seen on the ground, 114 in the first innings, 97 in the second. Of late, variation in bounce and the formidable West Indian fast attack has put a premium on batsmen's courage. England's Mike Gatting had his nose shattered by a ball from Malcolm Marshall in a one-day international in 1986 – as the England captain of 1935, Bob Wyatt, had his jaw broken by a bouncer from Martindale. In the Test that followed Gatting's misfortune, Patrick Patterson, a burly Jamaican on debut, urged on by a fanatical crowd, bowled, according to John Woodcock of *The Times* 'as fast as a man can bowl'. In the 12 innings in Sabina Tests in the 1980s, West Indian opponents have been dismissed for less than 200 seven times and passed 300 only once. Its last double-centuries were those of Rowe and Turner in the 1972 Test.

Yet, for all that, only two bowlers have ever taken ten wickets in a Sabina Test, both tall, slim, fast and Jamaican. Hines Johnson had 5 for 41 and 5 for 55 against England in 1948 on his debut aged 37; Courtney Walsh returned 6 for 62 and 4 for 39 against India in 1989.

As with all other West Indian Test venues, a private club, Kingston, developed Sabina and it owns most of the land. For international matches, it has come to an agreement with the Jamaica Cricket Association which acts as agent on behalf of the West Indies Cricket Board of Control. The additional land purchased to the north and south and the new stands recently built on it belong to the JCA which has entered into covenants with Kingston protecting the club's rights. But the club is still responsible for the upkeep of the ground and the preparation of the pitch, rolled since 1953 by one of the few remaining electrified rollers. Purchased on the recommendation of Allan Rae who saw one in operation at Brisbane on his 1951–52 tour of Australia with the West Indies, it has required little attention since. Like his father, Ernest, before him, Rae has been the virtual governor of Sabina for over 30 years, as well as Test opener and president of both the JCA and the WICBC.

Like all other West Indian Test grounds, Sabina was the centre for all sporting events in Kingston until the construction of the National Stadium in 1962 but cricket is its *raison d'être* and it is cricket that has filled it for over a century. When packed and the match intense, the noise from the most

Improvised viewing arrangements at Sabina Park.

excitable crowds in the West Indies can be deafening, the decibels seemingly magnified by its claustrophobic situation.

For years, their lunch intervals were enlivened by the impromptu performances of Lennie, a much-loved character and natural comic who would come on to the ground, uninvited but encouraged to give his hilarious imitations of the sporting heroes of the day – from Sobers to Pelé to Mohammed Ali. A big match at Sabina has not been quite the same since his death in 1987.

Situated in the heart of an urban residential district and skirted by the busy South Camp Road on its eastern side, Sabina Park is equidistant between the city centre, the modern business area of New Kingston and the main market at Halfway Tree. It is, therefore, easily accessible and, through the years, thousands who have made the journey to celebrate what is as much the national sport as the national obsession.

Kingston, Jamaica				
Ref/No	*Season*	*V*	*T*	*Result*
193/1	1929–30	E	4	Draw
241/2	1934–35	E	4	WI-1 & 161
298/3	1947–48	E	4	WI-10w
369/4	1952–53	I	5	Draw
382/5	1953–54	E	1	WI-140
386/6			5	E-9w
403/7	1954–55	A	1	A-9w
407/8			5	A-1 & 82
451/9	1957–58	P	3	WI-1 & 174
489/10	1959–60	E	3	Draw
526/11	1961–62	I	2	WI-1 & 18
529/12			5	WI-123
583/13	1964–65	A	1	WI-179
629/14	1967–68	E	2	Draw
680/15	1970–71	I	1	Draw
693/16	1971–72	NZ	1	Draw
714/17	1972–73	A	1	Draw
732/18	1973–74	E	2	Draw
776/19	1975–76	I	4	WI-10w
802/20	1976–77	P	5	WI-140
824/21	1977–78	A	5	Draw
899/22	1980–81	E	5	Draw
949/23	1982–83	I	1	WI-4w
985/24	1983–84	A	5	WI-10w
1016/25	1984–85	NZ	4	WI-10w
1038/26	1985–86	E	1	WI-10w
1120/27	1988–89	I	4	WI-7w

West Indies: P 27, W 14, D 10, L 3

Port-of-Spain, Trinidad
QUEEN'S PARK OVAL

The Queen's Park Oval is, by universal consensus, one of cricket's most beautiful settings. It is also the largest Test ground in the West Indies, with its expansive stands capable of accommodating 25,000, surrounding a perfect oval of an outfield. It occupies an entire block of over ten acres. On one side is the busy Tragarete Road, linking Port-of-Spain's north-west with the city centre, and the middle-class suburb of Woodbrook; on the other, the plush and peaceful residential district of St Clair, with its expensive, mainly ambassadorial homes. The imposing hills of the northern range form a breathtaking backdrop.

The Oval, as it is simply known, has been the home of the Queen's Park Cricket Club (QPCC) since the club moved from its previous location on the nearby Queen's Park Savannah, less than a mile away, in February 1896. It was then part of the government's St Clair Farm, ten acres and ten perches that were probably a cow pasture. The deed by which the land was leased obliged the club, among other things, 'to keep the land in good heart and condition and always in sound turf', a requirement so quickly and diligently adhered to that Queen's Park was able to host the English teams touring the West Indies early in 1897 at the Oval, one under Lord Hawke, the other under Arthur Priestley. For the former, Sir Pelham 'Plum' Warner, one of the game's legendary figures who was born in Trinidad, was the first man to score a hundred on the new ground, 119 against the club. The latter met a representative West Indies team, the Oval's first international match. Every team to the Caribbean since has played at Queen's Park which has staged more Tests than any other West Indian ground, 38.

Its enhanced capacity (no other venue holds more than 18,000) has made it the most profitable and, before the Antigua Recreation Ground was added to the Test circuit in 1981, the Oval was usually favoured with the extra match in any series of five Tests.

The club paid particular attention to providing accommodation for the public from its earliest days. In addition to its pavilion, that remained virtually unchanged from its erection in 1896 to its replacement by a larger, two-storied structure in 1952, there was a ladies' members stand and a temporary public stand on the western side, all filled to capacity, by the time Priestley's team visited. Since then, it has constantly added to the stands, no one doing more for this expansion than

Queen's Park Oval, Port-of-Spain, during the 1901–02 tour of the West Indies by a team of English amateurs led by R. A. Bennett. Taken from the album of E. R. Wilson, who headed the bowling averages, the photographs show (top) Wilson bowling towards the northern end; and (bottom) the old pavilion to the south.

Sir Errol dos Santos – a man of considerable power and prestige in government and business circles – who served on the club's committee for more than 40 years, latterly as president, a position he also held on the Trinidad and Tobago Cricket Council for 19 years and on the West Indies Board for a term. A man of dynamic energy, even into his 90th year when he finally retired to England, it was through his initiative in raising money that Queen's

Park rapidly developed, from the 1940s, into one of the world's finest cricket grounds.

Second decks were added to stands on the western side, one named in his honour, while large, raised, open stands were constructed on the popular eastern side through sponsorship from brewing companies and banks. In the 1940s – also through sponsorship – a large detailed scoreboard, based on the one at the Sydney Cricket Ground, was constructed and has been refurbished in the interim so that it remains one of the most informative anywhere.

Queen's Park has always been, first and foremost, a cricket ground. But it has been more, the only facility for major open-air events until the National Stadium was opened in 1981. So it has also staged international soccer, hockey, boxing and cycling for which a banked, concrete track circles the ground, between field and stands. The largest crowds it has ever witnessed were for soccer, in the 1970s when the magic of Brazilian star, Pelé, with his club, Santos, attracted an estimated 35,000, and in 1988 when as many as 30,000 turned out for a World Cup qualifier between Trinidad and Tobago and Honduras. The club maintains hard tennis courts and squash courts in the area of the large car park adjacent to its pavilion.

But it is cricket for which the Queen's Park Oval is best known – and the quality of the cricket played has been usually dictated by the variety of pitches that have been used.

The natural turf was prepared in the early years before the presence of the mole-cricket in the soil, that ravaged the grass roots, rendered a proper pitch impossible. So, in time for the visit of Arthur Somerset's MCC team of 1911, a clay strip was introduced over which matting was laid. It remained thus for over 40 years before a strong lobby, mounted by the Queen's Park, Trinidad and

West Indies captain, Jeffrey Stollmeyer, for the installation of a proper, turf square was heeded.

The original matting was woven of coconut fibre, coarse in texture and, as a result, lively. It encouraged bowlers to be fast and batsmen to cut and hook. It could be occasionally dangerous, depending on the surface on which it was laid out, but, when good, batsmen of quality could enjoy themselves as Patsy Hendren and Les Ames amply demonstrated during Queen's Park's first Test in 1930 when they added 237 for the fourth wicket in an England victory by 167 runs. Hendren's unbeaten 205 remains the fourth-highest Test score on the ground.

Efforts, all futile, were made in the 1920s for a reversion to a turf square but the only change came when the former Australian Test player Arthur Richardson was brought to Trinidad by Queen's Park to coach in 1935 and introduced matting made of jute, rather than coconut fibre. This was then being used extensively in Australia and proved to have far less bounce than its predecessor.

The first Test played on it – in which Richardson was one of the umpires – brought the West Indies' first, and most dramatic, Test victory at Queen's Park.

England collapsed in their second innings on the last day of the four-day match but it was only off the fifth ball of the very last over, bowled by one of Trinidad's greatest cricketers, Learie Constantine, that the last wicket fell, Maurice Leyland given lbw in a decision that has always been the subject of controversy. It was to be the last Test at the ground for 13 years as the Second World War intervened and also the last outright result before Stollmeyer finally had his way and the matting was eventually done away with in 1954, to be permanently replaced by a turf pitch.

The jute matting proved a boon for batsmen and

yielded prodigious scoring feats in the inter-island matches of the war years. Trinidad amassed 750 for 8 declared against British Guiana in 1947 when Stollmeyer himself recorded what remains the biggest first-class score on the ground, 324, and Barbados 619 for 3 declared against Trinidad the previous season when two of the famous Ws, Clyde Walcott (314) and Frank Worrell (255) added their fourth wicket record of 574 unbroken. Results were difficult to come by and successive draws were recorded in the Tests against England in 1948, the first after the war, and 1954 and the two against the first Indian team to the West Indies in 1953.

In the 1948 match, Andy Ganteaume and Billy Griffith collected maiden Test centuries of bizarre statistical value. Ganteaume's 112 for the West Indies was his one and only Test innings; he was simply never chosen again. Griffith, the reserve wicket-keeper doubling duties as assistant manager, was pressed into service by a spate of injuries and, opening the innings, his 140 was his first and only century even at first-class level.

The Test of 1954 finally settled the demise of the jute matting. It produced 1528 runs for 24 wickets, all three Ws scoring centuries in the West Indies' 681 for 8 declared and Peter May and Denis Compton responding in kind in England's 537. Four great England bowlers – Trueman, Bailey, Laker and Lock – each conceded more than 100 in the first innings. Within a few months, the bulldozers were excavating the square and soil brought from the south of the island was being laid, as Badge Menzies, the groundsman at Georgetown's Test ground, Bourda, and Son Waldron, renowned as a wizard at pitch preparation in Barbados, were brought in as consultants. But time was short and very little grass was evident for the debut Test of Queen's Park's new turf pitch on Australia's first West Indies tour of 1955. There was another glut of

runs, this time 1255 for only 23 wickets, centuries in each innings for Walcott, one for Weekes that was his fourth in successive Tests on the ground and one by each of the top three in the Australian order, Colin McDonald, Arthur Morris and Neil Harvey, as nine West Indian bowlers were tried.

Pakistan's inaugural tour of 1958 ended the Oval's sequence of high-scoring draws, the West Indies winning one, Pakistan the other. Since then the ground has been the scene of several remarkable matches, few dull, on pitches that progressively favoured spin bowling as the alien soil became more and more worn.

The West Indies were beaten there nine times out of 22 Tests between 1957 and 1978, by all opponents except New Zealand who drew both their Tests on their inaugural tour of 1972. Against that, the West Indies could count five victories. Time and again they were undone by spin – the strength of the opposition's as much as the weakness of their own. Ironically, the most outstanding individual feat by a spinner was by a popular Trinidadian, Jack Noreiga, a 35-year-old off-spinner in his one and only series who took 9 for 95 in India's first innings of the Second Test of 1971, a match that brought India their first victory in the Caribbean. Just as strangely, the best match figures produced in an Oval Test, 13 for 156 in England's 1974 last-Test victory that levelled the series, came not from a specialist spinner but from the all-rounder Tony Greig, adapting his style to off-breaks to suit the conditions.

Two of the West Indian defeats were caused by miscalculations by their captains who twice gambled with declarations and lost. Garry Sobers was the more generous and England scored the 215 he set them in 165 minutes for the loss of three wickets, the only result in the series of five Tests. It was a move for which Sobers was pilloried

throughout the Caribbean and has never been for-given. Clive Lloyd's against India in 1976 was somewhat more realistic but his bowling was inexperienced and India reached their target of 406 for the loss of only four wickets, the highest ever scored to win a Test. One of the architects of India's second victory in the Caribbean, and at Queen's Park, was Sunil Gavaskar, eulogized in local calypso after his prolific tour of 1971 as 'The Real Master'. In his four Tests at the Oval between 1971 and 1976, Gavaskar scored four centuries, one in each innings of the final 1971 Test in which his second innings 220 remains the Oval's highest individual Test score.

By the 1970s, it was evident the soil introduced back in 1954 was in need of a transplant. Pitches, invariably slow, had become unpredictable in their behaviour with a will of their own over which groundsmen had no control. Spin usually held sway and the West Indies selectors rarely entered a Test without two or three in their team, choosing to open the bowling in the two Tests against Australia

A classic view of Queen's Park, where the imposing northern hills form a breathtaking backdrop to the largest of the West Indian grounds.

in 1973 with Clive Lloyd. Yet Colin Croft, in only his second Test, destroyed Pakistan's powerful batting with his 8 for 29 in 1977, the best return by any West Indian fast bowler in Test cricket. While Roy Fredericks was bowled by Abid Ali's shooter the very first ball of the 1971 Test and the ball usually turned and skidded through, Doug Walters could still thump a century between lunch and tea for Australia in 1973, Vivian Richards dominate the high-class Indian spinners (Bedi, Chandrasekhar and Venkataraghavan) with centuries in the back-to-back Tests of 1976 and Gavaskar regularly stake his lengthy claim to the territory in the middle.

The mood grew with each passing season that it was time the square be dug up again (Sobers and Australian captain Bobby Simpson suggested as much as far back as 1965) but Trinidadians, recalling the dreary draws of the past and the frequent results and excitement since, resisted until 1980 when new soil was laid.

That has changed its character somewhat, allowing a heavier and more even covering of grass. There was more encouragement for the fast bowlers which is a feasible explanation for the fact that the West Indies have won four of the eight Tests played since and had much the better of three of the four draws – and that Trinidad has placed two fast bowlers in the Test team (Tony Gray and Ian Bishop) in recent years for the first time since the 1940s.

Two of the draws were among the most exciting ever witnessed at the Oval. In 1984, captain Allan Border followed an unbeaten 98 in the first innings with an unbeaten 100 in the second that allowed Australia to scrape to safety with nine wickets down; in 1988's magnificent match, in which no team ever held the advantage, Pakistan were 31 short of a winning target of 372 when last man, Abdul Qadir, played out the last five balls. In those years, the West Indies discarded their previous policy of choosing a spinner as a matter of course for the Queen's Park Test and their formidable fast bowling has usually done the job for them. Malcolm Marshall's 11 wickets for 89 against India in 1989 were the best returns of his celebrated career; only the Trinidadian leg-spinner, Wilfred Ferguson, against England on the mat in 1948, had taken as many for the West Indies at Queen's Park and only the great England left-hander, Bill Voce, had taken as many as a fast bowler, back in 1930.

A lively, cosmopolitan people, numbering just over a million and a half, Trinidadians are celebrated for their culture, as originators of calypso music and the steelband, and for their love of sport. The Queen's Park Oval was frequently filled to capacity for Tests in the past but the public, as everywhere else, has switched its attendance to the one-day international for which they now cram the ground. Yet their interest in Test cricket remains intense, even though they no longer come in their previous numbers.

Like Guyana, Trinidad's main ethnic groups are of African and East Indian descent and, as in Guyana, the Indians turn out in their numbers in support of Indian and Pakistani matches at the Oval. It is a situation that can lead to tension but the only serious crowd trouble during an Oval Test occurred in the second of the 1960 series against England and was unrelated to ethnic rivalries. The real reasons for a riot that halted play for the day and placed the tour in jeopardy were plentiful and diverse. Prominent among them were the hot and uncomfortable conditions, the plight of the West Indies who were routed for 112 by Trueman and Statham, the run-out dismissal of a local player in his debut Test, Charran Singh, and strong drink.

Volatile the Trinidadian may be but his cricket means too much for him to allow his, or his neighbour's, emotions to spill over into violence that would disrupt play. No section of the Oval crowd captures the spirit of Trinidad more aptly than that known as the 'Concrete Stand', latterly renamed the Learie Constantine Stand. Situated at the northern end, it is populated by avid fans, there from first ball to last, well stocked with their food and drink, vocal, witty and, often, biting in their freely offered advice. As the match nears its end, they break into the chorus of 'Oh, dear, what can the matter be?' and 'Amen, Amen'. A character, with the colourful nickname of 'Blue Food', has been leading the cheers at the fall of a wicket or the scoring of a boundary with a blast on his conch-shell horn for more than 30 years.

Cricket in Trinidad, as anywhere else in the West

Indies, is as much a social occasion as a sporting one, the Test eagerly anticipated.

Since 1981, the Trinidad and Tobago Cricket Association has taken over from the Queen's Park Cricket Club as agents for the West Indies Board in staging of regional and international matches. But credit for the development of the West Indies' most spacious and, arguably, most beautiful cricket ground is the club's, and the club's alone.

Port-of-Spain, Trinidad				
Ref/No	*Season*	*V*	*T*	*Result*
191/1	1929–30	E	2	E-167
239/2	1934–35	E	2	WI-217
296/3	1947–48	E	2	Draw
365/4	1952–53	I	1	Draw
367/5			3	Draw
385/6	1953–54	E	4	Draw
404/7	1954–55	A	2	Draw
450/8	1957–58	P	2	WI-120
453/9			5	P-I&1
488/10	1959–60	E	2	E-256
491/11			5	Draw
525/12	1961–62	I	1	WI-10w
528/13			4	WI-7w
584/14	1964–65	A	2	Draw
587/15			5	A-10w
628/16	1967–68	E	1	Draw
631/17			4	E-7w
681/18	1970–71	I	2	I-7w
684/19			5	Draw
694/20	1971–72	NZ	2	Draw
697/21			5	Draw
716/22	1972–73	A	3	A-44
718/23			5	Draw
731/24	1973–74	E	1	WI-7w
735/25			5	E-26
774/26	1975–76	I	2	Draw
775/27			3	I-6w
799/28	1976–77	P	2	WI-6w
801/29			4	P-266
820/30	1977–78	A	1	WI-I&106
823/31			4	WI-198
896/32	1980–81	E	1	WI-I&79
950/33	1982–83	I	2	Draw
982/34	1983–84	A	2	Draw
1013/35	1984–85	NZ	1	Draw
1039/36	1985–86	E	2	WI-7w
1041/37			4	WI-10w
1096/38	1987–88	P	2	Draw
1119/39	1988–89	I	3	WI-217

West Indies: P 39, W 12, D 17, L 10

St John's, Antigua
RECREATION GROUND

When the Antigua Recreation Ground became the West Indies' fifth, and the game's 52nd, Test match venue by hosting the Fourth Test of England's 1980–81 tour of the Caribbean, it was an occasion for joyful celebration for the people unequalled even by the island's attainment of independence from Britain nine years earlier.

Such cricketing elevation was as significant to the 75,000 Antiguans who inhabit their 108-square-mile island as had been the attainment of political sovereignty. Like the other Leeward and Windward Islands, Antigua had been excluded from the mainstream of West Indies cricket, left to play among themselves while Barbados, Guyana, Jamaica and Trinidad provided the players for the Test team and staged the Tests.

Only with the coming of the Shell Shield in 1966, the first annual first-class competition, were the 'islands' given a proper chance to join the fold and it was not long before the quality of their players became obvious. The emergence of two particularly outstanding Antiguans, fast bowler Andy Roberts and batsman Vivian Richards, stimulated the drive for even more cricketing recognition. Included in that was Antigua's concerted effort to have its Antigua Recreation Ground – to Antiguans the ARG – granted a Test match.

There were factors other than the exploits of Roberts and Richards that won the Board's approval. Antigua is excellently located at almost the dead centre of the Lesser Antilles with an international airport, frequent connections to neighbouring islands and an infrastructure that could cope with the demands of hosting a major sporting event. Enthusiastically, and financially, supported by the government and the business

Antigua's Recreation Ground during the England tourists' match against the Leeward Islands in February 1986. The Roman Catholic cathedral is on the left.

community, the Antigua Cricket Association put forward an undeniable case and two 'dummy runs' finally swayed the Board.

The first was a one-day international against Australia in 1978, the first match of such importance ever given to the smaller islands. Nearly 15,000, standing four deep in the open areas and many flocking in from neighbouring islands, watched. The second was the fifth 'Supertest' of World Series Cricket's only overseas tour the following year between Kerry Packer's powerful West Indian and Australian teams. Both went with hardly a hitch, as the Antiguans knew they would. Confidently anticipating Test status, they built two new stands and dedicated them to Roberts and Richards. When confirmation of the 1981 Test came, another two-tiered structure, the largest on the ground, was added, dwarfing the other more modest wooden stands and bleachers.

With the inevitable advertising signs circling the boundary, the ARG was hardly recognizable as the open pasture on the outskirts of the neat little capital, St John's, that greeted the first English touring teams under A.F. Priestley and Lord Hawke in the late 1800s. It had seen little physical development until the government undertook upgrading of the pavilion in the 1960s for a venue

that was most aptly named. It was, and remains, precisely that: a ground for recreation of every conceivable kind, from cricket to the annual carnival, from political rallies to calypso contests.

Contrasting landmarks surround it. Across the road, west on the town side, is the Roman Catholic cathedral. On Michael's Mount, a hill to the south, is situated a casino and hotel that overlook the ground. Across the road to the east is the island's jail, the inmates of which have long provided a ready source of manpower for preparation of pitch and ground, performing the duties, almost willingly, under the redundant eye of a warder. For years, he happened to be Malcolm Richards, the prison's deputy superintendent, himself one of Antigua's finest fast bowlers, at a time when Test cricket was beyond his scope, and proud father of Vivian.

Public excitement ran high for the inaugural Test of 1981, but such grand occasions often turn out to be disappointing anti-climaxes. Richards, however, sensed – indeed shared – the mood of the people. By now rightly regarded as the world's finest batsman and adored by the Antiguans as no political leader could be, he chose two days prior to the Test as his wedding day, marrying his childhood sweetheart, Miriam, at a ceremony that seemingly brought out the entire island, from Prime Minister to postman.

If some feared that the date was dangerously close to such a momentous match, Richards further embellished the moment with a thrilling century, 114 with 20 fours. Peter Willey had earlier claimed the honour of scoring the first Test century on the ground, an unbeaten 102, but that did not matter to Antiguans whose capacity for enjoyment was simply magnified by the heady sequence of events.

And how they celebrate in an atmosphere at the ARG that closely resembles that of a country fair. Every boundary, every wicket, almost every incident is greeted with a blow from the resident trumpeter, stationed in what is known as 'the Rude Boys' Stand'. Loud speakers from food stalls and bars at the back of the main stand blast out the latest calypso hit to signal another West Indian triumph on the field – always switching into silence as the bowler starts his run.

And there has been plenty to celebrate in the four Tests they have seen. Pelham Warner commented, with good reason, that Antigua's pitch was 'one of the best we played on' during his tour with Lord Hawke's 1896–97 team. He got 110 then and nothing much has changed since in that regard. There have been 13 centuries in all, the West Indies have never been dismissed for less than 400 and several batting records have been broken.

The inaugural Test, spoiled by the loss of a day to unseasonal rain, and the next in 1983 against India that produced 1254 runs for 24 wickets, were drawn. In the latter, there were four West Indian centuries in an innings for the only time in a home Test, Gordon Greenidge and Desmond Haynes

adding a record 296 for the first wicket before Greenidge retired 154 – 'not out' as it was later ruled – to fly back to Barbados where his critically ill two-year-old daughter died two days later.

The most recent two Tests provided Antiguans with even more reason to celebrate. Not only did the West Indies win both sweepingly – by an innings and 36 runs over Australia in 1984 and by 240 runs over England in 1986 – but Richards was in rampant mood in both. Aided and abetted by a new Antiguan star, Richie Richardson, he scored 178 in a record third-wicket stand of 308 against the Australians, Richardson marking his first home Test with 154. Two seasons later, impatient for a declaration in the West Indies' second innings, he lashed seven sixes and seven fours in an unbeaten 110, arriving at his century from 56 balls, the fastest on Test record.

As Pelham Warner knew so many years ago, the ARG is an uncompromising place for bowlers. Only two, not dissimilar in style, have managed more than five in an innings in the four Tests. Colin Croft, the awkward Guyanese fast bowler, claimed 6 for 74 from 25 overs in the 1981 Test against England, and Carl Rackemann, the big Australian, had to work even harder for his 5 for 161 off 42.4 overs in 1984.

The groundstaff from across the road have done their work thoroughly over the years. And the ARG is, after all, the home of one of the greatest batsmen of all time.

St John's, Antigua				
Ref/No	*Season*	*V*	*T*	*Result*
898/1	1980–81	E	4	Draw
953/2	1982–83	I	5	Draw
984/3	1983–84	A	4	WI-I&36
1042/4	1985–86	E	5	WI-240
West Indies: P 4, W 2, D 2, L 0				